Valley of the Shadow

VALLEY
OF THE
SHADOW

After The Turmoil
My Heart Cries No More...

Erich Anton Helfert

CREATIVE ARTS BOOK COMPANY
Berkeley • California • 1997

The maps, from *The Sudeten Question*
by Dr. Fritz-Peter Habel, are used with permission.

Valley of the Shadow is published by Donald S. Ellis
and distributed by Creative Arts Book Company

For Information contact:
Creative Arts Book Company
833 Bancroft Way
Berkeley, California 94710

For ordering information call:
1-800-848-7789
Fax: 1-510-848-4844

Cover Design by Roger L. Lee
Graphics and Book Design by Pope Graphic Arts Center

ISBN 0-88739-117-6
Library of Congress Catalog Number 96-86114

Printed in the United States of America

To Anne,

Claire and Amanda

"…yea, though I walk through the valley of the shadow of death,
I will fear no evil: for Thou art with me…"

23rd Psalm

Acknowledgments

This book is the outgrowth of decades of reflection and remembrance. It could not have become a reality, however, had it not been for the encouragement and emotional support of two of the most important persons in my life: My late mother Anna Maria, who had the unwavering conviction that I should some day put our joint experiences into printed words, and my loving wife Anne, who not only stood by me during the intermittent writing process over the past several years—which proved to be an emotional release and catharsis—but who also provided thoughtful, patient, and most capable editorial advice. I will always be grateful to them.

My sincere appreciation also goes to a number of our friends who read and extensively commented on advanced versions of the manuscript. Among these are Dr. E. Walton Kirk, Cynthia Poett, Lila Vultee, and the late Ruth McCandless, an accomplished author. Dr. Fritz-Peter Habel, my high school classmate and expert author of documentary books on the Sudetenland, was especially thoughtful in advising me on valuable details of the complex historical aspects, and Dr. Heinz Henisch, author and also a native of the Sudetenland, contributed his special insights.

I am most grateful to Prof. Alfred de Zayas, author and expert on refugee and human rights issues, for his generous foreword, and to Dr. Dennis Bark, Senior Fellow, author and expert on Europe at the Hoover Institution, for his very positive assessment of the book.

My publisher, Donald Ellis, has been an enthusiastic collaborator in bringing the book to fruition, and my editor, Jennifer Ellis, was invaluable in helping to shape the manuscript into its final form through her deep insight and infinite care.

Author's Note

The events described in this story are true. The names of the people and some of the locations have been changed for obvious reasons. Young Anton and the author are the same person.

Table of Contents

Author's Introduction

The backdrop of this true story is an untold and largely forgotten episode of modern history, lost in the confusion and upheavals following the end of World War II. These events occurred over half a century ago in central Europe, both before and after the war, when the Sudetenland,[1] a region containing parts of the former Austrian Empire's provinces of Bohemia, Moravia and Silesia, with a German-speaking population of over three million, became a pawn on the chessboard of European power politics. It is only now, after the unprecedented changes in Eastern Europe during the early 1990's, that this portion of history is beginning to receive some public attention at a time when the fate and treatment of minorities and ethnic groups is increasingly recognized as an important factor in attaining regional and world stability.

The upheavals that caused the uprooting and expulsion of the Wildert family as described in this story are based in fateful political decisions made at the conclusion of the First World War. The victorious Allies proceeded to reshape the map of Europe during the peace conferences of 1918-19 according to U.S. president Wilson's acclaimed principle of national self-determination. In this process the old Empire of Austria-Hungary with its many nationalities was broken up into a group of smaller ethnic nation states. One of these was the newly created Slavic republic of Czechoslovakia, whose founding father, Professor Thomas Masaryk, prepared its launching from exile in the United States.

When they established the boundaries of the new Czechoslovakia in 1919, however, the Allied leaders agreed to Czech demands that their new state include a number of adjoining areas with very different ethnic populations. The largest among these

---

[1] See maps on pages 184-85

was the Sudetenland, a border region rich in resources and industry and populated by German-speaking Austrians, some with French Huguenot roots, whose ancestors had developed the land and lived there for more than 700 years. The statesmen making this concession disregarded both the misgivings of far-sighted historians and the outright warnings of a Harvard University advisory commission to the effect that forcing ethnically disparate territories together would create a geopolitical time bomb. The Allies rejected urgent pleas by Austrian, German and Sudeten representatives to hold a plebiscite on the choice of either joining Germany or the new Czechoslovak republic. As a consequence, more than three and a half million Sudeten Austrians were made to live under the rule of nine million Czechs, who had the reluctant support of two and a half million Slovaks within their new nation.

Even though Czechoslovakia's leaders, President Masaryk and his foreign minister, Dr. Edvard Beneš, had intimated that they would create a country on the Swiss model of tolerance and acceptance of ethnic diversity, they instead proceeded to build a nationalistic state. Tensions grew when the Prague government practiced ethnic, political and economic discrimination against these citizens of different nationality, installing Czech officials to administer the Sudeten territory and actively encouraging growing numbers of Czech nationals to settle there. By the middle of the 1930's frequent appeals by moderate Sudeten leaders to be granted some degree of democratic self-rule and economic equality within the structure of the Czechoslovak republic were invariably rejected out-of-hand by the government.

The plight of this minority population—who within their own territory represented an overwhelming plurality of about ninety percent—gave Adolf Hitler another opportunity to further his territorial ambitions while the irresolute future European Allies looked on. Hitler's series of bold and unchallenged actions to invalidate the provisions of the 1919 peace treaty, such as the occupation of the demilitarized Rhineland and the annexation of Austria, culminated in the Sudetenland crisis of September 1938. Hitler now demanded control of this territory, and under pressure from Great Britain and France the Czechoslovak government agreed to the cessation of the Sudetenland. The famous Munich Agreement temporarily eased the tense confrontation when Prime Minister Chamberlain of Great Britain appeased the dictator once more and agreed to the conditions under which the Sudetenland would be separated from Czechoslovakia and annexed by Germany.

Soon afterwards Hitler broke his own explicit pledge to forgo further territorial claims. The indecisive European governments again failed to act as he ordered the *Wehrmacht* to occupy the Czech provinces of Bohemia and Moravia, where the German forces met no armed resistance. Slovakia immediately proclaimed its independence as a separate nation, while the Czech government now headed by Dr. Beneš fled into exile in London. A gloating Hitler appeared in Prague to declare that the Czech portion of Czechoslovakia was now a "Protectorate of the German *Reich*." The region remained under harsh Nazi rule throughout the Second World War; there were incidents of persecution and terror, and many Czech citizens were pressed into serving the industrial machine that supported the German war effort.

During the war the Allies granted the Czech exile government in London full restoration of the former Czechoslovak republic once the war was won—with borders that would again include the Sudetenland. The provisions of the Munich Agreement were ignored. As early as the fall of 1938, President-in-exile Beneš developed plans for a future population transfer from the Sudeten region in the interest of ethnic purity. Shortly after the collapse of Hitler's Germany in May 1945, Dr. Beneš and his colleagues returned to Prague. Within weeks they initiated sudden expropriations and mass expulsions of the ethnic Sudeten population across the new border into eastern and western Germany, applying methods that caused direct and indirect casualties of about a quarter of a million people and by 1947 created over three million new homeless refugees. Also, many thousands of Sudetens, including anti-Nazi Social Democrats, were interned and maltreated in re-opened former Nazi concentration camps, and any survivors were eventually expelled, some after years.

Earlier, when negotiating the postwar status of Czechoslovakia the Allies had agreed to the concept of a gradual, humane resettlement of the entire Sudeten population, with adequate compensation for their property. But instead they stood by passively when the Czechoslovak government persisted in carrying out its hurried "final solution" of confiscation and expulsion, without preparation and under conditions neither intended in the Allied deliberations nor warranted by the unprecedented state of devastation and human suffering already extant in central Europe.

Within the span of two years most Sudetens had been stripped of their property and belongings and were marched or shipped across the adjacent borders into the four Allied occupation zones of East and West Germany. The remainder of the population was forced out soon after, leaving only a few thousand to an uncertain fate within Czechoslovakia. The Allies were left to cope with the staggering burden of a vast new influx of displaced persons into war-ravaged Germany, where millions of homeless residents and refugees were already causing intractable problems for the military governments. It was not until 1948 that the Iron Curtain descended around Czechoslovakia, soon after the Communists staged a forcible takeover of the democratic government in Prague.

Foreword

Humanity has endured many armed conflicts in the Twentieth Century, including two world wars. These actually constituted a single conflict that started in 1914 with the assassination in Sarajevo of Prince Franz Ferdinand, the Habsburg heir to the Austro-Hungarian throne, by a Serbian nationalist, and which did not end with the November 1918 armistice but rather with the unconditional surrender of Germany in May 1945. In a very real sense, it was a "Thirty Years War"—just as brutal and devastating as the earlier European conflict that started in Prague and concluded with the signing of the Peace of Westphalia in 1648.

As time wears on, it appears that a mythology of the so-called Second World War has taken hold, so that historians only focus on certain aspects of it and deliberately ignore others. To any observer not ideologically committed, an event such as the expulsion of 15 million human beings—in the process of which nearly three million perished—constitutes a major historical and demographic revolution. And yet, the millions of stories that accompanied this event have remained largely unknown and unpublished. No one has cared to listen, because the victims were not consensus victims or "politically correct" victims: they were Germans from East Prussia, Pomerania, Silesia, East Brandenburg, Sudetenland, the Danube basin, where their ancestors had lived for seven hundred years, centuries before the Europeans "discovered" and settled the American continent.

Our modern understanding of human rights teaches us that all human beings are equal in rights and dignity, that no one should be discriminated against because of his ethnic or religious origin. All people have a right to their identity, to their own culture and language. In an ideal world they would respect each other and minority populations would live in peace and harmony with their neighbors. Throughout history, however, races and ethnic groups have sought to subjugate others, religious leaders have discriminated against members of other religions, atheistic regimes have persecuted believers.

For the contemporary American or Western European intellectual the Second World War manifested some of the worst traits that humanity can bring forth—intolerance, persecution, genocide. Hitler's crimes against humanity surely constitute one of the nadirs of the history of Western man, crimes that were documented and condemned at the Nuremberg Trials.

War crimes and crimes against humanity, however, did not begin or end with the Third *Reich*. It is a sad commentary on man's inability to learn from the past that we have had to witness many aggressive wars after Hitler sent his armies occupying half of Europe. We have seen mass murder and "ethnic cleansing" occurring in other parts of the world, most recently in Cambodia, Rwanda and the former Yugoslavia.

The subject of Erich Helfert's book is not familiar to the American reader—but it should be, because he recounts an important story, that of the suffering of people much like us, of injustices that have been hitherto ignored by the press. Everyone knows the maxim "to the victor belongs the spoils," and to the spoils also belongs the writing of history. The principle of *vae victis*, however, in no way stops us today from wanting to know more. Fortunately, in a free society we can. Fifty years after the conclusion of the Second World War, it is surely not too early and also not too late to inquire into other aspects of that conflict.

The author tells us of the ethnic Germans of Bohemia and Moravia, who lived there for many hundreds of years in peace with their Czech neighbors. It was under the banner of self-determination that the Czechs were granted national independence in 1919. The three and a half million ethnic Germans of this region also demanded self-determination for themselves, and their plea was heard and endorsed by the American Delegation at the Paris Peace Conference. Indeed, the Commission under Harvard Professor Archibald Coolidge clearly recommended that the territories settled by these ethnic Germans be incorporated into

Germany and Austria. Unfortunately for all concerned—and for the peace of Europe—short-sighted politicians denied them self-determination at the Treaties of Versailles and St. Germain and forced them into the new experimental State of Czechoslovakia. The archives of the League of Nations are full of petitions sent by these ethnic Germans denouncing the discrimination, confiscations and indignities they were subjected to in the ensuing 19 years, until the unwanted union was dissolved by the Munich Agreement of 1938. If Hitler himself had not violated this agreement in 1939 by invading Bohemia and Moravia, and if he had not started—and lost—a war against the rest of the world, the Germans of Bohemia and Moravia, the Germans of East Prussia and Silesia would still be in their historic homelands.

To those readers who think that "the Germans" had it coming to them, I would suggest that there were a lot of decent people among them: common folk, farmers, industrial workers, secretaries, lawyers, doctors, university professors—just as innocent (or guilty) as we are. They just had the misfortune of being Germans at the time when a madman like Hitler assumed power and unleashed a war. They were as unfortunate as the Russian people who had to endure Stalin's purges, massacres and GULAGs, just as unlucky as the Cambodians who had to live through the genocidal regime of Pol Pot and his Khmer Rouge, just as accursed as the Iraqi people who still have to see how they survive the crimes of Saddam Hussein. The Germans, the Russians, the Cambodians, the Iraqis—they too are human beings like us, and just as deserving of respect and compassion. There is no justification to hold them collectively guilty for the crimes of dictators—none of whom were democratically elected.

To those who would doubt the descriptions in this book, I should say that there are tens of thousands of authentic reports in the German Federal Archives at Koblenz, some of them published in the 8-volume "Documents on the Expulsion," edited by the late Professor Theodor Schieder and the German-Jewish scholar Hans Rothfels, who emigrated to the United States in 1938, taught at Notre Dame University, and returned to Germany after the war to become Professor of History at the University of Tübingen.

And those who would discard German testimonies just because they are German should consider going to the National Archives in Washington and consulting the U.S. Army documents on Czechoslovakia 1945, showing that U.S. military personnel had been eyewitnesses to many instances where Germans were forcibly evicted from their homes, "frequently being stripped there or on the road of the few personal possessions they could still carry, and being beaten if resistance was shown."[1] As the U. S. Political Advisor Robert Murphy repeatedly reported to Secretary of State James Byrnes, U.S. military authorities were increasingly concerned over the anti-Czech sentiments which had developed among U.S. soldiers as a consequence of these frequent abuses committed upon defenseless civilians.[2] Indeed, American soldiers had to intervene many times to protect German women and children from excesses by the Czech militia.

But it was not only the period immediately after the end of the war during which atrocities and injustices were committed against the German civilian population. The crimes and abuses continued during "peacetime," well into 1946 and 1947. And for many Germans the end of the war meant not only spoliation and expulsion—it also meant internment, starvation and death. One of the worst camps in postwar Czechoslovakia was the old Nazi concentration camp of Theresienstadt in northern Bohemia. Conditions under the new Czech administration are described by H.G. Adler, a former Jewish inmate:

> Many amongst them (the new inmates) had undoubtedly become guilty during the years of occupation, but in the majority they were children and juveniles, who had only been locked up because they were Germans. Only because they were Germans...? This sentence sounds frighteningly familiar; only the word "Jews" had been changed to "Germans." The rags the

---

[1] *Foreign Relations of the United States,* 1945, vol. 2, p. 1286
[2] Ibid., p. 1291

Germans had been clothed with were smeared with swastikas. The people were abominably fed and mal-treated, and they were no better off than one was used to from German concentration camps.[3]

Erich Helfert's book illustrates many of these crimes and abuses and makes them all the more believable, because he is telling a personal story with real people and real situations. He forces us to rethink the stereotypes we know from television and the press. Yes, Germans can be victims too—not only victimizers. No, there is no monopoly of suffering in the Second World War—nor, for that matter, in any other war. Perhaps this story will one day be filmed. There are lessons worth reviewing, most importantly our common humanity, our capacity for both doing good and perpe-trating evil, our need to share our suffering and to find someone out there who listens and understands.

Alfred M. de Zayas

J.D. (Harvard), Dr.phil. (Göttingen)
Visiting Professor of International Law,
DePaul University, Chicago.
Author of: "*Nemesis at Potsdam*" (University of Nebraska Press),
"*The Wehrmacht War Crimes Bureau*"
(University of Nebraska Press),
"*A Terrible Revenge*" (St. Martin's Press)

---

[3] H. G. Adler, Theresienstadt, 1955, p. 214. See also Th. Schieder, *Documents on the Expulsion,* vol. 4, p. 76. Also personal interview with a German survivor of this camp

ONE

The Expulsion

His face was a hostile mask of unrestrained power, a power conceived by turmoil and nurtured by greed. Dvořák had returned, clutching an official document littered with stamps and scrawled signatures which, in the name of the new Czechoslovak government, declared him owner of the confiscated Wildert property. His dark eyes squinted behind gold-rimmed glasses, betraying covetous impatience to seize at last the villa and its valuable contents.

"You have fifteen minutes to take essential things, *Pane* Wildert!" His low voice was menacing as he spat out the words in heavily accented German. "I repeat my warning—it is strictly *verboten* to take anything valuable! Your wife and your son will also follow my colleagues' orders. *Rozumíte*—eh, you understand? You will be taken to a worker's flat near your company. You will be evacuated from there when the time comes!"

Dvořák paused for effect. Emboldened by his own officiousness, the stocky gray-haired bureaucrat, dressed in his best suit, postured and waved his hand in an imperious gesture. He had power now and he savored its intoxicating tingle. He brimmed with the smug self-righteousness of nationalistic fervor and retribution. Two companions hovered behind him, their eyes eager.

The hall clock struck a quarter to twelve. Its resounding triple chimes assaulted the senses with shimmering vibrations. Friedrich Wildert glanced at the paper in Dvořák's hand, then lifted his eyes to meet the usurper's impertinent stare. He had a tall, gaunt frame and a noticeable stoop marred his former erect bearing. The vested business suit no longer fit his shrunken body;

only the fine English fabric, now worn, was a reminder of long forgotten better times. The upheavals of the dark weeks preceding and following the Allied victory had drained Friedrich of emotion. His ulcer burned and he pressed his left side.

Somehow he found it easier to face this kind of reality than coping with one nerve-shattering close call after another during the Allied bombings and the Russian invasion. The worst anxiety came as soon as the war ground to an exhausted end in early May 1945, when the new Czechoslovak government began in great haste to expel the region's native German-speaking population across the newly established border with Germany a few miles to the north. Most inhabitants of the Wilderts' own neighborhood disappeared in several sudden spasms of displacement. With lingering regret Friedrich wished again that their recent family suicide attempt had not failed.

So Dvořák has managed to get the villa after all, he thought. That man knew what he wanted, as did all the other vultures! Friedrich carried an official document certifying that a new Czech management needed him to arrange the transfer of the German-owned company he had managed for twenty-five years. This piece of paper so far had spared him and the family from evacuation. Now it was obvious the certificate did not protect them from the loss of their own home until they would also be herded across the border. Anger and frustration smoldered behind the impassive demeanor Friedrich learned to display as a protective shield, ever since all that was normal had crumbled along with the ruins that were everywhere.

He must have good connections, this self-important postal clerk! Angrily Friedrich recalled that in the headlong rush by Czech nationals to grab the area's expropriated homes Dvořák and his postmen were particularly well informed about the value and contents of the properties located in the better sections of the city, many having delivered mail there before the German takeover of the Sudetenland seven years earlier. Now they were closing in and some already lived in neighboring properties.

"*Rozumíte, Pane* Wildert?" Dvořák's hoarse voice was impatient. Friedrich nodded curtly and turned to Maria, clad in the black of mourning, gently touching her arm, and then to Anton, their fourteen year old son who gaped uncertainly at the exchange.

"Let's go." Anton glanced at his father's drawn face, surprised by the calm but firm tone in his voice. Although pale and thin from growing up on wartime rations, he was already tall enough to look directly into his father's eyes, although he rarely did so out of respect and because he was touched by the deep suffering he discerned in them. Still uncomfortable with his own long limbs, protruding ears, and the aquiline nose he inherited from his mother, Anton was often plagued by shyness and felt out of place, although he had managed to deal with some of the difficult situations of the past year in ways that surprised him.

Now he struggled with waves of estrangement, fear, and excitement all at the same time. Thus began another part of the drama, an ongoing series of episodes that forced him to alternate between searing flashes of grown-up reality and danger and escape into youthful daydreaming and play. It was often difficult for him to decide how he should react, what feelings were appropriate, and what was expected of him when facing overwhelming change in everything he knew.

With his parents, Anton had watched as part of the city's population was forcibly led away during the past several weeks. His friends from nearby houses had been among the stream of unhappy humanity trudging in the street below them, prodded into the unknown by soldiers' rifle butts. Laden with sparse bundles of belongings, most of the expellees were women, children and elderly people pushing baby buggies and tugging carts, many crying silently as they walked. Only a few able-bodied men were among them, as most men drafted into the *Wehrmacht* and later into the pitiful *Volkssturm*[1] in the final months of the war were missing, taken prisoner, or dead. How strange it had been to see the cumbersome groups passing by! Waving furtively from the large picture window that overlooked the quiet street and the main road leading north, the boy felt awkward not to be among these people, many of whom he had known since childhood. He

[1] Peoples' Front, a militia of older men and teenage boys

tried but could not imagine what their feelings must be or what fate awaited them across the border.

How still the neighborhood had become! Where were his friends now? Anton only half comprehended the stories his father reported to the family: tales of despair, suicide, and hopeless drifters that trickled back from the war-ravaged province of Saxony, across the recently re-established border with Germany. There the occupying Russians could or would do little for the tens of thousands of new refugees dumped in the area without a place to go.

The latest rumors were that the Russian general in charge of the Saxon region had finally insisted that the fledgling Czechoslovak government halt the mass expulsions into his area until he brought some order to the growing chaos. The evacuations had indeed ceased abruptly ten days ago, but for how long? Would he ever see his friends again? When would he and his parents be marched across the border? What would it be like to go, and where would they stay?

Anton felt the firm nudge of his father's hand on his shoulder. He bounded up the curving staircase, as always taking two steps at a time, to fetch the bundles his mother had packed and repacked in careful preparation for this moment. The Wilderts were the lucky ones, having had the chance to prepare—so many others had been taken by complete surprise.

Friedrich and Maria followed slowly, ascending the carpeted stairs for the last time. They looked at each other without words, relieved in a way that the waiting was over. Maria fought back her tears as she thought of Johann, her elder son, who was killed in the neighboring province of Saxony during the last days of fighting, a month or so before his seventeenth birthday, a boy soldier in makeshift uniform. He was better off than the living, she kept saying to herself, he was spared the cruel journey into the unknown. Nevertheless Maria had tried to argue Friedrich out of their suicide attempt a few weeks ago. When they went ahead but did not succeed she knew instinctively that somehow they must keep going, for Anton's sake. The boy had already picked up two of the sacks in the guest room and wrestled them down the staircase, almost eagerly. As he reached the bottom step Dvořák's piercing stare confronted him.

"These must be inspected so nothing valuable leaves the house!" Dvořák drew himself up to his full medium height and motioned his companions to the center of the hall. The men stopped examining the furniture and Maria's collection of porcelain statuary and sidled over to seize the bundles from Anton. Dumping the contents on the carpet they began to spread apart the clothes, linens and utensils Maria packed so carefully. Anton watched anxiously as eager hands rifled through the family belongings. He turned to look at his parents as if to seek help, even though he knew they could do nothing. Friedrich and Maria descended the staircase with the remaining bags and stopped halfway, watching the search in silence.

Not averting his eyes from the piles on the floor Dvořák snapped, "There are too many items of men's clothing! This suit is confiscated!" He stooped to retrieve one of Friedrich's suits and tossed it aside.

"My son will need some of my husband's things; he is outgrowing his own," Maria pleaded from above in passable Czech.

Dvořák merely shrugged and firmly shook his gray head. "Is confiscated." Then he turned to face Friedrich and Maria and with a quick wave of his hand ordered them to turn over their last bundles to the greedy searchers. Again the contents were unceremoniously dumped on the floor. Friedrich flushed a deep red and took one step forward, but Maria pulled his sleeve in warning.

Dvořák ignored the Wilderts, intent on missing nothing in the shifting piles before him that might be worth taking. Even used clothing was invaluable in times when goods could not be bought at any price and barter was the only way to meet daily needs.

Friedrich clutched his left side and struggled to remain calm. A consuming inner fury made him dizzy. Over and over he told himself that he should be glad he was not being pushed around at the point of a gun, as other intruders had done to him before. Yet there was enough spirit left in his tired mind to kindle a flare of searing resentment against being robbed in the name of authority, without recourse. But he also knew that to resist meant death, or even worse, internment in the newly re-opened concentration camps. He repressed his anger and stood motionless.

Anton watched the men finish the examination. Satisfied that they found no gold or jewelry in the bundles they seemed pleased with the booty they had appropriated: Friedrich's best suit, a pair of shoes, some ties, a new shirt, and a fine set of bed linen from Maria's dowry. This was a part of the drama the boy could not have imagined. In fact, everything was so strange and unlike his secure childhood and its dreams of the future that he had to cope with the unknown on a daily basis. By now he learned to fear the capricious use of power by strangers, and every time he witnessed it he was choked by helplessness. Romantic boyhood visions of bravery paled against the overwhelming reality of experience.

In such moments Anton felt a new and disturbing sense of eerie detachment, of looking on—just as if these frightening things were happening to someone else. The same strange feeling came over him again as he watched the men pursue their painstaking inspection.

"You may put these things back in the bags now." Dvořák's voice sounded almost magnanimous.

Without responding the Wilderts crouched on the floor to retrieve the diminished piles of their belongings and stuffed them back into the strong sacks Maria had made from the boys' old tent. The three intruders looked on in icy silence. The careless way the men had treated her neatly packed necessities momentarily offended Maria's housewifely instincts. But all the time her mind clamored, to no avail, for the meaning of what was happening to them. She was swept up in a surging emotion of finality, the hurt of having to leave the prosperous house where—it seemed a lifetime ago—she happily raised her two boys. One of them would never be hers to embrace again. Inconspicuously wiping her eyes she tried to concentrate on tying up the bundles.

The repacking finished, the Wilderts went to the hall closet to retrieve warm overcoats and hats and put them on over their regular clothes despite the heat of the morning. They learned from observing the refugees streaming past that the more they could wear, the less they would have to carry. The men watched closely but did not interfere. As final preparation they carefully pinned white armbands to their coat sleeves above the left elbow, feeling conspicuous and even more helpless. This strictly enforced symbol of subordination was a glaring mark that conveyed the same ominous meaning as the yellow stars which the Nazis forced their Jewish victims to wear when they ruled the land. Wrapped up uncomfortably the Wilderts dragged their belongings to the front entrance of the villa and out onto the stone landing of the stairs that descended to the garden path.

Anton ran to the empty garage to fetch a small blue wooden wagon he and his brother played with as children. The cart had been rebuilt and strengthened long ago in the company's workshop for use as primitive transport. Its new wheels were fashioned of bent iron rods, as rubber tires had become unobtainable. The cart bounced noisily on the fieldstone path as Anton pulled it toward the front steps. He dropped the handle, cast a furtive glance at the silent Dvořák above and hastened back once more for his bicycle with the patched balloon tires. The worn rubber grips and pitted chrome of the handle bar felt familiar and comforting.

"What is this?" The sharp voice of authority lashed out at the boy. "This is not allowed!"

Anton gripped the handles tightly. Clutching his bike he stood rigidly, feeling trapped. Above him, in a blur, he saw his father and mother holding on to each other beside the pile of sacks, and with them was the sinister stranger who acted so possessively about what had been his home, his world, his things.

Moments of charged silence lingered. Finally Dvořák shrugged and gestured condescendingly, "I'll make an exception this time."

Anton leaned the bike against the stone wall and slowly climbed the steps, avoiding Dvořák's stare. Father and son dragged the bundles down and piled them onto the small conveyance in an awkward heap. They secured the load as best they could with several loops of old clothesline. Maria who watched their efforts from the landing, joined them when they tied the last knot.

Her face was drawn and pale, marked by the recent sorrow over Johann's death. The black mourning clothes and hat contrasted sharply with the pallor of her skin. But she set her features into a stoic mask, behind which she hid her private agony of grief and fear. In the confrontations of recent weeks her natural talent for acting and her barely adequate knowledge of the new language of the land proved helpful. By this time, however, her innate love of the dramatic had been satiated with the shocks and strain of the roles the upheaval forced her to act out in this real-life drama.

Maria carried her handbag and the small suitcase with the family photographs and essential papers that were the last to be rifled through by the intruders. Friedrich picked up the handle of the blue wagon, but Anton hastily took it out of his hand. "Please let me pull this, *Vati*, you can push my bike." Guiding his son's bicycle with one hand and clutching his scuffed briefcase in the other, Friedrich turned and slowly walked toward the white garden gate. As he followed the path he tried to understand why he felt so relieved. Was he so numbed by the torrent of events that he no longer cared? Had not his worldly status been represented by this stately home filled with tasteful furnishings and valuables?

The sudden loss of his first-born son a few weeks ago sapped much of what strength remained in his weakened body. Over the past year he watched his world collapse under shattering blows to familiar values and with episodes of intense personal danger. Haunted by unremitting Nazi government pressure to increase his company's output, debilitated by poor food rations and a gnawing stomach ulcer, Friedrich's mind had long been racked by an insistent subconscious drumbeat, growing louder and louder, ominous and suggestive: "End it all, end it all, and get some peace!"

Some weeks past this sinister urge won him over. Together the three of them attempted suicide, but at the last moment fate intervened. Now he seemed not to care any more. He went through the motions of the final act of the drama, lacking a script, like a stricken ship in stormy waters, drifting wherever the winds would take it. He was tired. Friedrich stopped and took one last brief glance at the villa and the front steps where Dvořák posed in a domineering stance, hands folded across his chest, a faint twitch at the corners of the thin-lipped mouth.

The bastard is pleased with his coup and feeling very much at home already, he thought. Friedrich's anger flared up like the random sputters of brightness a flickering candle tosses vainly against the dark. But just as suddenly he smothered it and the heavy shadows closed in again. He saw his wife follow him, her mask intact except for the moisture brimming in her eyes that were dark wells staring blankly ahead.

Maria also turned back once more. She was determined not to look at Dvořák—she would not grant him this final satisfaction of the conquest. Instead she let her eyes roam over the facade of the villa, the curved bay windows, the climbing roses on white lattice, the comforting red-brown tile roof drawn down deeply over both sides, like a woman's hat. It had been a fine home, she thought. Then, capriciously, her mind seized upon the once so familiar feeling that she would have liked it much better had some of the villa's rooms been larger. More spacious rooms would have shown off her lovely furniture to greater advantage. But the men, her late father and Friedrich, insisted on setting the final dimensions of the plans. All those years she had been quite determined to rebuild the place eventually, and she never let Friedrich forget that her wishes were overruled. Well, there would be no plans to rebuild the house now—indeed, no plans of any sort. It was all over. Why was she even capable of such thoughts after all that had happened? It was strange, the ideas that surfaced under stress! She suddenly remembered the insistent, haunting way a simple folk tune plagued her mind for months on end after the unexpected death of her father, whom she adored. What tune would it be this time, after Johann and after today?

Anton maneuvered the top-heavy cart along the curving garden path toward the gate, past the green front lawn with its neat flower beds and trimmed fruit trees, past the colorful blooms and mosses in the rock garden along the fence. The iron wheels made a hollow grinding noise, and he was too busy guiding the clumsy vehicle to stop and turn around. Friedrich opened the gate, pushed the bicycle through and helped Anton lower the cart one step down to the sloping sidewalk. The hard wheel rims struck the granite pavement sharply. Maria followed behind, deep in thought. One of Dvořák's men stepped forward hastily to catch up with the Wilderts. He was under orders to take them to their temporary quarters. From habit Anton closed the garden gate securely for the last time, hearing the familiar click of the latch snapping into place. He felt no emotion, only numb remoteness. The boy peered once more through the grate of white pickets and saw Dvořák still standing on top of the stairs, staring after the departing family.

Their guard jerked his head to the left, the direction they were to go, up the slope past the silent villa on the corner. They turned left again onto the main street that led toward the distant center of the city and the outlying industrial district. Perspiring in their heavy clothing from the warmth of the day they plodded slowly alongside the stone walls crowned with white picket fences and ornamental iron, verdant with cascading shrubs and trees—stately barriers that framed the lifeless villas of their expelled neighbors. They had already been marched across the border, only five miles away, which now seemed an endless distance to the Wilderts.

This was the street where—just seven years ago—the crowds had cheered the armed German takeover. It was also the street where during the past few weeks they first witnessed the desperate shuffle of retreating German soldiers, then the massed armored might of the victorious Russian army, and finally the despair of endless streams of expellees. Over seven short years this thoroughfare, now deserted, had been the stage for vivid displays of the ebb and flow of human folly.

The cart's noise made Anton self-conscious at first, but he soon grew used to the echoing grind and clatter. Hardly any traffic stirred on the cobbled pavement, but when a solitary Russian army vehicle rumbled past it briefly drowned out the cart's irritating "rroing-rroing-rroing." The street had been Anton's route in his daily walk to and from school. Officials suspended all classes in early April because of the ever more frequent American daytime air raids and the surprise low-level intrusions by Russian fighter bombers. On the left he recognized rows of jagged impact holes gouged into the pavement and running straight up the wall of one of the villas.

He thought of the plane that suddenly roared in low over the horizon, close to the ground, dark and ominous, bright red stars marking wings, sides, and tail. Its powerful twin engines whining the attacker spat little orange flames from the cannons that flanked the gleaming glass-topped body, sending crazy spurts of stone chips and dust scattering as the bullets crashed into the cobbled pavement. Anton and his friend flattened themselves against the nearest stone wall at the sight of the enemy aircraft and with boyish excitement watched it thunder past so low that they glimpsed the pilot's helmet. Unhurt, they scrambled up to run home, both scared and fascinated that the Russian plane fired at them and others in the open. But that was long ago, or so it seemed to the boy. Now he was being led with his parents along an empty street, caught up in an inexorable drama that had plunged him from the excitement of adventure into the depth of raw fear.

The family and their guard approached the crest of the gentle hill, crowned by modern apartment blocks on one side and a semicircle of small shops set in a landscaped plaza on the other, with more apartments and houses rising behind. Shell holes and pockmarks left by random bullets littered many facades. The cruel steel treads of hundreds of heavy armored vehicles had maimed pavements, sidewalks and decorative grass strips when they lumbered through the area. Several streets joined the main road and led off in five directions, giving the wide hilltop intersection the name "Star." Most of the stores were shuttered and lifeless. The few still open had empty show windows plastered with the latest decrees and rulings of the new Czech government, blazing in crudely printed black and red. Very few people moved about—and fewer yet who wore white armbands. The street car tracks that swung in a wide arc through the intersection were rusted; no trolleys served the suburb after the last bombing raids decimated much of the old downtown area. A Russian patrol in brown uniforms idled near the kiosk in the small neglected park, smoking, their gray slotted submachine guns pointing to the ground. They took no notice of the family.

The blue cart bobbed and clattered over the marred cobblestone pavement, causing mad echoes to bounce off the lifeless buildings. The Wilderts traversed the Star and followed the main street with its trolley track descending toward the industrial basin. In former times Anton would have turned left at the Star to walk to his school located in the older parts of the suburb. He missed the familiar pattern of daily classes. How he yearned to play with his schoolmates, teasing the girls—they called them "the women" in condescending pre-puberty swagger—and savoring their terrified shrieks when sneaking up from behind and placing shiny brown inch-long "May bugs" to crawl in their hair. Anton always arrived home from school with disheveled clothes and scuffed bare knees, evidence of boisterous goings on with his pals. Johann patiently tried to be a steadying influence on his rambunctious younger brother, but with little effect.

Anton fought back his tears at the thought of his brother. While he often caused Johann to be angry with him, for good reason, he secretly harbored an abiding respect for Johann's common sense, maturity, and guidance, something he would rarely admit openly. In fact, the two boys, born on the same day three years apart were close like twins, sharing their feelings, thoughts and dreams, often talking late into the night. How he cried when Johann left for the front in December, and how hard it was to understand that he would never come back and be his good friend again. The boy shivered with the chill of loneliness.

They neared the bend in the street from which parts of the wide Elbe river valley became visible, where ancient volcanic hills gracefully framed the horizon in many shades of hazy green. The distant fields, meadows and vineyards were lush, a verdant garden-like setting of pleasant color patterns undulating with the soft curves of the river and the gentle slopes of the valley. Near the bottom of the hill, in stark contrast, lay the familiar expanse of walled factories built long ago, dreary masses of brickwork, soot-darkened with age, topped by massive smokestacks now cold amidst a maze of rail-yards and glistening piles of coal from the nearby mines.

Some of these vast chemical and manufacturing complexes burned uncontrollably for days after the last knock-out bombing raids during the spring, a macabre spectacle Anton watched with tingling fascination. The distance spread a deceptive veil over the ruinous wounds struck by bombs that rained from hundreds of aircraft, wounds reopened by the final sporadic strafing and shelling of the victorious Russian forces. Yet somehow the buildings of Friedrich's company, located at the nearest edge of the industrial district, had escaped much of the heavier damage.

This was the street Friedrich had followed every day to and from his office, an enforced walk ever since the company car and driver were commandeered during the first year of the war. Anton had visited his father often and knew the way well. But instead of continuing downhill their wordless guard once more jerked his head, signaling to turn left at the next intersection. None of the Wilderts had ever entered the narrow side street. The pavement ended abruptly and the blue cart became harder to pull in the loose dirt and gravel, the narrow wheel rims straining against deep ruts. Friedrich passed the bicycle handle to Maria and helped Anton tug the cart slowly up the sloping road. Both sides of the street were lined with small, modest bungalows built just before the war when industrial expansion had made more housing necessary.

Once dotted by dairy farms and vegetable gardens, the neighborhood now had no trees or greenery to soften the ugliness of pitted brick facades and stained, peeling stucco. Unfinished when the war began, this part of the city had a forlorn, neglected look made worse by the scars from stray bombs and shells that struck some of the houses. The recent evacuations left very few people in the area. No life stirred as they passed house after silent house.

Their bored guard trudged a few steps ahead of them, keeping up a steady pace. As they trekked behind the Wilderts' spirits sank. Under the stress of having to leave their home they had given little thought to what conditions they might realistically expect. The street began to slope downward again, revealing more of the dreary monotony of the rows of small houses. A tiny green field opened the view to their right, and in the distance they again saw the hazy jumble of factories, the smokestacks, and the long lines of steel masts linked by strings of suspended gondolas, rows of dark dots receding in the direction of the nearby coal mines. The raw industrial ugliness felt oppressively close in the drab surroundings.

At last their sullen guard stopped, pointed to the left and entered a paved front yard that opened beside a neat bungalow. Set back from the street stood a small two-story apartment house flanked by storage sheds. The gray utilitarian building was devoid of any adornment or plants to soften its plain, box-like appearance. Though shabby, the simple structure and its surroundings at least looked clean. The man crossed the paved yard and approached the front door in the center of the house. As the Wilderts climbed the two stone steps to the entry and followed their guard into the tiny hall they noticed an apartment door slightly ajar, from which an old woman's curious eyes peered through the crack. Opening further, she glanced at the Wilderts' white armbands, but spotting the guard she closed her door hastily.

Climbing the narrow wooden staircase past scuffed and faded gray walls they came to the upper floor landing where a small window overlooked the drab front yard. Their guard officiously removed a ring of jangling keys from his pocket, selected the right one and opened an apartment door after breaking the stamped paper seal taped across the lock and frame. The bold Czech inscription on the seal read: "Confiscated."

The man spoke up for the first time in broken German. "You will stay here until evacuation!" After they had entered he added menacingly, "I warn you, we have inventory of everything here! You have trouble if take anything! *Rozumíte*?" He glowered at his charges. Friedrich flushed as if he had been struck in the face. His repressed fury flared at the thought that the brazen warning came from one of the men who just helped themselves to all of his property. He felt Maria's steadying touch on his arm and he wrapped himself again in the mantle of stoic blandness.

The Wilderts stood in a tiny room, a kitchen and living area combined. There was just enough space for a coal-fired stove, a sink, a hot plate, some cupboards, a sofa and a table with three plain chairs. Next to the window, on a narrow shelf above the head of the hard sofa was an old-fashioned radio. From the living area a door led to an equally tiny bedroom, crammed with a double bed, a wardrobe, a chest of drawers, a small mirrored dresser and a padded chair. Tucked away in the far corner stood a forlorn baby crib.

The place was spotless, the furniture plain but lovingly maintained. Hesitantly Maria opened the doors and drawers of the wardrobe. They still held the neatly stored belongings of a young couple and child: linen in a tidy stack, some clothes, towels, and personal things. It was obvious that the family had not been allowed to take much with them during their hasty expulsion. How were they driven out? Where might they be now? Maria stepped back into the kitchen where she found sets of dishes, pots and pans, and cutlery. She felt like an intruder in a small world suddenly frozen after the mysterious disappearance of its inhabitants.

Their guard was watching. His expression of bored indifference changed briefly only once, when he assumed the unaccustomed posture of authority that circumstances bestowed on him. His propped-up self-image was quick to deflate when the Wilderts did not react to his bluster. Less sure of himself now he grumbled curtly, "You will be contacted," and turned to leave. The family listened to his heavy steps descending, and then they were alone.

Anton stepped to the kitchen window and gazing out at the drab view thought of the moments of terror and the seemingly endless drama that brought them to this place. What further shocks were to come?

TWO

The Occupation

September 1938

"One, two, three, *Sieg Heil!*" Over and over young voices shouted the slogan, breaking shrilly with exuberance. Curious about the shrieks outside Anton opened the side panel of the picture window on the upper floor of the Wildert villa and saw three of his neighborhood friends sitting on the low fieldstone pedestal of the white picket fence, clapping their hands rhythmically as they chanted their "*Sieg Heils*" in the warm afternoon sun. Anton closed the window and hurried downstairs into the front garden, his long blond hair flying. His friends were still chanting when he bolted out of the white picket gate.

"Haven't you heard, Anton?" squeaked Helmut, a schoolmate who just that month started the second grade with him. Anton looked puzzled.

With childish superiority Helmut proclaimed, "The Germans will soon be coming, and then the Czechs can't kick us around anymore."

"How do you know that?"

"It was on the radio, *Dummkopf!*" Anton gave Helmut a half-hearted shove, and Helmut pushed right back, pleased to know more than his friend.

"What's going on here?" Johann, Anton's ten-year-old brother joined the group from the back garden, curious about the noise in the street. Helmut, impatient now, repeated the news as briefly as he could, eager to resume his chanting. Anton began to shout along with the others, but his brother hastily pulled him away.

"They aren't here yet, and we'd better be careful," Johann

warned. The serious dark-haired boy gazed uncomfortably up and down the deserted neighborhood street. "What if the Czech police hear you and put you in jail! Don't you shout in front of our house! Go home and holler there, if you want to." Helmut and the others frowned, not sure what to do. But Johann was older and stronger and obviously determined to put an end to their fun. After a reluctant pause they shrugged and ambled away, still chanting, but with less zeal. Anton trotted behind his brother back into the front garden.

"Silly kids," Johann muttered, "don't they know it is dangerous to speak up against the authorities?" His eyes brightened. "Hey, let's find out if there is more news!" The brothers raced back to the open front door, bounded up the curving staircase to the living room and switched on the radio. Impatiently twisting the knobs as they waited for the tubes to warm up they tried several stations. At last they tuned in Radio Berlin. Flourishes of martial music blared from the loudspeaker. Then the deliberate, slow cadences of the announcer's voice filled the room.

"This is the *Grossdeutsche Rundfunk*.[1] We repeat again our special bulletin that the *Führer* has just returned from Munich, where he achieved another glorious success in his final conference with Prime Minister Chamberlain of Great Britain. A formal treaty was signed today to unite the Sudetenland with the German Fatherland. This agreement will finally put an end to the oppression of our three million Sudeten brothers by the Czechoslovak government in Prague. Soon the unjust border will be gone and the Sudeten population need no longer pay homage to a foreign regime." Rousing martial music resumed as the boys looked at each other excitedly. So it was true!

Even as children they became aware of the growing tensions between the Czech administration and the native Sudeten population. The pressures of the last few months felt almost tangible, the atmosphere prickly with danger. There had been clashes between Czech police and Sudeten civilians, and also between Sudetens and some of their Czech neighbors. There were injuries

[1] Greater German Broadcast Service

reported in some of these incidents and the government in Prague repeatedly issued stern warnings to the Sudeten population to refrain from all political activity—especially any demonstrations in support of Hitler's demands.

Every day their parents warned Johann and Anton not to join any gathering of people, to avoid talking about such matters with anyone, and always to come straight home from school or errands. Dinner was a time of discussion among the family as Friedrich relayed the latest rumors flooding the business community and the occasional real news he learned from the owners of his company who resided in Germany. In recent weeks the conversations touched on little else. The boys sensed that their father was worried not only about what was happening in the Sudetenland, but also about the broader developments in Germany.

"Why does he scream so much?" Friedrich said incredulously whenever the radio vibrated with the dictator's ranting bombast. He often spoke of his fear that the Sudetenland might sink ultimately into a political quagmire far worse than the oppressive conditions now prevailing.

Those circumstances were bad enough. Discrimination against the Sudeten population increased steadily. Anton and Johann overheard their two maternal uncles complain that their university training in Prague, already difficult because of the requirement to use the complex Czech language, would become worthless if they were not given the chance to use it in meaningful employment. Even before the boys were born, Friedrich saw his own promising career in one of the largest Czech industrial enterprises jeopardized. One day he was informed that unless he became fluent in the Czech language and also modified his Austrian outlook he would have no future with the firm. He reluctantly resigned and accepted a position with a much smaller local company owned by a wealthy family of German industrialists where he rapidly rose to the top, managing all Sudeten operations for the absentee owners.

The brothers also learned about the expanding role of Nazi sympathizers among the frustrated Sudetens. Such agitators found the festering discontent fertile soil in which to plant and nourish the seeds of radical change, pushing onto a reluctant majority the beguiling idea of finding common ground with their ever more powerful German neighbors. The leader of the emerging Sudeten German party, Konrad Henlein, frustrated by Prague's intransigence made no secret of his growing alignment with Hitler, whom he extolled as the only means to achieve redress of the population's grievances. The few remaining moderate Sudeten representatives pleaded in vain with the Prague government to find a palatable *modus vivendi* for the Sudetenland within the structure of Czechoslovakia. But events now rapidly overtook them. Everyone anxiously awaited Hitler's next move.

The boys ran downstairs into the front garden when they heard the car doors slam and saw their parents return from a visit to the shopping district. They eagerly told them about the news broadcast. Friedrich looked chagrined; he had already learned about this startling development at the office and talked about little else with Maria while being driven home after meeting her in the city.

"Let's be careful until the Germans are actually here," Friedrich cautioned the family as they ascended the stone steps to the front door landing. "I have my doubts about being taken over by Hitler's Germany, but there's nothing we can do. We'll have to lie low and wait to see what develops." His somber face betrayed his worries. "If only Prague gave us fairer treatment! Now we'll be at the mercy of the Germans, and Lord knows what they're up to, with that fanatic inciting them . . ."

"But Friedrich, things are terrible here—something has to give," Maria said pensively as they entered the hall. She struck a hopeful note, "Perhaps Hitler will bring back prosperity. Think of all our unemployed and how the Czech authorities ignore them—things can only get better."

"You know how I feel, Maria. Every time I was over there I saw the German frenzy to forge ahead. They're getting stronger and more single-minded all the time. I'm afraid they'll roll over anyone who stands in their way. And you can be sure they'll dominate us, too. Look at how they took over Austria and wiped out all independent leadership! We'll just wind up having different rulers—except this time our new masters will speak our language!" Friedrich suddenly looked very tired. The hall clock chimed six, the sounds lingering in the silence.

A beaming Nannerl appeared at the top of the staircase. The young live-in helper followed the political developments with great enthusiasm, eagerly participating in one of the Sudeten youth groups that favored an alignment with Germany. "Oh what great news!" she gushed, "soon we'll be free and united with Germany—I can hardly wait!" Friedrich smiled wanly but said nothing while he helped Maria out of her coat.

The door to the lower stairs opened and old *Herr* Sattler appeared, exuding uncharacteristic liveliness. "Soon we'll share the progress of the Third *Reich*!" the white-haired caretaker cackled gleefully. Momentary surprise passed over his lined ruddy face when he saw Friedrich's wary expression, but he squarely confronted the tall executive without any pretense of his normal deference and blurted, "Our *Führer* will make all of us equal, marching in step to build a greater Germany! And that will also include the so-called "better people"—isn't that so, *Herr Direktor*?" He drew out the last two words in a vaguely challenging tone while continuing to stare boldly into Friedrich's eyes.

Friedrich set his features in noncommittal blandness and replied evenly, but not without authority, "Indeed, a new era has begun, *Herr* Sattler, and there are bound to be many changes. Meanwhile, we still face great risks until the Germans arrive. I suggest we all be very careful about what we say and do. The Czechs are still in control for now. Good evening, *Herr* Sattler."

Sattler nodded curtly and averted his flushed face after hurling a venomous glance at Friedrich. Mumbling to himself he opened the basement door and descended to the caretaker apartment to rejoin his wife. Sattler was a life-long Socialist who quickly embraced the ideology of the new order filtering across the frontier. The Wilderts knew that the retired gatekeeper had become very active in the most fervent group of Nazi sympathizers and would seek every advantage such membership promised in the coming Nazi regime.

"We'll have to be careful of how we act and what we say around the Sattlers from now on." Friedrich grimly turned to

Maria who stood in troubled silence, obviously distraught by the confrontation. Sighing in frustration he added, "God help us, having an informer's eyes and ears in our own house! Listen, any talk of politics or opinions about Hitler and the Third *Reich* must remain strictly among ourselves, and no exceptions! The less said, the better. And this also goes for you, boys, and for you, Nannerl! Do you understand me?"

Anton gaped at his father, his eyes wide and anxious as he tried to comprehend the urgency in his voice. He managed to nod his head without really understanding. Johann saw the serious expression in Friedrich's face, took a deep breath and responded gravely, "Yes, *Vati*, I will be careful."

Nannerl, shaken by Sattler's fierce stare, felt a chill running down her spine. Her bubbly enthusiasm disappeared. Almost inaudibly she mumbled, "Certainly, *Herr Direktor*, I'll be very careful about what I say to anyone." Her full loyalty was with the Wilderts, where she was treated as one of the family. Brightening a little she sought reassurance, "But it *is* good news, isn't it?" Friedrich looked at her briefly without replying. She knew him well enough to gather from his quizzical expression that the situation was not as simple as her impressionable young mind pictured it.

Nannerl prepared a cold supper and the family asked her to join them at the dining table. As they ate the hushed conversation quickly returned to the dangerous times ahead.

"I wonder when Hitler will send in the troops," Friedrich mused while he carefully buttered a slice of crusty bread and reached for the platter of assorted meats and fragrant ham. "There's no firm news, but I expect it will be quite soon—this tension can't go on much longer."

"We still haven't heard from Walter," Maria said with a worried tone in her voice. Her bachelor brother, the youngest of five brothers and sisters had been drafted into the Czech Dragoons a year earlier to serve the obligatory military tour of duty expected of every able-bodied citizen, whether Czech or Sudeten. She sounded alarmed, "If there's any fighting he will be in danger!"

"I don't know, but I hope that with today's treaty the chances of armed conflict are pretty small," Friedrich responded calmly and added, "I'm sure Walter will be home before too long—he won't be needed by the Czechs any more!" Friedrich paused and grimaced. "But he'll very likely wind up in the *Wehrmacht* once the Germans take over." He shook his head as he thought of the irony of it all.

The boys ate silently. Anton absorbed himself in arranging and rearranging bits of bread, meat and salad on his plate with the fork in his left hand, while resting his chin on the other, something not normally overlooked. Johann kept watching his father, hanging on every word, and did not even think of nudging his brother about his table manners.

"Hopefully I'll know more tomorrow. I'll call some of my contacts to find out what they think," Friedrich suggested. He added firmly, "It's quite clear to me that we must be extremely careful not to get involved in any dangerous situation. The Czech authorities are nervous and edgy, while some of our people are becoming too headstrong and pushy for their own good. You all know there have been some nasty incidents. Let's just mind our own business and see what happens."

He turned to Johann. "You were right, Johann, to send the boys home when they chanted out front. The Czechs will see this behavior as a threat and it might put us in danger. Such carelessness could become very unpleasant for us."

The door to the dining room opened and Martha appeared, out of breath and still in her tennis clothes. Maria's younger sister, a pert and coquettish twenty-nine-year-old brunette, lived in the downstairs apartment of the Wildert villa after a brief unsuccessful marriage. Her new job as an insurance representative allowed her enough time to pursue sports and linguistic interests, and she made the most of opportunities to meet eligible men in adult education classes and on the tennis court.

"What great news!" she gushed as she took her seat at the dinner table. Unfolding her napkin she gave everyone a cheerful smile and blew a kiss to Anton, her favorite. "We talked for hours at the tennis club. Everyone is so excited. Sorry for being so late and crashing in like this, but I simply couldn't miss anything!"

Looking around the table she noticed the subdued atmosphere. She raised her eyebrows in surprise and Maria spoke up. "We've been talking, too, Martha. We have some real problems to worry about. You should have seen old Sattler's nasty attitude—it was like a bad omen of things to come. We'll have to be very careful from now on." Friedrich repeated his warning about avoiding any political talk outside the immediate family. Martha ate heartily, nodding to his words, but he couldn't tell if she was really listening. He shrugged almost imperceptibly and looked across the table at Maria who quietly understood.

The talk turned to Germany and its growing strength. "Hitler has written a book, *Mein Kampf*,[2] in which he supposedly lays out his philosophy and goals." Friedrich could not help a wry chuckle. "My friends who tried to read it tell me they couldn't get past the first page because it is so poorly written. Still, I suppose we'll have to get a copy and try to understand what this man is about. After all, he will soon be our leader, too."

Maria demurred, "I can't believe the book is that boring when you think how well he talks on the podium, or at least how convincing he seems to be to his audience." She warmed to the subject, put down her fork and gestured for emphasis. "I must admit I find his voice strangely compelling, even hypnotic. What strength he radiates! But I don't like it when he starts screaming and raving. The man is a puzzle! Yet he's so effective at what he does—look how far Germany has come along under his leadership!"

They almost forgot Nannerl, who ate quietly at the table. She listened attentively to the conversation, thoughts whirling in her mind. Now she spoke up with growing excitement. "We've been told about his early life in our group meetings. He's a simple man, from very humble beginnings, but he's become a great statesman in such a short time!" She rested her chin on her hands and gazed rapturously at the mental image. "He has beautiful pale blue eyes and they say he is quite charming to the ladies. I'd love to see him in person some time, even if only from the distance!" Her voice fluttered with excitement.

[2] My Struggle

"Oh yes, for sure," Friedrich interjected curtly, "but the real question is, what he'll do in the future when he has finished rearming the expanded Germany? Where will he stop? I hear that in his book he openly talks of armed conquest—he certainly uses strong language in his speeches against other countries and their leaders. He shook his head, frowning. "I can't get rid of the feeling that there'll be another war before long, and we'll be right in the middle of it. We may live to regret what happened at Munich in the last two days. I just don't believe we will have 'peace in our time,' as Mr. Chamberlain put it."

Friedrich fell silent and gazed moodily into the distance, his dinner now forgotten. "The other problem is the way Hitler and his henchmen treat all people who disagree with him or whom they don't like," he continued. "My colleagues in Germany tell me that many Jews have been driven from their businesses and homes and placed into some kind of holding camps. No one knows any details, and if they do know I guess they're afraid to talk about it. When I was there last I could see how much of a police state the place has become. I had the feeling of being watched all the time; no one trusts anyone." He grew agitated. "There is so much brutality and hatred in the air over there!"

Nannerl was again eager to share her knowledge. "We've been told in our meetings that the Germans plan to resettle all Jews in a territory of their own, and some have been moved to collection camps as the first step. But they didn't say where that place would be." The girl's excitement ebbed as a sudden realization hit her. Her voice trembled. "But they can't just move people out like that and take away all their property, can they?"

Friedrich responded sharply. "I think the Nazis will do what they want and not hesitate for a moment! *Herr* Hitler has proved all along that he acts as he pleases. Some people believe he's capable of anything and they are not taking any chances. Don't forget that in the last few weeks several Jewish families from our neighborhood left for Switzerland and England. They certainly weren't traveling on holiday—in fact I'm sure they won't be back. Didn't you notice that the Blum villa in the next street is deserted? When I saw *Herr* Blum last month he was most evasive about his plans. He only said something about the whole family wishing to visit their relatives in Switzerland."

"You are just being too negative, Friedrich!" Maria tried to inject a note of calm. Looking at her family seated around the table she smiled hopefully. "Maybe Hitler's bark is worse than his bite—he can't just upset everything! Why not give him a chance to prove that he intends to be peaceful and only wants to correct the wrongs that do exist. We don't really know enough about the situation to make hasty judgments, do we?"

Friedrich shook his head grimly. "Well, I wish I had your faith, Maria, but I am not at all comfortable about what's going on over there, and even less about what's going to happen right here. You saw how old Sattler's attitude has changed already, and that was just our first glimpse of a whole new way of life! I know that in the Nazi system people watch each other and report to the authorities whatever somebody does or says that is not in keeping with the party line—or worse, when they just don't like a person or are simply envious. People who've had no success in everyday life and carry a chip on their shoulder will seek importance through the party and by dominating others. Look at the higher-ups in Germany! Most of them have no real education or achievements—other than success in grabbing power! It'll soon be the same here, and we'd better face it."

Friedrich paused, upset with the fearsome vision only he could see so clearly. An uneasy silence fell over the family, punctured only by the tinkle of glasses, dishes and cutlery as the others continued eating supper. Then Friedrich again brought up the present danger. "I earnestly want to impress on all of you once more that there must be absolutely no talk of these subjects outside of this family. We must be careful as never before. We must not say anything remotely critical of the new order nor the conditions it may bring. This includes talking with friends and neighbors, and especially the Sattlers. From now on we can trust only ourselves, no one else." He faced his sons. "Even your schoolmates and close friends might report to their parents something you told them of our conversations, and there could be serious problems for us. Do you understand what I am saying, boys?"

Johann followed the discussion with rapt attention, trying to comprehend issues far beyond his grasp, while Anton's mind wandered frequently in a childish way. Yet both boys sensed their father's deep anxiety and nodded eagerly in response. Johann, more mature, felt a chilling hint of danger as the seeds of distrust began to sprout in his mind. Anton's innocence was merely touched as by the shadow of a passing cloud. Nannerl's face bespoke sudden insight. Her smiles vanished and she put her arms around the boys in a protective gesture as she led them from the room.

The days that followed were filled with more rumors and tensions. Sudeten organizations sympathetic to the German takeover began to assert themselves openly. Soon neighborhood committees sprang up to enlist everyone in the city to put up suitable decorations on houses and buildings as a festive welcome for the German forces. Vast quantities of freshly printed swastika flags, portraits of Hitler, rolls of bunting and stacks of posters quickly materialized, with slogans proclaiming *"Heim ins Reich!"* and other Nazi rhetoric like *"Ein Volk, ein Reich, ein Führer!"*[3] The stacks of blood-red, white, and black supplies smelled sharply of solvents, the ink barely dry on the coarse paper.

Unmistakable orders circulated that it was a patriotic duty to lavishly decorate every house-front facing a street. The Wilderts complied, along with their neighbors, and filled the bay windows of the villa with the stark symbols of Nazi power. Czech police and soldiers were nowhere to be seen—everyone decorated with impunity even though the prickly sensation of risk still lingered on. Tensely the whole population awaited the arrival of the conquering liberators—or would they be liberating conquerors?

On the morning of the expected German occupation windows and house fronts all over the city were decked out in the harsh colors of the new Germany. The garishly printed slogans assaulted the mind and eyes. Everywhere huge portraits of the mustachioed dictator arrogantly surveyed the swastika-littered scene. Friedrich made a final inspection of the appearance of all three

---

[3] Home into the *Reich*; One people, one *Reich*, one leader

levels of the villa, conscious of the roving bands of sympathizers who self-righteously judged the appropriateness or insufficiency of the decorations for the great day. Satisfied that the villa would pass muster, Friedrich and the family joined the crowds forming in the main street far down the slope of the hill. The boys begged to go and watch the troops marching in; Nannerl supported their pleas until Friedrich and Maria relented.

There was a festive and convivial mood as people filled the sidewalks in anticipation of welcome relief from the tensions of the past year. Women and children brought along flowers and cigarettes and the growing crowd of spectators carried fluttering small swastika flags to wave in greeting. Excitement swelled and ebbed, and necks craned in response, as those with a vantage view further to the north thought they could see signs of the approaching *Wehrmacht.*

At last the first column of troops appeared in the distance. As they drew nearer there were early outbursts of *"Heil Hitler!"* and *"Sieg Heil!"* with thousands of outstretched arms thrust from the multitudes flanking the route. But the excited onlookers silenced their shouts in sudden embarrassment when they realized that well ahead of the German forces marched a small company of Czech soldiers, down-trodden but stoically keeping rank, eyes averted, stepping in unison toward an uncertain fate. The hushed spectators remained quiet until well after the retreating formation passed. Maria touched Friedrich's arm and looked up into his impassive face, unable to overcome a nagging sense of foreboding. Friedrich struggled with his own dark thoughts. Even the boys stood stiffly, gaping at the forlorn soldiers while holding on to Nannerl's hands.

A distant roar of voices electrified the crowd; sweeping nearer it engulfed everyone. The shouts of the people soared as gray-uniformed soldiers rolled by on shiny modern tanks, trucks and motorcycles. They were proud and erect in bearing, the smiling, well-fed and strutting best of the new Germany. A forest of outstretched arms greeted them. Women threw flowers, girls rushed to kiss the soldiers, and blaring martial music stirred the emotions of the flag-waving, saluting multitude to a fever pitch.

On and on the stream of armed might surged past, slowing now and then to avoid colliding with enthusiastic spectators who dashed crazily between the vehicles. At last the flow thinned out and the throngs pursued the troops like children following the Pied Piper, streaming toward the city center and the celebration.

In the vast theater square a huge rally resounded with stirring military music, nationalistic speeches and endless outbursts of *"Heil Hitler!"* and *"Sieg Heil!"* Afterwards many residents of the city invited soldiers to stay in their homes as a gesture of hospitality. The Wilderts asked a dapper young officer to come to the villa with them and quartered him in Walter's room. As Friedrich predicted, Walter turned up the following day, still wearing the green Czech uniform, his conscription duty prematurely ended by the Munich Agreement.

There was much lively talk and banter at the family dinner table between *Leutnant* Schmidt of the *Wehrmacht* and Private Rohan of the Czech Dragoons, young men from opposing armies, yet both shared the same language and culture. Everyone understood the irony that but for a stroke of a pen at Munich these two soldiers might have been duty-bound to fight against each other had Hitler made good his threat to take the Sudetenland by force.

The days of hospitality passed in an agreeable whirl for everyone. Martha found the young officer attractive, while the handsome man did not hide his own admiration for her and they spent much time together. Young Nannerl now had two uniformed men to moon over. The boys and their friends played soldiers with real weapons—all bullets safely removed—and cheerfully dressed up in the oversize uniforms, belts and heavy helmets to pose for what they thought to be hilarious photographs.

One evening after dinner Friedrich sat alone with Lt. Schmidt chatting over cigars and brandy, trying to discover how the young man's generation viewed the future. "What do you expect from the *Führer* now that he has, in his own words, consolidated all German-speaking territories?" he asked, carefully cutting the tip of a fragrant Havana cigar.

"We'll soon be the most powerful nation on earth, and no one will be able to stop our progress," Schmidt replied heatedly. "We'll be able to deal with anyone who stands in our way, and whoever doesn't like it will have to face the consequences."

Friedrich smiled blandly at the young man's vigorous answer. "Are you saying that there might be war?"

"For twenty years the major powers dominated Germany after forcing us to sign that miserable treaty of Versailles! Now, if they want war they can have it—no foreigners are going to tell us what to do ever again!" Schmidt took several furious puffs on his cigar. "The *Führer* gave us the discipline and the strength to win!" His eyes were hard. After a brief pause he spoke calmly, a twitch of condescension in the corners of his mouth. "You people here have not been involved in the glorious changes and the cleansing which our *Führer* brought to Germany. You will not understand until you have been integrated."

Friedrich looked steadily into Schmidt's cold eyes, keeping his temper as he continued acting the role of the good host. He had heard enough to confirm the rumors about what Hitler's new order did to impressionable young minds, and he sensed in Schmidt the callous disregard for others that the Nazi propaganda constantly hammered into its subjects. He feared for his sons who would grow to manhood under such conditions.

At last Friedrich said smoothly, "*Herr Leutnant* Schmidt, I respect the fervor and conviction of your views, and I agree that those of us who haven't been close to the changes in Germany can only try to appreciate the full scope of the progress already made. I wish you the very best of success and happiness for you and your family." The two men talked for a while on lighter subjects, finished their brandy and Friedrich rose to say good night. The following morning Lt. Schmidt departed with polite expressions of thanks to all members of the Wildert household.

Left to themselves after the first flush of excitement of the occupation, Friedrich and his family speculated during the next few evenings about the changes the new regime would bring. They discussed the influx of German civilian officials from across the newly erased border to fill local administrative posts vacated by Czech incumbents.

"I've got the feeling we'll again be ruled by people other than our own kind. It's amazing how fast the profiteers are streaming in! Every opportunist in Germany must be looking to make his fortune at our expense. I heard that a high official from Düsseldorf has already taken over the Blum villa, and there are rumors that any remaining Jewish families will be moved out before long. These Nazis are enriching themselves with the property of the ones that fled, and plan to confiscate what the few others still own." Friedrich's face betrayed his disgust.

It was not long before the Sudetenland became a magnet for hordes of German tourists, most of them arriving in swarming travel groups arranged by the Nazi Party for its worker members. The government organization sponsoring such excursions into the region was called *"Kraft durch Freude"*[4] and the travelers used the opportunity to purchase what quality merchandise they could from the well-stocked stores of the region, things that were largely unavailable in the rearmament-oriented economy of Germany.

Soon waves of shoppers with ample German currency swallowed up most of the available goods, much to the irritation of the local residents who were pushed and jostled in the streets and shops by the boisterous visitors. Beleaguered restaurants served vast amounts of the rich Austrian and Bohemian dishes and desserts to the tourists, and the Wilderts saw many instances of gluttony and atrocious table manners. The family and their friends felt crowded out by the loud, singing multitudes who acted as if the province belonged to them.

Then came the day when Hitler broke the solemn pledge he made to Neville Chamberlain before the Munich Agreement by ordering the *Wehrmacht* to move again—this time to occupy all of the Czech heartland. Friedrich returned from the office gloomy with foreboding. He gathered the family in the living room and said gravely, "Today I'm convinced that *Herr* Hitler has taken a deliberate step towards war. He just broke his word. In the end we'll all have to pay for this—now that he has made us citizens of the Third *Reich*!"

---

[4] Strength through Joy

"Can you imagine the resentment and anger of the Czechs? They had to watch Hitler appear at their ancient *Hradčany* Castle in Prague, swastika flags flying, to review the strutting *Wehrmacht* that simply rolled across the Czech border the British and French were supposed to have guaranteed, without firing a shot! Having to give up the Sudetenland was a real blow to the Czechs—but at least one can argue that this brought German-speaking people together. There was also that treaty at Munich that made it legal. But this time the Germans occupied the Czechs in their own homeland. Hitler promised them they could live in peace—and now they've become what he calls a 'protectorate' under German rule!"

Friedrich covered his eyes, searching for the right words to express his burning anxiety. "Sooner or later the Western Powers will simply have to act if Hitler continues to challenge them. If another war does break out, then God help us all, for Germany can't win against the whole world—that was proven only twenty short years ago." Almost inaudibly he murmured, "We'll all be doomed."

Friedrich's urgent words struck home; the family sat in dejected silence. There was nothing more to be said. Dark and mysterious forces had taken over their fate and that of millions of others, pushing the world relentlessly toward the abyss.

THREE

The Conquerors

May 1945

In the darkness of early morning a numbing silence hung like a vast funeral drape over the city by the Elbe river. Paralyzed with dread and foreboding the inhabitants began to grasp the inevitability of their fate—the Russian army was relentlessly smashing its way toward them. They would be conquered within hours. No life stirred in the blacked-out streets. The cool breeze carried a nauseating odor of smoldering debris from the ruined heart of the city to the hills flanking the river, a pungent reminder of recent massive allied bombing raids that cut the vital rail links and turned much of the old town center into bizarre blackened ruins. The stench again evoked the gruesome spectacle of the vast chemical works and factories burning out of control for days, like seething lakes of fire. But now there was only silence.

Maria lay on the sofa in the living room of the hillside villa, wide awake, keeping her lonely vigil. The picture window faced the northern ridge of the Sudeten mountains, about five miles distant, where the road led into Germany. Marked by an ancient signal tower the pass was clearly visible in good weather. Now darkness obscured the familiar view. Soon the conquerors would cross this mountain range and descend into the valley to overrun the region. Maria remained alert as she strained for sounds of approaching danger, ready to warn Friedrich and Anton.

How many nights had she spent here in silent watch while her family slept in the bedrooms facing the garden? How often had she waited for the ominous growl of the air raid sirens to swell into wailing crescendos that echoed eerily in the night? How often had she heard the distant throbbing of hundreds of aircraft, burdened with deadly loads, while she waited for the terse radio announcements of the civil defense station, all the while doing her best to guess the target of the raid? When danger came close she would alert the others to take shelter in the basement of the villa. Although tired and overwrought from lack of sleep, Maria insisted this self-appointed role was her duty and her contribution to the family's survival.

The insistent, metallic "click-clack, click-clack" of an alarm clock sounded from the radio; the crude, ever-present call signal of the civil defense station had accompanied her vigil in nights past. The sound hammered away monotonously between occasional announcements and made the waiting for news—any news—even more anxious. Nerves jangled whenever the clicking stopped and, after an ominous pause of a second or two, the announcer's harsh *"Achtung, achtung!"*[1] assaulted the senses. The radio had fallen silent abruptly last evening after giving erratic reports about raiding Russian fighter bombers sighted here and there, and contradictory speculations over the latest positions of the advancing enemy forces. It would all be over soon.

As she lay there her thoughts kept returning to the spate of hopeful rumors that swept the city during the past week. It was just wishful thinking that led the inhabitants to expect that the American forces approaching from the west would push through to the Elbe river along its full length and occupy their city. Fragmentary reports suggested the Americans had already reached and crossed the Elbe to the north in Saxony. Now fervent hope alone spawned the opinion that it made sense for the *"Amis"*[2] to come this far upstream and enter the Sudetenland in order to conquer as much enemy territory as possible.

The disintegrating German forces were relieved to be taken prisoner by the *Amis*, laying down their arms whenever they could. Did the Americans not realize that they would be desperately welcomed by the civilian population, sought out as a protec-

---

[1] Attention, attention
[2] German nickname for American soldiers

tive shield against the dreaded "Ivan" pushing towards them from the east? Now that the western Allies had fought their way into the German heartland from the distant beaches of Normandy, what kept the Americans from coming just a little closer? What were the reasons that made the respected General Eisenhower hesitate to conquer the lion's share of the stricken Third *Reich* for the western Allies?

Two days earlier more up-to-date rumors began circulating, and soon proved correct with intense, burning reality. At long last the stunned residents of Aussig and the northern Sudetenland learned that, inexplicably, the Americans were halting their rapid advance and standing still to await the Russian thrust from the east. Forbidden Swiss and British newscasts, secretly monitored while huddling under a blanket covering the radio, confirmed the frightening news. Now the city lay in the path of a vengeful enemy and the dreaded Red Army's invasion was about to begin. In months past the refugees streaming in from the eastern provinces conquered earlier by the Russians told of mass rape, brutality and pillage, their eyes and faces marked by dread.

Maria shifted uneasily. Her churning thoughts made the tension of her lonely watch unbearable. She tried to calm herself with a silent prayer but lost the struggle in a flurry of emotions. In the darkness her gloomy fears hovered like insistent shadows.

Yesterday the family speculated at length about how they might escape the fury of the coming days. They weighed the chances of making their way to join Martha in the town of Eger in the western Sudetenland. Just before the war Martha met and married the young owner of a family business there, and she now had three young children. Her husband was drafted into the *Wehrmacht*, served on the Russian front and had not been heard from since Christmas. Martha and her children had the support of her husband's extended family, and the chances of being occupied by the advancing Americans were much better for them.

The family reluctantly admitted that they would be fools to try going to Eger, a distance of less than a hundred miles. With the obvious collapse of transportation, food supplies and communications, how could they possibly make their way and expect to survive? It made no sense to leave their shelter and what food supplies remained to throw themselves into the turmoil of a war-ravaged countryside.

Maria felt like a cornered animal darting to and fro in frantic search of escape, instinctively aware that there was no way out except by facing what terrors lay ahead. The atmosphere was heavy with foreboding and the eerie quiet of the room only fed her growing despair. Wiping her forehead and taking a deep breath, she rose shakily and walked over to the window, peering intently into the cool darkness. The occasional faint rumble of artillery to the north and east, quite audible yesterday, had ebbed away. Were it not for the icy grip of imminent danger it could have been a tranquil and lovely spring night.

Gone were the almost daily overflights of hundreds of heavy allied bombers. Gone was the macabre excitement of squinting at the glittering high-flying formations by day, of gaping in the darkness at the floating flares and fiery aerial "Christmas Trees"— colorful apparitions dropped by lead aircraft that became brightly shining markers of death and destruction over nearby targets. Gone was the vibrant droning of the multitude of heavy engines, the whooshing, whistling and crashing thunder of the bombs which made the house shudder and shake even when they exploded miles away.

The sky to the north turned lighter with the first tender hues of morning, outlining in sharp contrast the distant dark mountain ridge, the invasion route. Maria's thought of her elder son who was somewhere over there in Saxony, conscripted though not yet seventeen. Now Johann was caught among the tattered remnants of the *Wehrmacht*, tossed like sand against the overwhelming armed might surging in from both east and west. Her eyes filled with tears. "Oh God, please keep him be safe," she whispered, "watch over my son and bring him back to us."

Distant noises jolted her alert. She listened intently. An ominous low rumble drifted in from the direction of the pass road— perhaps she imagined it? But there it was again! A cool northerly breeze wafted through the window, carrying with it more distinct sounds from the mountains. Maria intently focused all her energy on listening. What she heard must be the throbbing of heavy motors, the clanging of metal and the shuffle of thousands of boots! This is it, she thought. As she held her breath she felt her heart pounding violently.

The noises swelled and became a steady drum roll moving nearer and nearer. Maria turned and swiftly tiptoed to the bedroom where Friedrich slept fitfully. She did not need to switch on the light. Accustomed to the faint light of early morning, she gazed at her husband's drawn face. The exhausted man needed every bit of sleep he could get. Since there was nothing they could do but wait she decided to let him rest a few minutes longer.

Maria left quietly and walked into Anton's room. The boy was sound asleep and she shook him firmly. "Anton, Anton, you must get up, I think the Russians are coming!"

Sleepily rubbing his eyes he slowly crawled out of bed. He always found it hard to wake up and trotted drowsily behind his mother into the living room. There they opened another section of the wide window, pulled up two chairs and stared out into the obscure distance, trying to fathom the origin of the steady droning.

The sky was beginning to glow with the pink and gold of dawn—a soft, deceptively beautiful backdrop for the ominous events that were still hidden from them. There could be only one explanation for the pounding noises to the north: a massive column of vehicles and men was nearing the outskirts of the city, with large numbers of trucks, tracked vehicles and soldiers on foot pouring in along the main road which passed less than half a mile from the house.

The villa stood halfway up the slope on one side of a wide valley; scattered wooded estates covered the other side. The main road on the distant valley floor led through a built-up area flanked by three-story row houses. These blocked the view of the street itself, and even if it had been light enough Maria and Anton could not have seen any movement.

Anton was seized by a strange exhilaration, a sense of high excitement mixed with intense fear. As he stared into the distance he imagined being seated in the family's box at the civic theater. The window became a vantage point from which to watch exciting happenings on the stage, except this time deadly reality was about to unfold before him. With boyish curiosity and impatience he peered intently in the direction of the noises, hoping to catch a first glimpse of what caused the frightening sounds. Mother and son sat transfixed, listening, straining to see, oblivious to the danger. The dull roar of engines, the rumble and banging of metal, and the muffled trampling of feet grew into a steady din that reverberated from the slopes of the valley. Still they could see nothing unusual.

The morning light now revealed the familiar outlines of the neighboring houses, the curving residential street below and the small green meadow opposite. On the left they could see a portion of the street which joined the main road a good mile further north near the soccer stadium. The Russian invaders would have to come that way.

Maria turned around when she heard her husband's footsteps approaching. The tall, stately man joined his family by the window. His face was thin and drawn, marked by the pain of a chronic ulcer. "This is the end," Friedrich murmured after a few moments of silent watching. "May God have mercy on us."

Suddenly Anton burst out with a shrill cry. "Here they come!" A truck heavily laden with soldiers rumbled into view, emerging from behind the grey villa across the meadow. Their hearts racing, the Wilderts braced themselves for their first glimpse of the enemy.

In an instant they realized that what they saw was not the spearhead of the conquering Red Army, but a battered gray vehicle with the familiar black and white Baltic cross markings on its side, piled high with men wearing the field grey of German uniforms. Stunned, they watched the overloaded truck grind past. Behind it followed a ghostly procession of ragged soldiers on foot, on bicycles, in mud-caked automobiles, on more battered trucks, and on horse-drawn carts. Heavily bandaged figures staggered along or swayed limply with the motion of their impossibly crowded conveyances. More fortunate comrades supported the wounded. Even from a distance the posture of the shuffling men and youngsters betrayed the strain, shock, and grinding fear of desperate flight. Clothed in tattered uniform remnants these soldiers no longer carried weapons; what rifles, grenades and bazookas remained had been thrown away many miles back.

Anton stood riveted with a lump in his throat. These broken men were running for their lives! Now he understood that all along he and his mother had heard the despondent cacophony of a defeated army, shrinking and melting away before the relentless onslaught of a victorious and avenging enemy.

"It's a replay of Napoleon's defeat in Russia," Friedrich muttered, "only this time we are not reading history books. God help them and us."

Full daylight illuminated the stark scene with merciless reality as the growing multitude of desperate men spilled into the quiet residential area like water swirling over an embankment too confined to hold a deluge. Steadily and single-mindedly these men surged westward, straining away from dreaded Russian captivity.

Onlookers poured out of their houses with buckets of water, makeshift bandages and what little food they could spare. Anton also ran into the street with water and bread. As he approached the moving mass of soldiers, a truck piled high with listless wounded men screeched to a halt, jarring its sullen cargo. Leaning heavily out of the window the dust-caked driver rasped at the bystanders, "Which way to the western road? For God's sake, make it quick!" His voice pitched and broke, his tired eyes were dark hollows flickering with fear. Nodding impatiently to the shouted directions he gunned the groaning engine and roared on in a cloud of blue smoke, not taking time to accept food and water.

A sickening smell of sweat, open wounds, decaying leather and exhaust fumes hung in the air, assaulting the senses with the cruel atmosphere of defeat. Anton felt the soldiers' collective urgency like a physical force. He had never seen grownups act in utter desperation and reduced to primitive urges. Unable to understand the full impact of their plight he strongly sensed the horror gripping the men moving past him. The avengers were hard on their heels, unforgiving, huge in numbers, well-equipped and armed to the teeth.

He imagined that these fleeing soldiers must have felt first-hand the shattering blows of the Russian rocket launchers which Uncle Walter talked about during his last leave from the Russian front. With awe and graphic detail the soldier had described the horrors of the "Stalin Organ," a devastating weapon that unleashed dozens of rockets, howling and screeching like banshees, to explode in a deadly hail of fire and destruction.

Anton watched the masses of defeated men hurrying past him. Withdrawn into their own world of private fear, few reacted to the activity around them. Gone were the loud, arrogant cogs of Hitler's war machine he had seen glorified so often in scores of propaganda films and newsreels. Many of these soldiers were old; hardly any were in their twenties or thirties. Clearly among them were numerous members of the *"Volkssturm,"*[3] mostly aging civilians pressed into service during the waning months of the war. Some were very young men, even boys, conscripted like Johann to fill out the thinning ranks of the *Wehrmacht.*

Anton could not bear to look the soldiers directly in the eye, afraid to perceive their desperation which was like that of hunted animals. The boy tried to imagine how it felt to be adrift, without shelter and destination, driven only by the urge to flee from the pursuing enemy. He had read about such events in books describing great historic defeats and upheavals, graphic accounts that stirred him deeply. But this moment of reality was so overwhelming, so frightening, that his mind refused to grasp it.

Some of the soldiers passing him seemed no older than he and their gaunt faces reflected experience far beyond their years, molded by suffering that even grownups found unbearable. Anton sensed a barrier between himself and these children in the guise of uniformed manhood. A few of them stopped long enough to have a drink of water out of his bucket and he asked anxiously if by chance they had come from the little town in Saxony where Johann was last based. The young ex-warriors barely took notice of him, their eyes averted and distant, until one finally shrugged, "Look, we are from all over, everything is in a mess. What does it

3 People's Front

matter now, anyway . . ."

Anton continued to scan the tired figures of the soldiers, hoping without hope to spot his brother among them. He wished so much that Johann would make his way back. During his last furlough some weeks before Christmas, Friedrich made Johann promise that whatever happened in the inevitable collapse he would head straight for home and not get caught up in some last minute grandstanding. Anton kept looking and searching as if in a trance, but his brother did not appear.

Only when his bucket was empty did he tear himself away to run back to the house for more water. When he returned to the street corner he noticed that the neighbors had disappeared and that the flow of vehicles and men was slowing down, as if hindered by an obstacle. Warned by a tingling sense of danger he felt vulnerable and exposed. Cautiously he looked about for the cause of the delay. Peering around the street corner he saw that a group of uniformed young men had suddenly appeared, halfway down the block to the left. They strutted arrogantly and wore large pistols in their belts. Rifles were casually slung over their shoulders, muzzles pointing down, revolutionary style. Their uniforms looked to Anton like the desert-colored outfits of Field Marshal Rommel's Africa Corps, but the familiar insignia and shoulder boards were missing. Instead, these militiamen wore wide armbands striped in red, white and blue, the Czech national colors.

The boy shrank back against the high ornamental stone wall and fence and stood still, holding his breath, half hidden by a large shrub with cascading masses of pungent yellow blossoms. Pressed against the wall he watched anxiously as the young soldiers issued sharp commands in German, colored with the distinctive Czech accent. Waving all vehicles to a halt they shouted, "*Nix* automobile for you, German pigs!" This they repeated over and over, brusquely ignoring the pleading gestures of the unarmed drivers and their charges. *"Raus, mach schnell,"* [4] they ordered, "you Nazi swine can walk to hell if you want!"

Shuddering alarm gripped the column of men still oozing west-

[4] Get out and fast

ward, as the fit and the wounded clambered to the ground. Having little strength left to protest they awkwardly resumed their trek, prodded by the raised weapons and threatening gestures of their new adversaries. One by one the militiamen drove away the empty vehicles.

Fearful of being spotted Anton hugged the wall in retreat and tiptoed around the corner. Once out of sight of the armed men he ran at breakneck speed back to the house. Breathlessly he reported to Maria and Friedrich what he had seen. "The Czechs will show their muscle," Friedrich murmured wryly, "now that it has finally become safe to do so! Remember the endless calls for Allied help from Prague radio yesterday, when Czech partisans apparently picked a fight with what's left of the German army?"

"I feel sorry for these soldiers; they are just trying to get away. Imagine the wounded being made to walk!" Maria sighed deeply as she thought of Johann. How terrible it would be if he were assailed like this while fleeing. Neither Friedrich nor Maria dared put their fears into words.

The family continued to watch in silence as the stream of retreating German soldiers diminished to a trickle. The street was now strewn with the debris of war, flung away as the men were forced to dismount and lighten their burdens. There were no more vehicles, only some stragglers on bicycles or on foot. The vigorous new militia grew ever more confident and effective in their demands and soon confiscated even the bicycles.

Silence again returned to the neighborhood which was now bathed in the brightness of a sunny spring morning. The daylight heightened the lush green of the gardens and trees, and the lovely pastel shadings of abundant blossoms and flowers bespoke the magnificent spring of 1945. The exceptionally beautiful season was an irony, as if nature herself wished to emphasize the gulf between the suffering inflicted by man's folly and the blessings there for the asking. Many times Maria voiced her feeling that nature seemed to be giving them all a final embrace. It was a beautiful farewell setting, a last hint of what could have been before the maelstrom tore away all that was familiar.

"They should be here any moment now," Friedrich said, his

voice hoarse with tension. Fear of the reality of imminent hostile conquest gnawed at his nerves and the eerie pause increased his apprehension. It seemed foolish just to stand and wait, but what could they do? Running away was out of the question, and hiding even less so.

Friedrich looked at his wife. Maria gazed into the distance, embroiled in her own thoughts. He could see the strain in her expression and wondered helplessly what he might be able to do to protect her once the Russians arrived. He wanted to console her and give her confidence, but he had none himself.

Many refugees from the east relayed horror stories of plunder and looting, murder and rape committed by drunken hordes of Russian soldiers intent on mass brutalization of women, girls and even children. Resistance was impossible against such armed and battle-hardened men.

Suddenly he remembered the old small-caliber handgun that had been around the house for years. No one in the family had ever fired it, not even Walter the soldier. The revolver and a few bullets had been well hidden so that the growing boys could not get their hands on it. Where was it now? But then Friedrich visualized soldiers approaching, their pistols and machine guns levelled, and imagined himself trying to hold them at bay with a little pop gun that he wasn't even sure would go off. It was ridiculous!

Friedrich pulled Maria close and faced her with a fearful gaze, his voice choking, "When they do get here and we see them coming to the house, you must hide and stay out of sight, regardless of what happens." He had to clear his throat. "I'll meet them at the front door, although I really don't know what I can do. Perhaps it is better for me to be down there than to have them break in the door and start turning the place upside down." He paused heavily, wanting to add, "I hope to God they'll leave you alone!" But he could not utter the words.

Maria nodded gravely, her large brown eyes reflecting the dignity and inner strength he loved so much. Friedrich sensed that she often thought about this personal horror, and he felt sick as he fought to suppress the image of his wife being violated by brutal warriors. He groped for her hand and pressed it firmly.

Anton kept watching and straining from his post by the window to discover signs of the approaching Russian army. A deceptive calm descended on the area, a tense silence not unlike the still of the night that carried every sound from afar. Then a new and ominous distant rumble jarred their nerves. The noise grew louder and louder. Joyous shouts resounded in the street where the excited Czech militia saw their Russian cousins drawing near. The Wilderts clung to each other as if rooted to the spot, their pulses hammering, seeking strength from closeness as they faced the onslaught of the enemy.

FOUR

The Bullet

April 1945

Johann Wildert stared into the distance, straining to see if he could make out any signs of the approaching enemy. The soil smelled damp and fresh; light April showers breezed through earlier in the day. To the west a small river meandered lazily between sloping banks of grass. Bounded by stands of mixed forest, the horizon reflected dark rectangles starkly outlined against the bright sky. In the other direction softly rolling fields extended as far as the eye could see, bathed in the warm rays of the late afternoon sun.

Johann kept watch from the corner of a walled graveyard behind a small rural church in central Saxony, which stood on a low mound half a mile from the nearest village. Shielded by the crumbling moss-covered stone wall he had a fine vantage point from which to observe the seemingly peaceful countryside. But soon the advancing American forces would emerge from the western forests and cross the narrow river, while the Russians would surge towards them over the level fields to the east. From the scant news passed on by his platoon leader and by the commanding officer, *Leutnant* Pritzke, Johann expected that one or the other enemy would close in on them in a matter of hours. The end was inevitable and he felt trapped.

The under-strength company of *Panzer Grenadiere*[1] stationed in the nearby village would be caught in the middle. The unit was a motley collection of wounded veterans and green recruits like Johann, garnered from every conceivable source of manpower still remaining as the disintegrating *Wehrmacht* drew its last gasps.

---

[1] Armored infantry

Johann would be seventeen in another month, one of the youngest draftees in the company. He barely knew how to handle the old army pistol and the two hand grenades issued to him along with mismatched uniform segments. There were some others like Johann, but a few of the young recruits had received a smattering of basic training, or experienced a taste of battle while serving with anti-aircraft batteries on the "homefront."

The older veterans maintained a condescending attitude towards these boys, willing to share hard-won combat experience as needed but bluntly warning them not to pull any feats of last-minute heroism that might endanger the whole outfit. Cynical and convinced the end was near these old hands had survived by their wits and were taking no chances. They would do their duty as long as necessary, but left no doubt they would try to save their skins when the final collapse came.

Johann craned his neck upward to the tiny window near the top of the church steeple where there was an experienced lookout posted. "Can you see anything, Georg?" he called out.

Georg's face appeared in the opening. "No, nothing at all. The *Amis* are certainly taking their time!" He sounded weary.

The tense waiting resumed. Occasionally there was the faint, distant rumble of artillery, puncturing the silence of the rural idyll. This agricultural corner of Saxony represented little worth fighting over. The villages and towns lacked strategic importance and the shallow river posed no defensible barrier.

Earlier that morning Lt. Pritzke assembled the company at the village schoolhouse and gave them a brief lecture on the importance of the day. It was April 20, 1945, Hitler's fifty-sixth birthday. The lieutenant read them a message from the battalion commander, a fanatical Prussian major who managed to crowd into the few sentences a dozen hollow-sounding phrases about personal sacred duty to the *Führer*, the enduring glory of the National Socialist cause, the promise of a last-minute offensive being plotted in the *Führer's* bunker in Berlin that would stop the advance of the enemy, and the need to defend every inch of holy German soil with Aryan blood.

The men and boys impassively pretended to listen, each thinking in his own way about how to survive the final combat. Calls for heroism seemed to belong to a distant past—the grim reality of their current predicament was obvious. An overwhelming force of well-equipped enemies was inexorably advancing towards their inadequate outpost, squashing along the way the crumbling remnants of men and equipment that dared oppose them. In the face of such odds heroism was suicide, and the stoic listeners knew it.

Lt. Pritzke maintained his noncommittal expression while reading the colonel's incongruous phrases. He ended the message with a most perfunctory *"Heil Hitler!"*, stretching out his arm stiffly for a brief moment in the political gesture that not long ago, by order of the Party, had supplanted the traditional Army salute. Professional soldiers like the lieutenant were offended by this latest sign of subservience to the all-powerful Nazi fanatics who maneuvered the country into the suicidal madness of "Total War." Many gave the new salute as little importance as possible.

Lt. Pritzke went on with a review of the situation, his grim expression exaggerated by a black patch over his empty left eye socket. The latest field radio messages suggested that the Americans were less than twenty miles away, slowly advancing in their direction with armored units. In their path there remained only the mauled remnants of a *panzer* division trying to make a feeble stand at a larger town to the west. These defenders might delay the arrival of the Americans by a day at the most; ammunition and fuel were running desperately low.

The sparse news from the volatile eastern front was confused and ominous. Lt. Pritzke admitted that nobody was certain how far the Red Army pushed westward during the last twenty-four hours. Fighting was fierce where units of the *Wehrmacht* were still intact. Repeated orders came from the distant army headquarters to defend the territory at all costs. The lieutenant speculated that there was a high-level policy of holding off the Russians as long as possible while allowing the western Allies to advance.

"It's very likely that the Americans will arrive first. It is our duty to engage them, but I will not give orders that could mean we'll be wiped out." The lieutenant had difficulty choosing his words. Fingering his black and silver Iron Cross he hesitated for a moment. "What I am trying to say is that I want to, ah, minimize casualties while maintaining our honor." His voice trailed off. The veterans understood; the young officer was no fool.

"If the Russians do get here first, we may have no choice but to fight. Let's hope that there are still enough functioning units between us and them so we don't have to face that problem. Our supplies are tight, as you all know. We only have twenty-two bazookas and enough rifle ammunition for about thirty rounds each. There are no hand grenades left except those you've been issued. Food rations may last us another day or two at best."

He paused and looked at the sullen, tired faces around him. With considerable effort he raised his voice, managing to give it a semblance of the clipped stridency of command that now belonged to another era. "I plan to send out patrols at dusk in both directions to probe the enemy positions. These patrols must just reconnoiter and avoid all hostile contact. They will defend themselves only as required and break off any action as soon as feasible. Based on what we learn I will make my next decisions. We can't count on help from anyone, so we must act on our own."

Again Lt. Pritzke looked at each of his fifty-two men. How many would survive the trap that closed around them? He knew that he would order them to surrender as soon as his sense of honor permitted. Where that point was, and when his conscience would allow him to give that final order he did not know. He found himself hoping that the circumstances would decide for him. He shook off his troubled thoughts and announced the orders for the day, including patrol assignments and lookout duty. Then he encouraged the men to rest as much as possible, both to minimize food requirements and to strengthen themselves for the fighting to come. At last he dismissed the company to quarters in the village.

Johann still stood by the wall of the graveyard; the worrisome impressions of the earlier meeting lingered in his mind. He squinted into the sunlit distance once more, saw nothing but the peaceful landscape, and decided to join his platoon in the cool church. Lt. Pritzke assigned him to a three-man patrol that would go west for a mile or two at nineteen hundred hours, in order to explore the clumps of forest on the horizon. They would have to wade across the shallow river and make their way through the dusky fields. Another patrol was assigned to a similar mission further to the northwest.

Johann still had a sufficient boyish sense of adventure left to be momentarily excited by the prospect of stalking cautiously through the open fields and probing the dark stands of trees. But he soon reminded himself how serious the situation was. This was no time for games. He recalled the solemn promise he gave his father not to risk his life needlessly, and resolved to be especially careful tonight.

The cool church smelled of dampness and decay. Johann sat down next to Wolfgang who would later accompany him on patrol. Wolfgang volunteered for this assignment. He was a year older than Johann and had received his basic training; afterwards he served for six months in an anti-aircraft battery that protected a synthetic fuel plant near Aussig, the target of frequent massive Allied bombing raids. Wolfgang and his young gunner comrades endured their baptism of fire many times over. Miraculously he escaped unscathed when a bomber scored a direct hit on his battery emplacement, disabling three of the four long-barreled guns and causing heavy casualties.

After a brief leave spent with his parents in Aussig, Wolfgang was ordered to Saxony in early April. A reshuffling of units brought him to the small village where Johann served, and a few days earlier the remains of his platoon merged with Lt. Pritzke's company. Johann and Wolfgang had known each other in preparatory school and met occasionally during the required activities of the Hitler youth organization. Both were glad to find someone from home. They used their free time to talk about nostalgic family memories, school days and shared worries about the future.

"Have you heard from your family yet, Johann?" Wolfgang concentrated on cleaning his rifle which he had taken apart expertly, wiping and oiling the mechanism.

"No, I wrote to them on the eleventh, but the field mail is getting slower by the day," Johann responded moodily.

He also impatiently awaited a response from his girlfriend to whom he had written a passionate letter the same day. Erika was his first romance; she affected him enough so that he often lapsed into the bittersweet longing of young love, especially when he lay awake at night, unable to sleep. With his eyes closed he liked to visualize her pretty face and her sparkling, teasing eyes, ardently wanting more of the shy kisses they exchanged on his last leave. This he decided was none of Wolfgang's business.

His friend broke the silence. "I just had a long letter from my father." He paused, fiddling with the trigger. "Things aren't too good at home. Food is getting scarce and the latest air raids knocked out the city center and the old town. The main railroad station was totally wrecked this time. Trains and supplies are having trouble getting through."

"Has your own place been damaged?" Johann had never been to Wolfgang's home, but he knew the family lived near the center of the city in a modest apartment complex.

"No, thank God, but incendiary bombs hit the building next door. The roof burned off, but they were able to keep the fire from spreading. Dad writes he was glad not to live right downtown. It must be a total mess! There's so much rubble that dead bodies have to be left where they are, and the stench is awful."

"I feel sorry for the women and children." Johann vividly recalled the increasingly frequent air raids he lived through while still at home. The feeling of helplessness had been overpowering when he sat with the others in the basement of the villa, listening to the steady grinding roar of vast formations of aircraft, approaching closer and closer, followed by the whistling of the bombs and crashing impacts that shook the ground and made the house creak and tremble. Even when the explosions were far away, loosened wall plaster fragments rustled in whispering cascades during the moments of quiet between thunderous convulsions. Of course he never experienced a close hit, such as the one Wolfgang escaped, but the distant pounding was scary enough.

"I think we're better off out here," Wolfgang mused while he reassembled his rifle. "At least we've got something to defend ourselves with." He patted the barrel that now glistened with fresh oil. "When I was with the anti-aircraft battery it felt good to shoot back, even though I doubt we ever hit anything, they were flying so high. But just doing something was better than sitting and taking it."

"I wonder how we're going to manage here," Johann said pensively. "Don't you feel trapped? We've hardly got weapons to fight with." He pulled out his pistol and wearily examined it. "I don't even have a rifle!" After a few moments of troubled silence he added, "Wolfie, did you ever fire a bazooka in combat? The *Leutnant* said we have only twenty-two of them left— how long can we hold off scores of *Ami* tanks with these?"

"No, I haven't—although they showed me how to do it. We aren't likely to be asked to do it with so few around! Let's leave it to the others—though I've got the feeling the older guys aren't going to make a big stand against the *Amis*. In fact, it would be stupid to resist now." His voice dropped to a confidential whisper. "I have no intention of becoming a hero myself, Johann. The war is lost, everyone can see that. I'll go through the motions but I'll keep my eyes open for the first chance to be taken prisoner by the *Amis*, unless I can make my way home before that."

Johann was surprised at Wolfgang's openness in revealing his thoughts of surrender. The long years of conditioning about duty and honor, continually hammered home by the Nazi youth movement, left their mark on his impressionable young mind which still lacked the cynicism of experience. Yet he found that he could not disagree with his friend. He swallowed once or twice, then decided not to respond. The Nazi regime also taught him to hold back his innermost feelings for fear of betrayal—wariness was instinctive by now. In his mind he saw his father earnestly admonishing the family to be careful about what was said to outsiders. Yes, he would be careful and keep his thoughts to himself.

"I wonder what's going to happen to us when the war is lost." Johann surprised himself by speaking so easily about the impending collapse, a certainty that was numbly expected by most people. He knew that despite the arrogant efforts of the party leaders to trumpet an ever more elusive vision of "final victory," the fiery storm clouds of the *Götterdämmerung*[2] boiled up relentlessly, casting dark shadows of abysmal defeat.

Nearly seven years earlier his father predicted that an ill fate would eventually devour them all. Johann remembered that the first time Friedrich said this was on the day when Hitler's *Wehrmacht* strutted into the Sudetenland, and the second time was shortly thereafter when Germany occupied the heartland of Czechoslovakia. Vivid images of these events remained in his memory. Now he was a soldier himself, separated from his family by many miles while he waited at this forgotten outpost to be overrun by the enemy.

"It'll be brutal, you can bet on that." Wolfgang set aside his rifle, after checking the few remaining bullets in the scuffed leather ammunition packets strapped to his belt. "Haven't you heard the stories the eastern refugees are telling? When the Russians come there will be rape, murder, and plundering. With the *Amis* it'll be better, but they are no angels either . . ." He sighed and added wistfully, "I just wish the *Amis* would hurry up! Let's hope the eastern front holds out for a while longer."

Johann was thinking ahead. "Once they occupy us, what will happen? Can we go back to school some day? How will all the damage be repaired?" He tried to picture a return to the normal life he had known only for a brief time beyond his tenth birthday, and continued to ask questions he knew could not be answered. "I'd like to attend the university once I get my *Matura*[3] from prep school—do you think that it'll be possible? I really want to study chemistry. How about you, Wolfie?"

His companion did not respond for a while. He seemed preoccupied, thinking troubled thoughts and staring absently into the distance. At last Wolfgang answered. "I'd like to become an engineer, like my father." Once more he hesitated, then drew out his words. "But I think there'll be a lot of confusion and upheaval for a long time before we can get back to studying." He still avoided looking at Johann and his eyes again had that faraway expression.

---

[2] Twilight of the Gods; German epic of tragedy

[3] Graduation certificate required for university admission

Almost as an aside he added, "With your family's means you and Anton should have no problem studying whatever you like—that is, assuming you can keep it all."

Johann was surprised at the mention of family wealth. He did not know Wolfgang well enough to have ever discussed such matters with him and they had not visited each other at home. Yet Wolfgang sounded so knowledgeable—and why did he use such a strange tone when bringing up the Wildert family resources?

"What are you talking about—whether we can keep it?" Johann again could not catch Wolfgang's eye.

"Well, I don't want to alarm you—but I've got the feeling that our land and property may somehow be used to settle Czech claims from the war and the German occupation." Wolfgang paused once more and stared at his feet, his face averted.

"What is that supposed to mean?" Johann became impatient with the way his friend was stalling.

"Don't you remember that in 1938 the Czechs had to let go of the Sudetenland when Hitler demanded it? Sure, the treaty of Munich made it legal. But now the Third *Reich* is collapsing. Don't you think the Czechs will want the Sudetenland back? And they'll expect some compensation for having been occupied themselves, won't they? Where will that come from?"

How did Wolfgang get such ideas, Johann wondered, not sure what to say. His friend appeared to have so much insight, yet he was reluctant to volunteer specific information. But of course, Wolfgang had just been home on leave only three weeks ago! Did he learn all of this then? Johann was still troubled by the odd expression he observed in Wolfgang's eyes. They sat in awkward silence.

At last Johann could stand it no longer. "Dammit all, you sound like you know something that I should know, too! Would you kindly tell me what this is all about? After all, you've just been home, haven't you?"

A grim shadow passed over Wolfgang's face. Then he set his jaw firmly. Indeed, he did have a great deal of information, but he was not going to share any of it—how could he possibly reveal the secrets he knew? But then his nagging conscience was beginning to act up again. Wolfgang took a deep breath as he sought to rid himself of the uncomfortable sensation. He tried to rationalize away the painful conflict in his mind with the soothing suggestion that at a time when chaos was about to descend everyone had to think of himself first—wasn't that the way it worked?

Wolfgang could not loosen the grip of the disturbing memory of recent talks he had with his father who told him of having made contact with the growing Czech underground network. This was a most unexpected turn of events. Wolfgang recoiled from the startling realization that his parents were secretly collaborating with the other side. But they had indeed become involved with the clandestine group that prepared for the Czech takeover of the Sudetenland, after the collapse of Nazi Germany. Reluctant at first, he soon began to see the wisdom of securing personal advantages by such collaboration during the inevitable upheaval that lay ahead. He learned from his father that the exiled Czech government in London planned to expropriate and expel the native Sudeten population from the territory as soon as the hostilities ceased. He had further learned that in exchange for a promise of favorable treatment and money, his father had agreed to provide the Czech underground with information on the persons and properties of well-to-do Sudeten families—betraying his own people in order to secure better conditions for himself and his family during the expected uprooting.

Wolfgang's conscience kept troubling him sporadically, even though his parents were most persuasive in explaining their actions as a means to better their own chances. They also confided to Wolfgang that the expanding Czech underground planned to find ways of eliminating Sudeten citizens with leadership potential. The network's rationale was that such persons might cause the refugees to rally around them after their expulsion from the region and demand the undoing of the injustice. The members of the underground were determined to neutralize anyone who could in some way serve the Sudeten cause, and this plan extended even to targeting the young offspring of respected families.

Wolfgang agreed to go along with his parents' collaboration by the time he left to return to his unit. But he still struggled to reconcile his conscience with the mission he had accepted. On the day of his departure he was shown a secret list of names, some of whom he recognized as the families of schoolmates. The long list represented persons marked for elimination whenever the opportunity arose. The Wildert family name was among them.

Johann became aggravated with Wolfgang's brooding silence and jumped to his feet. "I don't understand your attitude, Wolfie! Whenever I ask you a straight question you just keep staring. What the hell is going on?"

"Sit down, Johann; I am sorry to be so distracted." Wolfgang smiled wanly as he faced his friend squarely for the first time, his composure regained. "Surely by now your parents must also know that the Sudetenland will be retaken by the Czechs, who'll do their best to grab all the property they can. That's why I said I hoped your family could keep its wealth. In time the Czechs may even push all of us across the border into Germany."

Wolfgang paused uneasily, averting his eyes again. He took a deep breath, looked Johann straight in the face, and attempted to make light of the startling news he had just shared. "First the war and the occupation have to be over, before anything else can happen, right? I don't know any more—and all is speculation, anyway. At any rate, given half a chance we must try to get home as fast as we can." He nodded, seeking agreement, but his forced smile was unconvincing.

Johann stared at him with dismay. It took a few moments for the grave meaning of Wolfgang's revelations to sink in. Then he responded unsteadily, "I hope you are wrong, Wolfie. It'll be bad enough if the Czechs take over again—perhaps that's all they'll do. Right now I agree we must head for home—once we can get away." Johann suddenly felt very homesick for his family and for his girlfriend. He desperately wanted to be with them. He was afraid, shivering, chilled by the touch of an invisible evil presence. In vain he tried to rid himself of the ominous feeling. Nothing more was said.

The evening shadows lengthened. Inside the church the soldiers opened small cans of beans with their field knives and dug in their knapsacks for pieces of hard rye bread issued that morning. The cold food tasted like glue and cardboard, and they were glad to wash down the sticky mess with gulps of water from their field bottles.

The patrol made ready to leave. Kurt, their experienced leader, climbed the creaking wooden stairs to the top of the church steeple where Georg still kept watch. The lookout had seen no sign of enemy activity from his vantage point. Kurt carefully surveyed the scene and satisfied himself that the patrol would have little difficulty fording the narrow river and crossing the open fields once dusk approached. Kurt rang Lt. Pritzke on the field telephone to report that he and his men were ready. Pritzke repeated his strict orders to avoid all contact and to return with estimates of enemy position and strength, if at all possible.

At nineteen hundred hours sharp the patrol left the church and stalked through the graveyard into the open fields. Several times they paused to listen to the sporadic deep rumble of artillery audible to the west. Evidently the remaining *panzers* maintained their futile stand near the town, although it seemed that the *Amis* were content to draw the defenders' fire from a distance to exhaust their ammunition and fuel. It was only a question of hours.

With Kurt in the lead, followed by Johann and Wolfgang to the rear, the three young soldiers ducked through the open spaces as darkness enveloped them. They stopped by the steep river bank to survey the other side, then skidded down the grassy slope and sloshed through the knee-deep water, holding their weapons high. With wet and clammy boots they scrambled up the other side, then rested flat on their bellies. They stared toward the west where the last light in the evening sky turned a faded grayish purple, against which the dark trees stood out sharply. A chorus of croaking frogs mixed incongruously with the distant thunder of the guns. When nothing stirred they rose and stole their way through the fields and meadows for several hundred yards.

A shot rang out, cracking like a leather whip. The faint echo mocked them. Flattening themselves against the damp ground they held their breath, waiting. Could it be the other patrol—or was an advance unit of Americans coming their way? No further shots followed and after a long, tense wait Kurt pushed himself up on his forearms, turned his head and whispered, "You two lie low while I make my way to the edge of the trees. Follow me in two minutes if I don't signal." The agile soldier sprinted forward, cat-like, skillfully taking cover behind bushes and trees. Soon he disappeared into the darkness. Johann and Wolfgang waited, straining to hear. Nothing moved.

"I doubt that the *Amis* have come yet," Wolfgang murmured, "that shot sounded like someone in the other patrol got nervous."

At that moment the distant staccato of an American submachine gun rattled and echoed from the direction of the other patrol, followed by several muffled rifle shots and two unmistakable bursts of a German automatic. Johann hugged the ground, his heart beating wildly. The enemy had arrived—but perhaps it was only an advance probe? Wolfgang pressed himself into the moist grass behind his companion. Nerves taut, they both waited. The other patrol must have stumbled on some Americans scouting the terrain and drawn fire, but now followed orders and broke off. No further shots were exchanged.

In the intense silence Wolfgang's thoughts strayed from the present danger and returned to his preoccupation with the secret role he had accepted. Trembling excitement seized him when the sudden idea flashed in his mind that at this very moment he had an opportunity—a perfect opportunity—to serve his new masters. He again pictured the lengthy list he had seen, the many pages of names.

Spurred on by a surge of blind determination that drowned his doubts Wolfgang whispered hoarsely to Johann, "We must catch up with Kurt, let's go!" Johann pushed himself up, climbed to his feet and cautiously began moving toward the trees, now veiled in darkness. Wolfgang followed closely behind, his rifle pointing at Johann's neck below the helmet. Absorbed in his groping advance Johann thought only of how best to reach Kurt at the edge of the small forest.

A sudden, searing, blinding surge of white light enveloped Johann's mind and blacked out all consciousness. A convulsive sensation of release flooded Wolfgang, a simultaneous flash of overwhelming pleasure and pain. The shock of reality made him gasp when he saw Johann's tall dark shape collapse to the ground, his neck shattered by the impact of the rifle bullet fired from only inches away. He knelt down by the lifeless body, covered his face and sobbed. Inside him an insidious message hammered away, again and again, relentlessly, "Judas, Judas, Judas . . ."

Kurt sprinted back when he heard the crack of the rifle far behind him. Aghast, he crouched beside Johann, bent down to feel his pulse, then carefully turned him over on his back. In the darkness he could make out only hints of the massive damage the bullet caused, but his experienced eye knew that Johann was beyond help.

"What in God's name happened?" Kurt hissed sharply between heaving breaths, trying to keep his voice low.

"I had my safety off and as we got up the rifle fired by accident," was the sobbing reply. Wolfgang comprehended just a fraction of the enormity of his deed. The opportunity had been perfect. He let himself be driven to stage an accident, a tragic blunder by an inexperienced young soldier. Already he began to sense the explosive eruption of guilt and remorse that would envelop him. But he also knew instinctively that he must carry on, insisting that it had been a terrible mistake. With stunning clarity he saw that his life would never be the same again. The vision of having to live a lie gripped his mind in a steely embrace.

Casting cautious glances to the northwest where the earlier shots rang out, the two young men strained to carry Johann's limp body back toward the church, wading and stumbling though the dark waters, panting up the steep river bank, and hurrying the last few hundred feet through the fields to the walled graveyard. There they gently put him down on the age-worn stone slabs just inside the church door.

Kurt wearily reported the accident to his platoon leader, who angrily cranked the field telephone to notify Lt. Pritzke. The lieutenant hurried over from the village with the company medic. By the flickering light of candles they pronounced Johann dead, agreeing that an accidental bullet fired at close range killed him instantly.

With a heavy heart Lt. Pritzke knelt next to the body stretched out on the cold stone floor. He had been fond of the young man who never shirked his duty and was always ready to help others. Angrily he cross-examined Wolfgang, who was weeping openly now and repeated his story over and over, punctuated by sobs.

The lieutenant announced to the men who had silently gathered around that Johann would receive a proper burial early in the morning, assuming they were still clear of the enemy. He wrote down Johann's serial number and searched the dead soldier's pockets for papers and addresses to notify the next of kin. Then he pulled a letter from his own pocket which bore the delicate handwriting of a young girl. It arrived an hour earlier in the field mail and was addressed to Johann Wildert. He stared at the small envelope for a moment and gently placed it with Johann's belongings on the worn church bench.

The lieutenant straightened up, took a few steps to the door and stood still, gazing into the darkness. What a waste, he thought, what a stupid waste to try and fight on with children. Images of past battles flooded his mind, vivid scenes of victories and defeats, and the faces of countless dead and wounded. And now another young life had been snuffed out—to what end?

He could not answer his own query, and he slowly walked back to the village to await the inevitable.

FIVE

The Red Army

May 1945

The menacing and squat Russian tank rumbled into view, emerging from behind the gray villa where the fleeing German soldiers had surged forth earlier. Its gun turret slowly sweeping from side to side, the mud-brown vehicle loomed like a huge, ugly beetle. Rigid with fear and fascination Anton gaped at the monstrous apparition. It seemed to the boy that the bright red star on the turret was the creature's gleaming eye, staring at him coldly. The tank shuddered to a halt, surveyed the deserted scene and roared to life again, spewing blue exhaust fumes, its tracks and wheels whirring ominously. Two, three, and four more tanks lumbered closely behind in ponderous procession. Then followed the first personnel carriers, heavy armored vehicles moving along on rumbling tracks.

Piled high above the metal sides of the transport sat rows of Russian soldiers in brown uniforms, gazing watchfully about, their submachine guns ready. The powerful machines clattered onward at a deliberate pace down the center of the street and disappeared one by one behind the neighboring villa to the left. Above the din the three awed onlookers peering from the upper window of the Wildert villa heard barked commands in a half melodic, half guttural language that was new to their ears.

Soon foot soldiers poured forth, mixing with the tanks and vehicles that thrust onward with irrepressible force. The alert armed men walking alongside the massive column kept their snub-nosed submachine guns poised, ready for any opposition. There was none.

"My God, are they well-equipped!" Friedrich exclaimed as they watched the stream of men and machines swell and stream past them. He remembered the Nazis' ceaseless drumbeat of war propaganda about the "Russian Rabble." But the army they watched was no rabble; it was a disciplined force of professional soldiers with ample modern equipment—not unlike the German occupation forces that had come this way seven long years ago.

The officers' uniforms had an elegant cut, topped with large shoulder boards and round caps trimmed in red. Their jackets flared from wide leather belts, and slender boots complemented the tight-fitting riding pants. The brown-clad soldiers reminded the Wilderts of the tunics worn by Russian peasants, the loose-fitting but tightly-belted attire they had seen at the opera long ago. Most of the men were of stocky build, their helmets or peaked caps drawn down over their foreheads.

Anton stared in awe at the strange vehicles and weapons. The tanks, trucks and personnel carriers appeared new and well maintained. The men's belts bulged with huge pistols and ammunition packs. Submachine guns were everywhere, thick, gray, air-cooled barrels of slotted aluminum surmounted by large circular magazines. The boy wondered how heavy these lethal weapons were, and what it felt like to fire them in rapid bursts. He had seen guns in action in many war films and even witnessed live weapons demonstrations the *Wehrmacht* gave to youngsters like him to build up martial spirit. He recalled how those rifles and machine guns fired wooden blanks that shredded as soon as they spewed forth from the throbbing muzzles, making harmless piles of red and white slivers on the ground. The deafening roar was captivating and the boy loved the racket—but now he was staring at silent weapons held by determined men who would not hesitate to point at him and fire if he got in their way. The guns looked ugly and frightening.

The Wilderts lingered by the window, half hidden behind the drawn lace curtains and unnoticed by the conquerors. They saw hundreds of troops rolling and marching by with relentless determination, in loose but coherent formation, as if on display for unseen generals. On and on they came, a stream of men and equipment like a stage scene, impressive and vibrant with the power to destroy anything in its path.

The spectacle cast a spell of macabre fascination, masking for the moment the stark reality that this indeed was the enemy who at any time could, and would, exercise the ancient right of the victor to plunder and pillage. After many minutes of rapt attention Friedrich came to his senses and decided they should be less conspicuous. He carefully closed the heavier drapes over the transparent lace, pulling them very slowly to avoid attracting the soldiers' attention. Through narrow openings between the fabric panels the family continued staring at the spectacle unfolding before them.

Suddenly one of the columns of vehicles and soldiers slowed, veered toward them and spilled onto the meadow opposite the villa. This was as close as any of the marchers, friend or foe, came that morning. Holding their breath, the Wilderts watched dozens of Russian soldiers maneuver trucks and horse-drawn wagons into position, their wheels gouging the green expanse. One of the trucks carried a field kitchen which was set up rapidly. Other wagons bulged with sacks and cartons of food supplies. Soldiers quickly staked a large tent into the ground. Soon officers and men milled about the new feeding station ready for the troops filing into the city.

Anton was absorbed by the activity below him. How often had he sat by this window to watch the owner of the meadow, a farmer from a village to the north, cultivate the soil of this last remaining rural enclave in the suburban neighborhood? The growing boy could sense the rhythm of the seasons as the solitary farmer skillfully sowed, grew and harvested grass and feed grains, coaxing his pair of stubborn oxen and cursing them colorfully in his gruff hill dialect. What strange contrast the present spectacle was!

"It is amazing," Friedrich whispered, putting his arms around Maria's and Anton's shoulders, "they must feel completely secure—they haven't even bothered to check out the houses around this space."

After having witnessed the despair of the routed German army the family understood that all the Russians need do was to march into the city—no resistance was offered or expected. A single thought spurred on the fleeing men and boys—how to get away from the Russians. Not a single shot was fired by the powerful intruders who set up camp coolly right before their eyes.

"This is too good to be true," Friedrich continued with a touch of relief while they stood motionless behind the drapes. "Perhaps it is a Godsend that they're stopping right here. Do you see the officers over there? They won't want ill-behaved men around them, will they?"

Maria took a few moments before answering, her eyes riveted on the alien activity below. "You're probably right, but I'm sure they will come to our house any time they please and we'd better be prepared to face them."

Friedrich nodded dully as oppressive thoughts again invaded his mind and smothered the slender ray of hope. "Yes, unfortunately. I've heard too many horror stories to believe we won't get hurt in one way or another."

Anton had a throbbing sense of danger while he peered at the milling men in their strange uniforms. Yet somehow to him the morning's events remained more of a thrilling adventure, an intriguing game rather than a sign of the fundamental change they would bring to his life. He was only half listening to his parents' gloomy comments as he concentrated on watching the soldiers. The men set down their weapons while going about their many tasks. Only a few guards on the sides of the field held their submachine guns ready, calmly keeping watch.

The villas surrounding this disciplined but potentially explosive scene seemed lifeless—yet many pairs of eyes, hidden from view, peered anxiously at the enemy soldiers. The atmosphere crackled with tension. Frightened civilians found themselves cast in the role of rabbits eyeing the fox, a predator supremely confident of his power, ready to pounce on whatever victim he chose.

Maria grabbed her husband's hand and held it tightly. She thought the deceptively calm scene far more terrifying than facing a direct onslaught. Friedrich sensed her feelings while he struggled with his own rising tension. He began to squeeze his left side to alleviate the cutting jabs of his ulcer.

In the meadow below the unconcerned soldiers made plenty of racket, banging their equipment, revving up engines and shouting to each other in melodic Russian singsong. To the Wilderts the noise seemed unreal. The scene was like a Kafkaesque dance of doom—burly soldier figures floating dreamlike in a ritualistic orgy of celebration before consuming their victims.

Anton gasped and pointed, suppressing a shriek. One of the soldiers, pistol in hand, left the group. The man ambled across the street towards them, approaching the white picket gate of the fenced-in front garden. Friedrich and Maria spotted him instantly. "Maria, for God's sake, quick—hide in the cellar! Run! Cover yourself with coal sacks if you hear someone coming. I'll try to deal with him!" Friedrich half shouted, half whispered, fearful of attracting the soldier's attention. His pulse raced wildly and the ulcer hurt more than ever.

He watched transfixed as the soldier came nearer, deliberate and menacing. Behind him he heard Maria's hurried footsteps tumble down the curving staircase. After a moment Friedrich swallowed hard, turned around and mustering what courage he had left, descended the stairs to position himself behind the front door.

Anton remained by the window and glimpsed the soldier leaping over the five-foot gate, not bothering to turn the handle. The boy's heart pounded. He ran to the master bedroom, remembering that his father had firmly told him to stay out of sight, whatever happened. He cowered in the corner where his crib once stood, hidden by the large armoire made of the blond burly wood that gave his parents' room such a warm and secure feeling.

Insistent pounding shook the front door. The sharp blows startled everyone in the house. In the caretaker apartment the old Sattler couple looked for cover, trembling with fear. The refugee women and children on the first floor fearfully hid as best they could.

Friedrich stood frozen behind the shuddering door, feeling terribly alone. Every blow jabbed at his insides. He knew he had to face the impatient intruder before he became even more dangerous. Drawing a deep breath he stepped forward and turned the handle. As the door swung open Friedrich stared into the muzzle of a large caliber revolver. A pair of intent, dark eyes pierced him as he tried to overcome the shock of the confrontation. His mind reeled, forgetting the pain of his ulcer, refusing to accept the enormity of this life-and-death encounter. Desperately he tried to focus on what action he might take. Confused, he let his instincts take over. He slowly lifted his eyes from the ugly black opening in the gun barrel and faced the intruder.

Reeking of leather, sweat and alcohol, the heavy-set Russian appeared to him like a giant outlined by the bright sunlight of the open door frame. The man rasped a few guttural words, his tongue heavy with drink. Stunned, Friedrich backed off a step or two while his fluttering brain registered with amazing clarity details of the man's unkempt appearance. The soldier followed him, the revolver always pointed at Friedrich's stomach. For a moment the vested executive and the rough, battle-worn warrior hovered in intense, primitive assessment.

Friedrich gathered all his courage and made a host-like gesture towards the man. The Russian seemed to understand and entered, gun extended, eyes riveted on his victim. Backing off further in small groping steps Friedrich tried, without success, to hide the terror that showed in his blood-drained face and widened eyes. He felt like screaming. The silent, possibly lethal encounter turned seconds into an eternity, and the steady ticking of the hall clock pounded like hammer blows in his ears.

Once inside the hall the primitive man seemed unsure. Friedrich's instinctive gesture of hospitality appeared to have a calming effect, although the intruder did not lower his revolver or lessen his vigilance. He slowly followed Friedrich to the upper floor of the villa, ascending the curving staircase which Maria had hurried down just moments ago. Together the uneven pair entered the dining room, a setting heavy with tradition, graced by a crystal chandelier and brocaded chairs, carved dark furniture, oriental rugs, and displays of fine china. At a loss, the soldier hesitantly responded to Friedrich's gesture to be seated, easing his massive body in the stained uniform onto one of the delicate chairs.

Perspiring from his efforts to stay calm Friedrich cast about in his mind as to what to do next. His eye fell on the carved humidor which held his most prized possession, about fifty cigarettes saved up painfully from meager ration allotments. In better times Friedrich smoked fifty cigarettes and more in a single day, but now this treasure would have to last him a long time. It occurred to him that the soldier might respond to a peace offering of a cigarette. He felt the man's curious gaze following his every move as he tried to assess what his nervous host might do.

Friedrich reached over to the side table for the humidor. As he did so he saw the soldier swaying slightly in his chair, the Russian's unsteady eyes following his movements. Carefully Friedrich opened the lid and extended the box to offer his guest a smoke. At the sight of the neat stack of cigarettes the man's stubbly face broke into a wide grin, his teeth dark with steel crowns. Clumsily he lifted himself to his feet, crashed down the revolver on the polished table and lifted his arm in a sloppy salute. A stream of guttural Russian floated on his smelly breath, the word *tavarishch* [1] repeated over and over.

With amazing agility the soldier grabbed both the humidor and his gun and retreated toward the door in a drunken dance. He thundered down the staircase, flung himself out of the front door and hurried along the garden path, jumping over the gate in one mighty leap. Friedrich was left standing in surprised disbelief.

Anton crept from his hiding place when he heard the heavy footsteps thumping down the staircase. He ran to his father who stood silently in the doorway of the dining room. As the boy looked up at him he saw Friedrich's ashen face, his hands limp by his side, shaking from the encounter.

"Well, thank God he is gone," he muttered with a hoarse voice, hugging Anton. "And so are all my cigarettes," he added forlornly. The boy knew what this loss meant to his father, who so often had tried to stop smoking.

Together father and son hurried down to the cellar. They called out to Maria who emerged from one of the storage rooms

[1] comrade

where she had managed to camouflage herself. Clinging to each other they knew that this was only a fleeting respite. The officers' presence in the Russian encampment across the street did appear to provide a degree of protection, for they had no further intruders. The Wilderts had no way of knowing what was happening in other parts of the city, or even in the immediate neighborhood. They felt as if they were living on a hostile island, cut off from all communication.

The family huddled in the living room facing the street and the meadow so alive with Russians. Talking quietly behind drawn curtains they tried to keep up their courage. In the early afternoon they ate some days old bread and oily margarine that they garnered before the invasion, in the last long food queue at the depleted neighborhood shops. As they sat, the smell of hearty Russian cooking wafted through the window. The soldiers had settled in well and were busy providing for their hungry stomachs.

After an hour or so the babble of voices from the meadow grew louder. Anton got up to peer from behind the drapes and saw groups of laughing and talking soldiers lounging about. They passed bottles from hand to hand. He turned to his parents and whispered, "They sure are drinking a lot!" An uneasy silence fell over the family, each wondering what would come next. The noises from the camp were a constant reminder of the danger, and their helplessness gnawed on their nerves. The episode with the soldier at last brought Friedrich face to face with one of the conquerors—a brush with brutal reality —and they knew that so far they had been exceedingly lucky to be spared.

Anton sat quietly, subdued by the tension he could feel all around him. He wondered idly whether they could have made any defensive preparations. The childish heroic idea of barricading the house and taking a last stand lingered in his mind for weeks. It was rooted in the many stories of heroism that had been fed him and his friends over the years by the party youth movement in their constant effort to mold thoughts and attitudes. But today the reality of what he could see around him with his own eyes sobered him. How was it possible for civilians to do anything in such circumstances? He began to understand that they were being subdued by an overwhelming force, and that anyone who tried to resist would be crushed like a gnat, not to mention the fact that they had no weapons with which to fight. He remembered Johann's letters telling them that there were not even enough rifles and ammunition for the young conscripts during the waning days of the war.

Friedrich went downstairs to check on the refugee women and children quartered on the first floor, and to see the old Sattler couple below. In each case he found cowed human beings consumed with foreboding and fear, mirroring his own feelings. There was nothing anyone could do except wait, wait, wait . . .

But how long could this waiting game go on? The residents of the area gathered what meager food supplies could still be scrounged up during the past weeks. These were mostly tasteless gray bread, coarse flour and dried pasta, some sugar and an occasional precious lump of margarine. Eggs, milk, butter, and fresh meat were things one could only imagine now, ration tickets or not. Those who dared—and there were heavy penalties for black-market dealings—bartered some of their bed linen, yards of cloth, garments, shoes, and other treasures for butter, eggs and meat from nearby villages. But in recent months the farmers had become reluctant to part with food, thinking of their own needs as the end drew near, many of them satiated with the finery from the city folk.

Miraculously the city's gas system still operated despite the heavy bomb damage. The Wilderts cooked simple meals from hoarded staples, supplemented by home-grown fruit and rabbit meat put up in vacuum glass jars stored in the basement of the villa. There was also a small pile of coal briquettes left to feed the central heating and hot water furnace. Electricity, though unreliable, was still on much of the time; the water supply was limited and taps ran only during certain hours of the day. Bathtubs and all kinds of containers were kept filled with water. Under these conditions the Wildert family and the other residents of the villa could probably manage for two or three weeks. Yet this degree of preparation, such as it was, depended on surviving the onslaught of the conquering army. The critical question was whether the

Russians would begin plundering, smashing and devastating the homes and apartments left untouched by the war, and much worse, violate the women and girls as they had done in other areas they had overrun.

The noises outside grew steadily louder. Fortified with food and drink the soldiers were moving and milling about and small armed patrols began reconnoitering the deserted residential streets. So far the Russians seemed content with observing the houses from the outside. Tensely, the Wilderts waited for some-thing—anything—to happen. And it did.

Thunderous pounding at the front door brought the family to their feet. This time they had not seen anyone approach or leap over the garden gate. The ominous hammering persisted. Friedrich made a wordless gesture toward Maria and Anton to hide again. Maria ran to the basement, anxious to resume her suc-cessful hiding place. Anton hurried into the small room, accessi-ble only through the kitchen, where Nannerl lived before she had to leave the Wilderts because of war-time restrictions on domes-tics. Downstairs *Frau* Sattler and the refugee women hid as best they could.

Once more Friedrich stood behind the throbbing door. He wait-ed as long as he dared to give everyone as much time as possible to take cover. With trembling hands he turned the handle. The heavy oak door swung open to the outside, pulled by a powerful arm. He faced the massive figure of a soldier who immediately thrust the muzzle of a submachine gun, slung low from his shoul-der, into Friedrich's stomach. Wincing with pain Friedrich stum-bled backward, arms raised. This time he knew with frightening clarity he faced an adversary far more dangerous than the first one. His mind reeled.

The man shoved impatiently with his weapon, uttering slurred guttural commands which Friedrich could not comprehend, his breath heavy with alcohol. The contorted stubbly face had the high cheekbones and elongated eyes of the Mongolian troops whose reputation for cruelty far preceded them wherever the Russians invaded.

Friedrich's heart thumped painfully and his mouth went dry;

his tortured brain raced to seek a way out. Instinctively he knew this one was intent on finding women, although his demanding words were unintelligible. There was nothing he could do; the intruder took over. No host-like attitude would help here.

Poking his victim with the submachine gun and kicking his legs, the intruder maneuvered Friedrich upstairs and began to look into every room. He was not interested in any of the valuable furnishings; his search was single-minded. Walking from room to room the soldier threw open any closed doors with a crash, and peered inside intently. Then he would turn around, muttering, and kick and push the ashen-faced Friedrich to the next room.

In the bedrooms the man slowly walked to the bathroom doors, flung them open and looked inside. For some reason he did not examine the large armoires, nor did he probe under the beds. Perhaps the unfamiliar furnishings made him overlook obvious hiding places, or it might have been the haze of alcohol clouding his mind. Occasionally he swayed and staggered, his speech slurring, only to pull himself together again with a jerk.

When he heard the soldier approaching the kitchen, Anton could stand the tension no longer and peeked out of Nannerl's room. The man spotted him and came closer. Towering over the crouched boy he gave him an endless stare that froze Anton's spine. Finally he turned away with a shrug. Anton never forgot the icy hostility of the armed intruder.

The search continued. His efforts having proved fruitless so far, the soldier burst open the last door in the upstairs hall. Behind it a narrow staircase led to the large, empty storage area under the peaked roof of the villa. Again he forced Friedrich to stumble up the steps, jabbing him with the weapon. Cleared out long ago under orders from civil defense, the roof storage was a barren, half-lit gabled space with exposed slanted rafters and roof slats. The man looked about the dusky expanse. A shaft of sunlight angling through the small windows illuminated the dancing dust specks. No one was there. Disappointed with the failure of his search he turned and slapped Friedrich hard with the back of his free hand, and cursed him in a rasping voice short of breath from the rapid ascent. The unsteady procession retraced its steps down the roof stairs and the curving main staircase.

Somehow the soldier overlooked the entrance to the first floor apartment which housed the refugee family. Instead, he turned to the door opening to the basement stairs and pushed his captive downward. Friedrich stumbled, lost his balance and almost fell headlong down the steep stone incline. The noise alerted the Sattlers in their quarters and they clung to each other, expecting the worst. But without stopping captor and captive went past their door into the basement area.

Maria heard the ominous steps approaching. Sensing that she might be discovered in her hiding place she slid quickly out of the storage enclosure, moved stealthily through the washing facilities and opened the back door leading to the garden. Taking cover behind verdant rows of berry bushes and ornamental hedges she fled into the furthest reaches of the open space. The rear fence was heavily shielded from view by dense clumps of greenery. She found a secluded spot to hide and listened intently, but there was only the loud hum of honey bees among the flowering bushes.

Breathlessly she waited, mentally preparing herself, if necessary, to scale the five-foot wooden picket fence and flee into the neighboring garden. That property belonged to an elderly retired judge, a long-time friend of the family. As she crouched uncomfortably, the astounding images of the morning burdened her mind. She was numb with fear for her husband and Anton, left behind in the house with the intruder.

Back in the villa the soldier poked furiously around the basement rooms, including the one which had been Maria's hiding place only moments earlier. He started to curse Friedrich, slapping him repeatedly across the face. Then he forced him to turn and reverse the course. As they neared the stairs they encountered *Herr* Sattler, who stood trembling in the dimly lit hallway, no longer able to bear the uncertainty of hiding.

The sight of the stooped, white-haired man momentarily distracted the soldier, and he missed the entrance to the Sattler apartment where the grandmotherly woman sat shaking and sobbing. Instead he pushed both captives up the steep stairway to the hall. There the enraged and frustrated Russian bellowed at the top of his lungs, brandishing the submachine gun at his victims. Anton crawled to the upper landing of the staircase and watched helplessly from above. This was different from his own scary encounter in the kitchen a few minutes ago. He was petrified to see his father and *Herr* Sattler in mortal danger. Anton wanted to scream, but his throat was constricted with horror.

Friedrich acted instinctively. Forcing himself to steady his shaking limbs he lifted his hand as calmly as he could up to his vest pocket. He pulled out his gold watch and unfastened the chain from the buttonhole. With a gracious gesture he proffered the watch on his outstretched palm. Taken by surprise, the soldier stopped shouting and stared at Friedrich's hand. His mind, dulled with drink, shifted slowly from the purpose of his search to the glittering object before him.

Friedrich knew that watches of any kind were coveted booty for the Russian soldiers. They universally shouted the word "tick-tock" when demanding watches from their victims. The soldier's face mirrored a mixture of greed, anger and hazy pleasure as he jerkily pocketed the prize. After a moment's unsteady hesitation he turned aggressively toward the old man, whose normally ruddy face had taken on the color of his white hair, and shoved the machine gun into his sunken chest.

"Tick-tock," he growled, "*dawai* [2] tick-tock." Mercifully Sattler had on him a large nickel pocket watch which he began to unfasten clumsily with trembling fingers. Before he could finish the soldier impatiently grabbed the timepiece and tore it from its chain. The double booty was sufficient to divert his attention completely. To his captives' amazement the soldier turned unsteadily and left by the front door.

Anton eased himself down the stairway when he saw him disappear. Peering out with the other residents he watched the intruder stomp along the garden path leading to the street, holding the watches in his hand, eyeing them admiringly as he went. At the gate the man stopped, rattled the white lattice and puzzled over the handle for a moment. Then he slid the watches deep into

[2] give me

his tunic pocket, slung the submachine gun across his back, put his hands on top of the gate, and with one mighty pull and leap heaved himself over, disappearing into the throng of soldiers across the street.

Back in the garden Maria did not know the outcome of the soldier's search. She stayed low, pressed against the weathered fence, the dense bushes hiding her from sight. The steady hum of the insects seemed incongruously loud, and in the eerie suspense she felt her heart beat more rapidly when she heard bursts of noise made by the Russian soldiers across the street. Through the openings in the fence she could see the back of the judge's villa and the deserted garden in between. There was also no sign of life at her own house. If soldiers were to appear at the rear door of the Wildert villa, would she have time to scale the wooden pickets? Could she even manage something her boys had so often done with boisterous energy? Calling for help made no sense, she thought. The neighbors were in danger themselves and female screams would only attract more soldiers.

All of a sudden she spotted the old judge emerging from the rear entrance of his villa, accompanied by a wiry young Russian soldier. She ducked lower into the bushes, hoping that her bright dress was not visible. To her amazement she observed the judge conversing with the young man, apparently in a friendly fashion. In a flash she remembered that the educated man spoke Russian fluently. Clearly he used his special ability to bridge the gulf in this first contact with the conquerors.

Not daring to stir from her hiding place Maria watched in frozen suspense as the two men strolled nearer. A moment later a sharp Russian voice sounded from a window of the judge's villa. The young soldier stiffened, turned abruptly and bounded back toward the house. Maria seized this opportunity to make herself heard. She rapped the fence with a small stone and called out, almost under her breath, "*Herr* Judge, *Herr* Judge, please come here!"

Judge Carstens, a man of dignified bearing and handsome in his old age, turned slowly and squinted in her direction for a few moments before he approached the fence cautiously. He had to come right up to the gnarled pickets to see the crouched figure huddled below him. *"Gnädige Frau,"* [3] he called out in surprise, incongruously choosing the formal Austrian address used even by long-time neighbors in his generation, "what on earth are you doing here? Are you all right?"

"Please help me if you can, *Herr* Judge," she breathed anxiously, "both my husband and son are caught in the house with some Russian intruders. I'm afraid they are looking for women—so far I've been able to get away. But they may come out into the garden any moment! Please help me!"

"Just one moment, please," Judge Carstens said hurriedly, "I asked one of the officers and his man to stay with us. I'll get him to help you. The Russian officers can be trusted." With this the old gentleman turned and hastened toward his house at a speed far beyond his age. Seconds later he returned with a young soldier who bounded ahead of him, brandishing his submachine gun.

"Russki soldier *nix* make people hurt!" the agitated man in the brown uniform shouted breathlessly. Bellowing in a wild mixture of Russian and German he insisted: "Russki soldier good, *vojna* [4] over!"

After leaping nimbly over the fence he raced across the green lawn toward the Wildert villa. Slapping his weapon he roared, "Stalin *nix* want people hurt, if hurt—I shoot!"

Just then Friedrich emerged from the rear door into the garden. Startled at the sight of an irate armed Russian soldier racing toward him he resignedly raised his hands. The young man stopped abruptly and grinned. *"Tavarishch,* me *nix* hurt you." He then saluted and gave the weary man a friendly but painful slap on the shoulder. Friedrich sagged with relief. He put his arm around Anton who had followed him through the rear door.

Grim-faced the soldier pointed to the Wildert house, *"Russki tavarishch nix* here?"

Friedrich shrugged."He's gone." Then he padded his vest pocket. "He has my tick-tock." The soldier frowned, turned around and took a quick few steps back toward the fence and angrily

[3] Gracious Lady

[4] war

shouted rapid-fire questions in Russian at the judge, who inter-preted Friedrich's halting description of the encounter. Frustrated at being unable to confront his comrade the energetic soldier finally gave up, bowed smartly to Maria who emerged from her hiding place, and scaled the back fence effortlessly to return to the judge's villa.

Judge Carstens faced the Wilderts squarely. "Do you realize that this man was ready to shoot his fellow soldier? The troops have strict orders to behave themselves, which seems amazing to me after all that has been done to their own people." The old man smiled philosophically. With obvious concern he addressed Maria. "Are you quite all right, *Gnädige Frau*?" When Maria nod-ded he continued, "I don't know how long the Russian officer will stay in my house, or how long the encampment out there will remain. But for the time being we are more protected than most just by having these officers around us. Still, I wouldn't count on anything for certain."

He bowed politely and began walking back toward his house. After a few steps he stopped, turned once more and said gravely, "*Herr* and *Frau Direktor*, if you need help, please try to draw our attention. I know the phones are out, so we will have to find other ways to communicate. As long as I can use their language as a shield I'll try to do so—and I will also help you, if possible. But we are all in God's hands. I'm afraid terrible times are coming." Judge Carstens' words trailed off as he slowly resumed his deliberate walk and disappeared from view.

SIX

The Early Days

Fear became a steady, oppressive companion. Still shaken by their experience with the Russian intruders, the Wilderts and the other residents of the villa stood in the main hall and talked in hushed tones about how close they had come to serious harm. Would their luck hold?

Friedrich cautioned, "We'd better keep out of sight—who knows if the officers will be able to control their men, particularly at night!" The old judge's clever move to quarter a Russian officer was but a small ray of hope, like the wisp of smoke spotted on the horizon by survivors of a shipwreck. Would he be near enough to help when trouble came?

The hours dragged on as if time were suspended. The Wilderts remained in the living room, subdued, drawing strength from being close even though they said little. The refugee family on the first floor and the Sattler couple below them also huddled together, trying to share the burden of uncertainty. It seemed that nervous waiting had become the only choice. They behaved with the enforced passiveness of caged animals; their keepers had all the time, all the power, all the initiative.

On this first night of occupation the fading light of evening soon gave way to darkness. Outside, the Russian soldiers settled into a steady routine of feeding troops in shifts with much noise and clatter, but now the activity gradually died down. As night fell the field kitchen closed. Some of the vehicles in the meadow were reloaded, sputtered to life, and began to leave, laboring with roaring engines to regain the road. Soon everything was quiet; only a few soldiers were left to guard the remaining supply carts.

The family pulled down the air raid blinds to darken the villa. Lights would be a beacon to marauding soldiers. Friedrich sent

Anton to ask the refugees and the Sattlers to do the same. The family shared a meager meal by candlelight, for the electricity had failed again. As they sat in the flickering semi-darkness the masked windows added to the feeling of helpless isolation. They prayed that the night would not bring more encounters with the soldiers. The judge's villa and the Russian officer now seemed miles away, separated by darkness and the dead telephone.

The tensions and shocks of the day had taken their toll and the Wilderts were leaden with fatigue. Friedrich suggested they should try to rest, but remain fully clothed just in case soldiers intruded again. They left the windows open in the dark bedrooms and Anton soon drifted off to sleep.

Friedrich and Maria held each other's hands as they lay on their bed, reassured by the warm touch. They could hear Anton's regular breathing through the open door. Too tired and dispirited to talk, they listened closely to the noises drifting in from outside, sounds that betrayed the drama of the night. They could hear much distant commotion, frightening screams, and the muffled roar of engines. The sharp crack of shots reverberated ominously. Violent things were happening close by. It was obvious that other sections of the city were less subdued than their immediate neighborhood.

The night hours stretched on agonizingly. All their senses were hyper-alert though Friedrich and Maria's exhausted bodies craved for the relief of sleep. No intruders interrupted their uneasy rest, and at last they dozed fitfully, only to awaken fearfully whenever the noises in the night flared up. They decided to take turns sleeping so that one would always be alert to warn the others if danger was near.

When the hues of dawn finally lightened the night sky Friedrich and Maria were much relieved to see outside again. Tired but glad the long darkness had passed without incident they removed the blinds from the living room windows. They were just in time to watch the last Russian vehicles leaving the meadow below them. Gouged and churned by hundreds of wheels, the green space was littered and raw, a desolate reminder of the masses of troops that passed through the previous day. Still, the Russian presence had been a form of security; now even this small protection was lost.

"We were very lucky to have the camp out there, but we'd better think of another way to get some help," Maria said resignedly. With a wistful tone she added, "Judge Carstens was so clever to ask an officer to stay with them—how I wish we could speak the language!"

Friedrich was deep in thought, pondering the problem. "It would be wonderful if we could find some released Allied prisoners to stay with us," he mused.

The idea seemed natural because Friedrich's company employed a number of French prisoners during the last years of the war and he always insisted they be treated well. These men might respond favorably to such an invitation, but the problem was how to reach any of them. It could not be done without venturing into the streets. No one dared to go outside, at least for the moment—and where were the prisoners now, anyway? Friedrich was certain they were released immediately by the invading Russians and it was likely they had begun their homeward trek already.

"I'm afraid this will remain an idea only." Friedrich sadly shook his head. "How could we hope to find them in this turmoil?"

As the morning wore on the family kept watch from their window but there was little to observe. Occasional patrols of Russian soldiers passed by without incident. The young Czech militiamen who acted so officiously during the German retreat were nowhere to be seen. Life stirred cautiously in the neighboring villas; some people even appeared in their gardens, only to retreat quickly when hearing the heavy-booted footsteps of Russian patrols.

Suddenly Anton spotted two figures walking past the villa down the gentle slope of the street. They were clearly foreign soldiers, and in a flash the boy recognized the cut and color of British uniforms. Pointing at the strangers Anton called out excitedly to his parents, "Look, these men are British soldiers or officers!"

Startled by this unexpected opportunity Friedrich exclaimed, "Anton, you had better muster all the English you learned in school, and try to talk these men into staying with us! Quick, run after them!" He remained by the window, anxious, feeling badly about sending the boy, but his own inadequate linguistic skills always caused much good-natured joking among the family whenever his sons showed off their expanding English and Latin vocabularies and tried to converse with him. Tense with frustration he muttered to himself, "Of all the times not to be able to speak another language . . ."

Anton bounded down the staircase into the open, raced along the garden path and bolted out of the white gate. He did not have time to be frightened at leaving the safety of the house and entering the street, so familiar and yet so strange. As fast as he could he ran after the two soldiers and caught up with them in front of the neighboring villa.

The men stopped and turned when they heard the boy's hurried footsteps. Anton glanced about warily, but no Russians were around. He stared intently into the strangers' faces and swallowed hard to overcome his nervousness. Between rapid breaths he gasped in halting school English, "Are you Englishmen and vill you like to stay in our house?"

Surprise swept over the men's faces. They looked at the stammering boy for a moment, then seemed to understand. The taller one twanged in what they later learned to be a South African accent, "Yehs, we are. Do you have a wireless that is working?" Responding to Anton's puzzled hesitation the man repeated, "Wireless—raydio—you know?"

Anton bobbed his head eagerly, "Yes, ve have radio, and ve also have food. Vill you like to stay vith us?"

The men conversed in rapid-fire dialogue that outstripped Anton's schoolboy vocabulary. Uncomprehending and confused the boy became anxious about standing in the street and kept looking in all directions.

Finally the tall soldier faced him. "Yehs, okay, that will be fine with us."

Anton hurried the Englishmen toward the villa, pulling at them in his haste to get off the street. Friedrich and Maria stood on the stone landing outside the front door, waiting nervously. They greeted the men warmly with handshakes and smiles, but in awkward silence as their tired minds yielded no English words of welcome. The boy beamed with pride at his success. For the first time he had done something important and his use of real English worked. He was pleased and a little less frightened than before.

The men were put up in his uncle's and his brother's rooms, and they delighted in taking long baths. The water had just come on again, and they did not mind the lukewarm flow the heating system provided.

A few hours earlier the electricity resumed, which meant the radio was working as the critical link to the world. It was a powerful American Lafayette receiver Friedrich imported shortly before the war, and Anton proudly demonstrated the set, feeling free of the severe war-time prohibitions against receiving foreign stations. As the soldiers concentrated on any English language broadcasts, the boy sat with them, straining to understand the rapid flow of news. It soon became clear that the collapse of Hitler's Third *Reich* was complete. Acting for the *Führer* after his suicide, Admiral Dönitz signed the unconditional surrender. The war was over and the monumental task of restoring order lay ahead.

The Wilderts' feelings contrasted sadly with the obvious delight of their foreign guests about their newly won freedom and impending homeward journey. To the family the events of the recent days were just preludes of doom, of overwhelming changes in everything they had known.

The soldiers sat by the radio continuously, tuned to an Allied military station that emitted bulletins and announcements in a steady stream. Tenaciously they listened for news on when and how they would be processed for return to their home country.

Meanwhile all the inhabitants of the villa shared a welcome sense of relief as a result of harboring these strangers in their midst. How fortunes shifted! Hapless prisoners only days ago, these young men suddenly became eagerly sought-after protectors as members of the winning side, able to shield their hosts from serious harm by their mere presence. As long as they stayed in the villa the worst excesses of any armed intruders could be averted. The second night of the occupation promised to be more restful for everyone.

Anton helped Maria and Friedrich prepare a full course meal for their guests. They opened some of the few remaining jars of rabbit meat, preserved fruit and other odds and ends they had hoarded, and they displayed a tasty array of dishes in the formal dining room. In honor of the occasion Friedrich poured a bottle of powerful berry wine, home-made from the bounty of the garden. It was a rare feast for everyone, both in setting and quality, yet the festive formality seemed incongruous after all that had gone before.

Anton served as a halting interpreter, his initial red-faced inhibition melting away with practice. A steady conversation developed, punctuated by occasional merriment over humorous twists in Anton's labored use of English, or over the few samples of prison camp German the men contributed. Warm feelings grew from this human contact; it was contagious for all, and the group savored a fleeting pause of tranquil pleasure and normalcy. The Wilderts began to relax a little, allowing a sense of security to displace the constant tension they felt. They were grateful to be harboring these civilized men in uniform under their roof. In turn the ex-prisoners relished this advance glimpse of their longed-for return to freedom.

The family learned that the tall lieutenant was from Durban, and the sergeant from Capetown. They were held as prisoners by the *Wehrmacht* for just under a year, after being separately captured in France during the invasion. Their treatment at the hands of the Germans had been rough but not unbearable. Conditions during the last two months had worsened, however, as supply shipments became disrupted in the massive confusion of the impending collapse; these shortages affected captives and captors alike. The conquering Red Army opened their camp and freed them—now they were anxious to get in touch with the western Allied forces.

Long deprivation brought a heightened appreciation of food; the men savored every morsel and left not a scrap on their plates. Anton secretly admired their deliberate style of eating and their polite table manners.

After dinner the South Africans asked to be excused and gratefully returned to the radio in the living room where they listened for further news about their repatriation. An hour later the electricity failed again and they went to their rooms, glad to stretch out comfortably in the soft, snow white linen of their beds, a treat they had missed for so long. The second night of occupation descended over the hushed neighborhood. Distant noises still echoed, occasionally startling the inhabitants of the villa, but the tension diminished greatly by the soldiers' presence. Everyone slept, restoring much needed energy.

In the morning they shared a simple breakfast of *ersatz* [1] coffee and coarse bread. While they ate the radio again broadcast in English and the South Africans soon resumed their vigil, waiting tensely for the critical announcement that would bring orders to begin their journey halfway around the world.

From time to time Anton tried to talk with the soldiers who must have been about twice his age. His beginner's English was being tested beyond its limits, but the serious young men, an engineer and a shopkeeper, enjoyed the company of the spirited boy. Often they shared a hearty laugh when some of Anton's sentences turned out especially convoluted.

Yet there was something wistful about the South Africans. They had experienced bloody fighting in fierce battles, preceded by the hazardous Channel crossing on D-Day. The many deprivations of prison camp were still vivid in their memory. This sudden leap into a hospitable setting had an air of unreality about it and they missed their own faraway homes and families even more.

Here they were, giving aid, comfort and a measure of protection to people who had been their enemies only days before. The Wilderts offered hospitality in an obvious trade for security. But why not accept? The family treated them as guests and shared their shelter and whatever food they had. The men were glad to partake of this brief respite, for soon they would be on their way home, traveling in spartan army conditions. Home! They could hardly believe it!

[1] substitute

The long awaited announcement resounded in the room. "All former Allied prisoners of war report immediately to the processing center that has been opened in the central square of the city!" the radio blared. "Further instructions for repatriation will be issued there. Repeat: All. . ." The soldiers jumped abruptly to their feet, electrified. "How do we find our way to the city center?"

Anton described the most direct route downtown, a walk of about thirty minutes. The electric trolleys connecting their neighborhood with the bomb-damaged core of the city had been knocked out of service early in the year.

"Perhaps you have bicycles we could borrow?" the lieutenant asked the boy. "We'll return them to you in the evening, since we are not likely to be moved out for a day or two at the earliest. You can trust us; frankly, we would like to enjoy your house for another night."

Anton hesitated. There was only one working bicycle in the house, with two others laid up because they lacked essential parts and tires. This old bicycle meant mobility and if it were lost there would be no quick way to reach neighbors and friends should that become necessary. What if the men had to leave the city immediately? Would they be able to return the bicycle? Anton tried to explain the predicament and the men understood.

Soon they emerged from their rooms, leaving them as clean as they found them the previous night. They were neatly dressed in their newly mended, cleaned and pressed uniforms. This was the first chore they insisted on doing when they came to the house the morning before. The family stood with them on the stone landing. "We expect to be back before dark," the lieutenant said, "and we should know by then what we will do next. Meanwhile we thank you kindly for your hospitality." After declining Maria's offer of pieces of bread to sustain them for the day the soldiers saluted smartly and said good-bye to their hosts. They shook hands with Anton and thanked him for being a good interpreter. Walking briskly to the garden gate they turned into the quiet street, their firm steps audible for a long while.

As he watched them leave Friedrich said wistfully, "I wish they would be back tonight, but somehow I doubt it very much." The

South Africans' departure left everyone with a keen sense of loss. The brief episode had been a curious reminder of the frequent happy, hospitable occasions the family enjoyed in normal times. To touch other lives—poles apart in background and circumstances—and to be able to do so in a civilized way was like a momentary flash of memory of life before the war. They knew this glimpse of peaceful times could not last as events continued on their inexorable course.

They returned to the living room and changed the radio dial to receive bulletins that poured forth one after the other in both German and Czech. The first announcements told of the re-establishment of the Czechoslovak Republic and of the arrival from exile of a provisional government which would take over authority from the Allied occupation forces. The political leadership was again in the hands of Dr. Edvard Beneš, who had returned to Prague via Moscow after spending the war years in London.

Then came messages addressed to all persons of German nationality, whether native to the Sudetenland or newcomers after the German annexation. A strict overnight curfew was put into effect, and every individual of German nationality was ordered to wear a white armband at all times, exactly fifteen centimeters wide, above the left elbow. The announcement threatened severe penalties for violation of any of these decrees. Other orders included everyone's obligation to return to work, to carry suitable identification at all times, and to register for ration coupons.

The ominous stream of rules and threats was chilling, especially the requirement to wear white armbands in the street. These white markers, like the yellow stars which Jews had been forced to wear under the Nazi regime, would instantly single them out as vulnerable, lacking any legal standing and leaving them open to attack. The Wilderts realized the weeks ahead would bring yet more dangers and untold difficulties from the new regime. Their preoccupation would continue to be with day-to-day survival.

Later in the afternoon, as the family continued to listen to the jumble of announcements, Friedrich looked firmly at Maria and said, his voice tense, "Like it or not, I'm convinced I must go to the office tomorrow. A lot of people in the company depend on me. Lord knows what I'll find, but I feel I must take the risk. I expect the new authorities will impose themselves quickly—but perhaps my position will give us some protection."

Maria protested sharply. "You'll have to walk for at least twenty minutes in the streets, Friedrich, with armed Russians and Czech militia swarming all over the city. It's too dangerous and far too soon! Please try to think of us as much as you think of the others!"

Friedrich persisted with a stubborn determination that even surprised himself. It was as if he wanted to influence events through what he perceived as dutiful activity—any activity—to break the tension grating on his nerves. Not too convincingly he tried to counter Maria's tearful arguments by saying that he would first go to look up Dr. Fisher, the research director of the company who lived only a few houses away. If he was well they could walk to the office together. He maintained that being in the streets with a companion would be safer, although deep down he did not believe it. Anxious to end the debate, he argued that whatever he did, he would have to wait until morning and there was no sense in discussing it further.

When evening fell the South Africans had not returned and the family realized they would never see them again. Only occasional traffic stirred on the street, mostly Russian army vehicles and soldiers. From time to time a few civilians passed by, and there were groups of the strangely uniformed Czech militia with their colorful armbands. So far they saw no one in the street wearing the white armbands the radio bulletins ordered. Obviously people were not yet venturing out of their houses!

The phones were still dead and the family deliberated whether to try and contact some of their neighbors in person, as the feeling of isolation was becoming unbearable. From time to time they checked on the refugees and the Sattlers below. But the other people in the house were caught with them in the same prison, unable to shed any light on what was happening elsewhere.

From the bedroom window Friedrich spotted some movement in the old Judge's garden. He quickly went downstairs into the basement and emerged through the rear door, crossing the open space cautiously after looking about him for a few moments. Judge Carstens glimpsed his neighbor, waved anxiously and came to the back fence, craving human contact as much as Friedrich.

"It doesn't look good at all," said the silver-haired gentleman, his shaky voice betraying grave concern. "There's much talk among the Russians in my house about an impending evacuation of all German nationals from this area, native Sudetens and otherwise. I'm not certain whether this means exile to Siberia—a terrible prospect—or some type of resettlement into Germany. I'm also not sure whether it's the Russians or the Czechs who are behind this plan, although I suspect the latter."

Lost in worried thought the judge paused, then resumed his account. "What I understand so far is that the Allies signed a treaty some time ago returning the Sudetenland to Czechoslovakia, in effect nullifying the Munich Agreement of 1938. But this time it appears that all of us non-Czech residents will be resettled, even though we represent more than ninety percent of the population and have lived here for generations, for many hundreds of years, as you well know."

The judge paused again. "It reminds me of the times in the 1930's before Hitler's takeover, when the Czechs put pressure on us to give up our Austrian identity. Now it seems we'll have to give up everything—our land, our homes, our belongings. We had better steel ourselves for terrible times to come. As long as they don't separate families—and there are even rumors about that—it may be bearable. But where in God's name will they ship us?" The distinguished old man fell silent.

Friedrich became more and more tense upon hearing the alarming news. He recalled the many troubled discussions with friends and colleagues during the last months of the war when they speculated about the implications of what they saw as certain defeat. At the time he tried to prepare his family for sacrifices—material losses like bombing or shelling of the villa, or plunder and injury by conquering soldiers.

But he had not prepared himself or his family for the frightening prospect of being cast adrift as disowned refugees in a war-torn land. Would they now share the fate of the streams of German refugees from East Prussia and Silesia, who months ago began passing through this area and were crowded into any available space? The authorities provided minimally for these hundreds of thousands of homeless and, under emergency decrees, quartered them in the houses and apartments of the local inhabitants, including the Wildert villa.

But all familiar authority had ceased to function. Who would be in charge now, and who would help them when their turn came? Would they indeed be sent to Siberia, men and women separated and children sent somewhere else?

His older son was probably trying, at this very moment, to find his way home from Saxony. Gnawing fears for Johann's survival racked Friedrich's tired mind, already churning with deep worry about how he could protect Maria and keep Anton safe. He bit his lower lip hard not to scream out loud under the weight of the burden that threatened to crush his resolve and carefully controlled demeanor.

Judge Carstens shook off his own fears for a moment when he saw the younger man's visible struggle. He had known Friedrich and his family since they built the villa fifteen years before. He watched the boys grow, patiently putting up with their childish noise and banter when they played in the adjoining garden with their friends. His neighborly feelings had grown into genuine regard for the Wilderts. Now it was his lot to alert Friedrich and his family to the tragedy that lay in store for them.

Swallowing hard the judge finally said ponderously, "In the cosmic perspective we individuals count for nothing. Higher forces have decided our fate. All we can do is to try to be strong. We have a duty to go on living and to prove ourselves as best we can. My wife and I have decided we will go wherever fate sends us—somehow God will help."

Friedrich replied with an uncertain voice, "I'd better go back and prepare my family and the others in the house for the bad news. I can only say respectfully, *Herr* Judge, I hope very much that for once you are wrong."

Judge Carstens did not reply and started to walk toward his

house, sadly shaking his head. After a few exhausted steps he turned around to face Friedrich once more. "You'll probably have to go to your office tomorrow. Please ask your wife to stay out of sight, but if she should need help have her send young Anton to the back fence. The Russian officer is still with us and I promise to do what I can to assist you and your family." He averted his face so as not to let the younger man see the tears welling in his eyes.

"Thank you again, *Herr* Judge, and may God bless you for all your kindness and concern; we shall not forget it." Friedrich also tried to hide his surging emotions and quickly walked to the back door.

Maria had prepared a simple meal. When she saw the distress in her husband's face she asked anxiously what he had learned from Judge Carstens. Friedrich told his wife and son the fearsome rumors, and for quite some time they discussed how they might deal with these uncertainties. Friedrich also went downstairs and reluctantly told the refugee family and the Sattler couple the news, which was received with tears and stunned disbelief.

Maria battled her melancholy feelings and tried to think of practical steps to take. She suggested that she put together a set of essential utensils, basic clothing and everyday supplies. These would have to be limited in weight and bulk to what they could carry if an evacuation order did come.

Friedrich was still preoccupied with the judge's worrisome words when Anton left for his room to get ready for bed. Finally he spoke up. "Maria," he said tenderly, "do you really think we should let ourselves be driven out as refugees, if it comes to that? What if the four of us are separated and we have to go to Siberia or God knows where?"

Maria slumped back in her chair, almost feeling the heaviness enveloping her husband. He was so tired of late, tired of struggling just to live and keep his family safe. "If it were just you and me, matters would be simpler—but we do have to think of Johann and Anton; they still have their lives ahead of them. Once Johann finds his way home, the four of us must face whatever lies ahead—if only for the boys' sake." She held back her tears while trying to sound brave.

"I wish I had your conviction," Friedrich sighed dejectedly. "I have the terrible feeling that we'll be treated like cattle, separated and left to rot. I'm not sure I have the courage or strength to face that." He did not dare tell Maria that he sensed his first-born would not return, and gripped his left side where the ulcer gnawed at his stomach.

"We can't lose our heads, Friedrich," Maria continued her show of bravery. "As long as we're alive there's always hope. We must believe that. Why don't you and Anton get some sleep while I begin sorting out what we may need to take with us."

With that Maria began to pick out some of the clothing essential to take during an evacuation and assembled it into four neat piles. Then she sat down at the sewing machine and from an old tablecloth made the required white armbands for the three of them, and an extra one for Johann. Being busy was good for her troubled state of mind; she could shut out disturbing thoughts by concentrating on sewing straight seams and measuring the precise width of the armbands as required by the official decree.

They spent a fitful night, often stirred awake by frightening noises near and far. Miraculously, no harm came to the inhabitants of the Wildert villa, and the immediate neighborhood remained unmolested on the third night of occupation.

SEVEN

The Messenger

On the morning of the fourth day Friedrich insisted that he must walk to his office, and Maria pleaded with him in vain. Resignedly she fastened the mandatory white armband to his left coat sleeve, taking great care to do it correctly. She shuddered at the thought of Friedrich displaying this stark symbol of vulnerability, and she won his firm promise to stop first at Dr. Fischer's house so that he would have a companion to walk with through the dangerous streets. Friedrich quickly downed his piece of bread and *ersatz* coffee and embraced his wife and son.

Closing the garden gate after him, Friedrich paused for a moment and looked cautiously left and right for any sign of trouble. He saw only a deserted neighborhood warmed by the morning sun, and turned right to start down the gentle slope. He stepped quickly, feeling vulnerable with the white armband glaring on his sleeve, all of his senses alert for danger. When he passed a neighboring villa he glimpsed a familiar figure waving to him from a partially opened door. He returned the greeting and resumed his brisk pace, encouraged by this forlorn sign of normalcy.

Soon he arrived at Dr. Fischer's house and rang the doorbell. His colleague, a slight man with a characteristic air of reticence, peered through a crack in the front door. When he recognized Friedrich he anxiously waved him in and quickly closed the door securely behind him.

"Thank goodness you're all right, *Herr Direktor!* Did the Russians bother you and your family?"

"We've been lucky so far. There were two incidents which could have become very nasty, but fortunately we were spared." Friedrich had a weary look on his face.

"We had our problems, too," Dr. Fischer said sadly. He related how drunken Russian soldiers plundered several rooms on the ground floor of the house. They broke more than they took and also demanded his gold watch at gunpoint. Luckily his attractive blond wife and golden-haired six-year-old daughter had hidden themselves well and remained unharmed. A subdued *Frau* Fischer and young Edda joined the two men in the hall. When Friedrich spoke of his decision to walk to the office and asked that Dr. Fischer go with him, she protested strongly as Maria had done, insisting it was far too dangerous to be seen in the street wearing white armbands. Edda began to wail.

Friedrich remained firm and cited several radio bulletins that had proclaimed all persons in the city were ordered to report to their respective work places as soon as possible. Ration cards would be issued only to those who complied. Dr. Fischer argued for a while and then reluctantly agreed to go along. His pouting wife fastened a white armband around his sleeve, and he gave her and Edda a long hug. He locked the front door carefully behind him after they left the house.

The two men stood for a while by the garden entrance, glancing anxiously about them. Everything was silent. They began to walk hurriedly along the familiar streets of the neighborhood to the main street that sloped down into the industrial district. They spoke little, each man steeped in his own concerns while keeping a watchful eye on the street around them.

When they turned a corner they faced a Russian patrol armed with ugly gray submachine guns. Though their hearts pounded wildly, Friedrich and Dr. Fischer walked past the soldiers warily. To their great relief the men ignored them.

The main street resounded with traffic, mostly Russian army vehicles, including horse-drawn carts that clattered loudly on the cobblestone pavement. Further down the slope they spotted a few civilians wearing white armbands which made them feel less conspicuous.

Suddenly they were stopped by three young men clad in the odd makeshift uniforms of the Czech militia who stepped out of a doorway, wearing the red, white and blue armbands of the

Czechoslovak Republic. With their weapons raised they demanded to see their identity papers. Friedrich and Dr. Fischer nervously produced their I. D. cards, which the makeshift soldiers
took a long time to examine in every detail. In Czech they
demanded their destination. Since neither man spoke more than
a few words of Czech Friedrich pointed toward the industrial district and said, timidly, *"robot."* [1] Their interrogators hurled a
stream of obscenities in reply.

Next the militiamen busied themselves examining their captives' white armbands. Luckily the women had taken great care to
sew them in the correct width, for one of the young men pulled
out a small pocket ruler and made a great show of measuring each
armband in two places to see if they adhered to the official fifteen
centimeters. When he was satisfied he spat on the armbands and
kicked each captive in the shins. Butting them with their rifles
the patrol ordered the pair to resume walking and laughed
viciously as the two frightened men hurried away.

Friedrich and Dr. Fischer observed similar scenes of interrogation along their route, but they were not stopped again and the
Russian patrols continued to ignore them. They passed more and
more bomb-damaged buildings and had to pick their way along
the rubble-strewn sidewalks littered with the debris cast away by
soldiers from both armies and obstructed by freshly deposited
rubble from random shelling during the Russian invasion. The
lingering stench of recent fires choked their nostrils.

At last they reached the curved iron gate that led to the walled-
in buildings of Friedrich's firm. The live-in caretaker greeted his
superiors eagerly at the porter's window, relieved to see their
familiar faces. Pushing open the squeaky gate the normally defer-
ential old man babbled on about the damage from stray shells
fired for no apparent reason by the Russian tanks thundering
past. A warehouse building was still smoldering, and many windows in the office tract were shattered, glass shards littering the
ground below. Black oily smoke billowed from a ruin across the
street, part of a factory complex that had already been badly hit

[1] work

during the final Allied air raids. It was a bleak scene of neglect and desolation.

The old caretaker told them that two Czech officials from the new regime were waiting in the executive offices. Several members of the office staff had come in earlier, including Friedrich's private secretary. About a dozen people had gathered in his large office, including the two strangers.

After watching tensely as Friedrich gave his assembled staff a subdued greeting, the Czech spokesman, *Pan* Novak, addressed the group. In fluent but accented German he announced that the company had become nationalized and taken from its German absentee owners. He would take charge of the new Czech management that was soon to be installed. For the present everyone was expected to work effectively to resume peacetime production and performance, and the relatively minor damage would have to be repaired as soon as possible. Those reporting for work would be issued papers that entitled them to food ration cards and earn provisional minimum wages in the new Czech currency which soon would be the only acceptable money.

After dismissing the group Novak and his colleague remained in the office with Friedrich. When they were alone Novak told Friedrich firmly that he and *Pan* Homulka, both businessmen, would use every means at their disposal to make the transition as effective and timely as possible. Friedrich's duty as the former chief executive was to aid them and not to withhold any information. He was still to be held accountable for the performance of the company, and his responsibilities included guiding Novak until he assumed all duties as Friedrich's successor. They would issue Friedrich a document that certified his importance during this transition period, protecting him and his family against immediate resettlement.

Friedrich listened apprehensively to the matter-of-fact way in which his future was decided. But the last statement struck him like a fierce blow. He was being told with certainty of what had only been rumors so far: Resettlement!

Stunned by the news he tried to question Novak, but the stone-faced man curtly refused to say any more. He only added that a few carefully selected senior employees might possibly be given similar temporary papers if Friedrich could prove a real need for them to assist in the transition. Otherwise they would have to take their chances along with the other employees. Novak and Homulka ended the discussion and said they would return the following morning to begin working on the takeover with Friedrich.

After the two men left, Friedrich reassembled the hushed group of dispirited employees around him. He advised them that under the current circumstances everyone must carry on as best they could. He hesitated, searching for words, then repeated, with an unsteady voice, Novak's reference to an impending resettlement of the Sudeten population. The group stood and listened in agonized silence.

Finally his secretary, *Frau* Habel, spoke up, barely able to control her emotions. "Perhaps they're only trying to bluff us to make us work harder. What do you think, *Herr Direktor?*" Before Friedrich could respond there was a blur of anxious voices. "It's true, it's true! We heard that in London the new Czech government prepared everything to expel us from our territory. They signed a treaty with the Allies that returns the Sudetenland to Czechoslovakia, and they'll be throwing all of us out..."

The cowed assembly lapsed into ominous silence. Friedrich felt nauseated but pulled himself together. This was the third time he had heard talk of a planned evacuation of the Sudetenland. He struggled for a measured response to give the hushed group, and did not believe it himself when he finally said, "Even if all this were true, an action of this kind cannot be carried out overnight. The war is over, after all. The Czech authorities would have to organize a great deal of transport, food, and housing. This should give all of us time to prepare for the ordeal. Certainly we should all begin right now to think about what essentials we might need to take along, just in case. In the meantime we must do as they say—after all, they are in charge now."

As he stood before his worried employees Friedrich's brain reeled with conflicting thoughts. He deeply felt the anguish of the people with whom he had worked for so many years. Yet he was helpless, as helpless or even more so than he had been when the Nazi dictates kept streaming in from Berlin, demanding the impossible of him and his associates. What could he now do to help them, when he could not even help himself? He was being forced to manage an orderly transfer of control to Novak and his team, only to be pushed out into the unknown himself.

Friedrich took a deep breath and said tensely, "You had all better go home and see to your families and property. Tomorrow we'll have to start working with Novak and Homulka. Please try to contact our associates who are not here today, if you can, and tell them to report for work tomorrow so that they will receive rations and pay. May God protect you all!" He watched as they filed out of the office. One or two tried to keep up appearances but most looked completely distraught.

His secretary stayed behind. With a shaky voice she reported that a number of employees had suffered greatly at the hands of the conquering Russians. Several of the women had been raped, some disappeared and were thought to be hiding. Worst of all, there were rumors that a few had taken their own lives. There were incidents of plundering and beatings, and others had been wounded while trying to prevent harm to their families.

Friedrich listened with growing dejection. He knew that his own neighborhood had been miraculously spared the more extreme consequences of the invasion and occupation. While he was grateful for having escaped major harm, his heart went out to those less fortunate. He felt helpless and angry as he realized that the Sudeten population was now paying for the follies and crimes of the Nazi system that imposed itself on them only seven short years ago. He recalled numbly that he predicted this outcome to his family at the time. The sharp jabbing pain in his left side throbbed and he thought of his family and the other inhabitants of the villa, wishing he had not left them alone.

"Thank you for telling me all this, *Frau* Habel. I'm so sorry for everyone who has suffered, but I'm afraid that things will get even worse. Now please be extremely careful on your way home and always try to walk in a group. If you like, Dr. Fischer and I will accompany you home."

She accepted gratefully and after a few minutes the threesome began the perilous trek, ever alert for trouble. They were spared, however, and the two men saw *Frau* Habel safely to her apartment, where she lived alone since her husband was drafted several years before. Friedrich and Dr. Fischer resumed their hurried walk along the main street, once making a detour to avoid a Russian patrol and skirting scenes of rough interrogation where civilians with white armbands were harassed and questioned by young Czech militiamen.

It was early afternoon when they neared their own homes under gray, overcast skies that reflected their mood. Before they parted Friedrich faced the trained chemist firmly and said with unmistakable urgency, "*Herr* Dr. Fischer, I must ask an important favor of you—in fact, it is a matter of life and death!" Friedrich waited a moment before explaining. "I want you to obtain for me some cyanide from your supply of chemicals in the company laboratory. If the rumors we hear should indeed become true, I want to have the option of taking my and my family's lives to avoid going into exile."

Dr. Fischer paled visibly and muttered, "But, but... *Herr Direktor*, how could you..., how could I...?"

Friedrich cut in sharply, surprised at his own vehemence. "Don't be a damned fool; this is serious business! This isn't the time for moralizing! The decision is mine, not yours, *Herr* Dr. Fischer, if we ever come to taking the stuff. But only you are in a position to provide me with enough cyanide of the proper strength to make sure we go quickly, without suffering. Will you do it?"

After a long pause the slight man sighed and replied gravely, "You can count on me as always, *Herr Direktor*. I'll have it ready for you tomorrow."

"Thank you, *Herr* Dr. Fischer, I knew you wouldn't let me down." They split up after shaking hands, and Friedrich walked the short distance to his home alone.

As he strode along rapidly he mused wryly over his colleague's response and the solemn assurance that he could be counted on. During the last year, due in part to marital difficulties, the man had become an absent-minded professor, as Friedrich often described

his diffuse behavior to Maria. Friedrich and his increasingly inef-
fective subordinate had repeated stormy confrontations, always
ending in the research director's abject promise that he would
improve the handling of both his job and his personal problems.

Now, ironically, this disturbed man became the key to
Friedrich's potential escape from a cruel fate he did not want to
face. Could he be counted on, just for once, and would he indeed
provide the proper chemical with the correct potency, as he
promised? Might they all suffer horribly after taking the potion if
Dr. Fischer failed him again? Friedrich wiped his brow as if to
hush the sinister thoughts crowding his brain. His only choice was
to trust the man, like it or not. Straightening his posture he strode
rapidly through the garden gate to the front door of the villa.

There was no one behind the carved door as it swung open at
the turn of his key. He had rung the bell from the garden gate in a
prearranged rhythm to announce his arrival. Foreboding seized
him when he heard muffled sobs from upstairs. At the sound of
his footsteps the door to the first floor suite opened, revealing the
pale faces of the two refugee women, their eyes filled with weary
compassion. *Herr* Sattler appeared from the door leading to the
basement stairs, wordless, the same doleful expression on his
face. Friedrich hesitated, not comprehending, and stared into the
faces that obviously bore a grievous message.

Then in a white-hot flash he knew. Last night's premonition
about his first-born son, the haunting feeling which he dared not
mention to his wife had become horrible fact—Johann was never
to return! With an agonized shout Friedrich raced up the staircase and found Maria in the bedroom. Sobbing and weeping
uncontrollably his wife lay face down on the bed.

"My son, my son, my beautiful son!" she screamed again and
again. Friedrich sat down beside her, too numb to show any emotion. Then he touched her gently on the shoulder and bowed his
head, his tears flowing freely.

Anton crouched by the side of the bed, overcome with grief.
How he missed his brother, and how he had counted on Johann's
return to resume the happy life the two boys once shared. Now
this was not to be—Anton simply could not understand why. He

had never known such anguish and sorrow burdening him like an enormous weight.

After a long time attempting to console his wife, Friedrich left the bedroom, responding to Maria's wish to be alone for a while. He tenderly took the weeping Anton by the hand and led him into the living room. There, between sobs, the boy told his father what happened that morning, about an hour after Friedrich left for his walk to the office.

The doorbell rang and Anton cautiously opened the front door after seeing only one person standing by the garden gate, wearing a white armband. The young man had slowly approached the house, walking hesitantly as if in a trance. Drawn by a dark instinct Maria joined Anton on the stone landing. As if under a spell herself she stared at the young stranger coming closer and closer. All of a sudden she screamed in agony, "Johann!" and drew back.

The young caller nodded as he mounted the steps reluctantly. Maria covered her face in shock. Shyly the messenger produced a handwritten envelope from his jacket and held it out to Anton who was unsure at first, then accepted it with a reluctant hand. "I'm afraid this letter brings very bad news about your son, *Frau Wildert*." He spoke softly, his eyes warm and compassionate. "I'm one of Johann's comrades from his unit." Tears came to his eyes as he added, "Johann is in God's hands. He died quickly and without suffering." After a long struggle to regain his composure he continued. "It was a tragic accident. This letter was written by his friend. He was with Johann when it happened. Please accept my sincerest condolences."

Maria stood frozen, the shock distorting her features, her eyes wide and uncomprehending. The young man looked at her with deep respect and said quietly, "I am so sorry for you. But I have to go. I was able to make my way here from Saxony, but I have many more miles to walk home. May God protect you and your loved ones!" The messenger turned to leave after bowing and pressing a quick kiss on Maria's limp right hand. Anton felt thunderstruck, unable to speak, clutching the letter.

Friedrich listened to his son's halting account without uttering a sound. He was at a loss to find words of comfort for the grieving boy and he reached out to hold him. Then he turned to the tear-stained letter he had taken from Maria's hand. It was written on two sheets of lined paper torn from a school scratch book. The adolescent handwriting bespoke intelligence and sensitivity. Friedrich hastily read the account of the tragedy, crushed by the realization of finality, of the unassailable fact that his older son had been taken from him forever.

The letter described the desperate situation of the under-manned company of *Panzer Grenadiere* on April 20, based in the south-central part of rural Saxony, waiting for the enemy to close in from both directions. There had only been sporadic gunfire, but everyone knew the final stand must come soon. It went on to describe how during an evening patrol Johann was walking ahead of Wolfgang, the writer of the letter and his close friend in the unit. Inexplicably, a shot rang out and Johann collapsed, mortally wounded. Wolfgang wrote that his rifle accidentally discharged, even though it was in good working order after he had cleaned it in the afternoon. He suggested the tragedy might be due to his inexperience and lack of training with weapons.

Wolfgang spoke at length of the awesome guilt he felt, since it was he who held the rifle at the critical moment. He could not bring himself to face Johann's parents just now, he wrote, because he blamed himself so much, and therefore he sent another friend as a messenger. Some day he would like to call on the Wildert family himself to ask their forgiveness. He assured them that Johann died in an instant and was spared any suffering, although he knew this was a very small consolation. Wolfgang added that he prayed for Johann's soul and for God's absolution for his care-less act.

Friedrich read the letter over and over, and finally rested his head in his hands, covering his eyes. Then he reached out again for Anton to hold him close, and they both sobbed.

Anton now felt an even greater sense of unreality about the events of the past few days. He recalled how his mother told him a month earlier of a vivid dream about a wide, peaceful expanse of fields and forests, in the midst of which she recognized a lifeless figure as Johann, sprawled near the green banks of a small meandering river. Maria struggled for a long time to rid herself of this frightening apparition, and Anton shuddered at her deep sense of foreboding when she described the scene. He could not have known then how realistic the landscape in Maria's dream had been.

During the evening the other inhabitants of the villa came to call to express their condolences. Their compassion was deepened by their own private fears for loved ones. The younger refugee woman worried about her soldier husband who was out somewhere to the east and had not been heard from for months. The Sattlers thought about their only son, an officer in the *Wehrmacht*, who had not yet made contact with them. They all came for a brief moment of shared sorrow.

Maria heard their well-intentioned words, but she was really far removed, recalling and savoring the thousands of pleasurable and bittersweet memories of a son she raised almost to maturity. The pathetic letter carried by the young messenger struck a grievous wound. Again and again her mind tried to escape the truth by returning to loving memories; it was her instinctive way of blanking out reality, of making harsh facts bearable.

The evening and night passed slowly for the Wilderts, each picturing the handsome youth at his best and wishing that the whole episode was only a dream. Wouldn't Johann walk up to the front door the next morning like the polite messenger, having found his way home through the turmoil and confusion?

Anton convinced himself so much of this forlorn hope that he checked Johann's room in the morning and cried bitterly when he found it empty. He began to have repeated vivid dreams of his brother's homecoming, unharmed and strong, like Ulysses returning from the Trojan War.

EIGHT

The Suicide

Feeling lonely after many days of confinement in the house and still trying to comprehend his brother's death, Anton wandered outside to see if there might be someone to talk to in the adjoining gardens. The phone was still dead and he longed to see his friends in the neighborhood, but he could not reach them unless he ventured out into the street. The boy living in the next house was several years younger, an only son spoiled by his parents and by a doting grandmother residing with them. Surely he would be kept out of sight at a dangerous time like this.

As Anton walked, he paused to admire the flowering bushes and patted the stately fruit trees whose thick trunks and branches bore the marks of his and his brother's climbing exploits. The garden looked as inviting as ever, lush with the colors of spring. It had always been a haven where they played carefree games of hide and seek, cowboys and indians, and trappers in the wild, pitched the small tent, and filled the air with the boisterous sounds of youth. Those childhood pleasures faded away as the shadows of the war and the final collapse draped their gray mantle over his life. Even though he was seeing and touching familiar objects he wondered if his vivid memories were just dreams.

As Anton came near the rear fence he saw Judge Carstens strolling in his own garden. The old gentleman waved to him and came closer. He said warmly, "Please tell your dear mother and father how shocked we are at Johann's death." His face was grave. "Assure them that I will come to call as soon as it is safe to do so. I am so sorry about this terrible event, Anton."

The boy managed to utter a choked, "Thank you, *Herr* Judge." He gave Anton a kindly nod and turned back into the garden. To reach the Wildert villa he would have to risk walking in the open street for two blocks.

The encounter stirred anew Anton's grief about his brother, and he ran to escape into the quiet of the house. He went to his room and tried to read, a favorite pleasure in normal times, but found he couldn't concentrate and he fidgeted until it was time for Friedrich to return from the office. Anxiously he waited by the window and when he saw his father appear he ran wildly to the garden gate. Friedrich looked grim and drawn. Without a word he hugged his son tightly and led the way into the house.

As they walked he kept his right hand buried in his coat pocket. Anton thought something precious must be hidden there, but he did not ask, for he sensed his father's heavy preoccupation. For the first time the boy realized that his father had aged greatly. The once stately man visibly stooped and his clothes draped loosely around his diminished body. It suddenly occurred to Anton how ill he looked during the frightening days a year ago, when Friedrich suffered a nervous collapse and temporary amnesia from exhaustion and unrelenting wartime pressures at the company. He never wholly recovered and today he looked ashen and distant. Anton began to worry about his father, plagued by a sense of foreboding.

As he followed him upstairs he saw that Friedrich still kept his hand in his coat pocket. Together they looked in on the grief-stricken Maria who rested in the bedroom. Friedrich stood by the bed for a moment, then bent down to kiss her. She gazed up at him and studied his expression for a long time, keenly aware of the toll of trouble and sorrow in his face.

Finally she sighed and rose from the bed. With great effort she said, "Somehow we must deal with our present problems. We can't let yesterday's events paralyze us." She still found it impossible to speak of Johann's death directly. "With God's help we'll try to face each day as it comes, as best we can. What's the latest news, Friedrich?"

Her husband looked at her with respect. He always felt her strength of character beneath a personality given to emotional swings and a love of the dramatic that sometimes caused minor arguments to grow into tearful scenes. Though she never had to struggle directly with the cares of a workaday world, she inherited unerring common sense from her father, a self-made businessman. Friedrich discovered this when he shared the trials of his own career with her and found her advice both insightful and practical. Now he worried about his own declining strength, gradually chipped and eroded away by the torrent of stresses of the past years. He was not sure of himself any more. With a touch of regret he realized that only his wife now seemed to possess the strength to face adversity.

When Maria finished dressing the three Wilderts sat down in the living room to consider the latest available information. Friedrich began by telling them what he learned through some business contacts and from the Czech overseers at the company.

"I might as well put everything on the table—Anton is old enough to face reality." He hesitated, his eyes questioning, and Maria nodded in agreement. "There's absolutely no question that all of us will be driven out, sooner or later. The only doubt remaining is whether it'll happen tomorrow, in a week, or in a month. We must face the fact that life will be one anxious moment after another. The Czech militia and the new officials in charge are beginning to assert themselves, and they do enjoy their new power! By making us wear white armbands they obviously intend to treat us the same way the Nazis used to treat the Jews."

Friedrich had to pause for a moment, wincing as he pressed his burning stomach. "We clearly have no rights anymore, and no one will help us. Officially the Russians remain neutral, recognizing Czech rule. But I'm sure they support them in practice. Apparently Beneš wangled some damned agreement from the Allies that awards them everything the Sudeten population owns here."

Maria and Anton leaned forward, hanging on every word as Friedrich continued angrily. "Where will they send us? Some are guessing it will be Siberia—the Russians need cheap labor after the heavy losses they suffered in the war. There's even talk that men, women and children will be separated. Others believe that we'll just be pushed across the old German border and abandoned."

Friedrich looked intently at Maria who sat quietly, with a stunned expression on her face. His voice rose as he said with great agitation, "The problem with being sent to Germany is that the war destroyed much of the housing and farming. Assuming we reach Saxony alive, what can they do with us there? Millions of other refugees from the east are already wandering around without any support. Sounds hopeful, doesn't it?" Friedrich had rarely been so sarcastic. He added heatedly, "Ugly rumors have it that the Czechs don't give a damn, they're just anxious to be rid of us and get their hands on the wealth of the region. Without food and shelter our lives could become tenuous, to say the least!"

Friedrich had to stop as he wrestled with the impact of his own words—his account rekindled in him the memory of his first reaction to the news, a leaden realization that untold deprivation and suffering lay ahead. "There are even rumors that the Czechs have already begun these so-called "evacuations." People in whole sections of the city are suddenly told by armed militia—often in the middle of the night—that they've got just fifteen minutes to get out of their homes. All they can do is grab a few essentials. People of all ages are being marched or trucked to the border and then abandoned. Many are taking their own lives—the older ones especially."

Friedrich became emotional. "Maria, Anton, we are facing the crisis of our lives. They may ship us to Siberia, they may separate us, or they may just dump us among the ruins across the border!" He paused to catch his breath.

"If we only had some idea of what will happen to us and when, the situation might be more bearable. But all we have to go on is uncertainty and rumors, rumors . . ." His voice drifted off and his hand trembled as he fingered his tie.

All this time Maria said nothing, her deep brown eyes riveted on her husband's anguished features while she listened to his despairing message. She was aghast at what she heard, but she also knew instinctively what he was leading up to. Now she spoke up. "True, the situation is terrible, but we still have one young life to account for. As long as there is any hope at all, I feel we must go on for Anton's sake."

Maria also noticed that Friedrich kept one hand in his coat pocket as if clutching some secret. Her words seemed not to have reached him, his eyes were fixed in the distance, and he did not respond. After a poignant silence that Anton found almost unbearable but did not dare interrupt, Maria pointed to Friedrich's pocket and said gently, "What have you got there, Friedrich?"

Mother and son watched in bewilderment as Friedrich slowly removed his hand and opened it to reveal a small green vial glistening on his palm. "The answer to our problems," he murmured, barely audible now. With great effort he faced Maria and Anton, his eyes pleading. "I had Dr. Fischer prepare cyanide for us. He also mixed some for himself, his family, and several others in the management group. I just hope he knew what he was doing this time—but since he will also depend on it himself, it may be all right."

Anton once again experienced the prickling sensation of fear while his mind tried to grasp this new turn of events. Maria's cheeks paled. She stared at her distraught husband and asked in a voice devoid of emotion, "Do you really want us to do this?"

Friedrich sighed, relieved that he finally revealed his secret without causing an outburst on her part that, with his raw nerves, he would have found difficult to handle. "If it means escaping a more horrible fate, I do indeed," he said hoarsely. "And God will surely forgive us for committing this sin in such a crisis," he added. The tone of his response revealed that he had weighed the step over and over in his mind, and was even prepared to set aside the tenets of the family's Catholic faith. Tired of struggling he hoped desperately that he could convince his family to give up, too.

Maria turned to her son. "Anton, what do you think about this? You have not yet had a chance to live your life. Would you want to take this step as a way out? You must try to imagine a life away from here, and having to battle with constant uncertainty; but you must also try to understand that as long as there is life, there is some hope." Friedrich watched his wife intently as she spoke.

Anton drew back as if he had been struck. His hands began to sweat and he turned red in the face. He tried to say something brave, but the whole idea was beyond his youthful experience. How should he respond to the choice he was being asked to make? "I . . . I don't think I am scared to do it," the boy stuttered. As he heard himself say this, the decision became even more unreal. He again had that uncanny sensation of detachment, looking on the scene as an observer, as if he were watching a group of strangers discussing a fearful matter. Yet all the while his young mind whirled to try to conjure up images of heroism, historical figures who defied death. If they could do it, could he not be brave, too?

But then, what did it mean to die? Did it mean going to sleep? What would it be like to drink the clear liquid? Would it hurt? Would he go to heaven, that old-fashioned place with the bearded saints, the harps, and the angels with their flowing white gowns and wings? Would he meet Johann there? What about his friends who went on living? Would they miss him? Would he miss them?

Anton had no basis for grasping the consequences of a life and death decision. He always admired stories about strong people facing danger and accepting death, but how could he know what it was like to be in their place? He could glimpse the feeling of glory, but not the harsh truth of pain and agony, and surely not the finality of leaving this life. After a confused pause he managed to mumble in an unsteady voice, "I . . . don't want to be separated and left alone. I would rather be with Johann . . . "

He was surprised at his own words and wondered whether he really meant to select this option; but he had given an answer, and was calmer now for having said something—anything. Unfamiliar feelings assailed him, elation, fear, sorrow, and doubt, all chasing each other in a mysterious ballet that transformed the reality of the moment into a theatrical performance, except that he was one of the actors. Anton sat dazed, facing his parents with questioning eyes.

Tears came to Maria at Anton's naive response. She knew he could not make such a decision himself, that he would be guided by what he sensed his father and mother wanted. Reaching out to hug him she held him close. Given Friedrich's obvious determination, she now felt the crushing burden of having to decide; the ultimate choice fell on her shoulders. What right did anyone have to ask the boy to die? How could this be reconciled with God's will? What if he were to suffer horribly from the effects of the poison? What if he somehow survived and had to face exile alone? The chilling thoughts made her tremble visibly. Then again, could she and her weakened husband face the future, if, indeed there was to be one? What kind of life would Anton have when he grew up? If they went into exile, would conditions become so unbearable that perhaps some day they might wish they had taken this way out?

Maria felt her resolve weakening as she held on to Anton and stared into Friedrich's grim face. His ominous words still pounded insistently in her mind. She began to admit to herself that she, too, was tired and afraid of the turmoil to come. The thought of bearing the guilt for Anton's death was at first abhorrent, but now insidious doubts about the future chipped away at her strength, hollowing out the foundation of her faith. A fateful temptation emerged, stronger and stronger...

Friedrich could see the silent struggle in his wife's face. He turned to his son and seized his opportunity. "Yes, Anton, we will all be with Johann. Dr. Fischer assured me that the cyanide is very strong and that we will not feel anything. It'll bring the end of our fears and suffering." They looked at each other and suddenly knew the decision had been made, that there would be no turning back.

Dazed by the decision, they moved in slow motion as they began to consider what still needed to be done. They would use the remaining food tucked away in the basement store room to prepare a last, formal meal. After dinner they planned to take the poison while lying side by side on the large bed in the master bedroom.

Friedrich rose purposefully, walked to the kitchen and returned with an extra long gas hose he obtained and hid there weeks before. Maria's face betrayed her complete surprise. Abruptly she now realized that her husband had thought about family suicide for a long time and had planned the act with great care. Almost eagerly Friedrich demonstrated that the hose easily reached from the kitchen to the bedroom. They would turn on the gas and take the cyanide immediately afterwards. If the poison did not work properly, the gas would certainly finish the job.

Anton moved about as if in a trance. He felt calm inside and quietly attended to his chores. Yet to him the whole experience was unreal. Drifting again into his vexing observer role he wondered whether to feel and act solemnly to fit the occasion, or perhaps to feel light-hearted in anticipation of seeing Johann again? He decided on being merry in a make-believe way, and soon he was humming his favorite melodies while he tackled familiar chores around the kitchen. Friedrich sent him to the basement to fetch the last glass jars of rabbit meat and fruit, a small jar of butter similarly preserved, and the final three bottles of berry wine from last year's garden crop.

Together the three Wilderts made ready their last supper, each of them pretending to concentrate on the preparations. They said little, only what was needed to get everything done. Friedrich did most of the cooking as had been his hobby on special holidays. Seemingly absorbed in his task he put his experience to good use on this final occasion, turning the meager supplies into a fine meal.

Meanwhile, Anton laid the table with heavy damask and the family's best silver, china, and crystal. They rarely used most of these items during the closing years of the war. For the final drink he selected three small hand-cut goblets.

Maria saw to it that she left the kitchen and the other rooms in immaculate condition, her housewifely pride not permitting disorder to survive her. Friedrich disconnected the gas burners and attached the long hose to the wall outlet, snaking it along the floor of the kitchen and the hall and over the oriental rugs into the bedroom.

At last they sat down to dinner. The blazing crystal chandelier scattered flecks of refracted color from its multi-faceted ornaments. With an even voice Friedrich began to say grace, something he always did on special occasions. "Thank you, Lord, for our last meal together." After a moment he added, "Forgive us our sins and have mercy on our souls, for we see no other way out of this crisis." His voice choked with emotion and his eyes remained closed. During a long period of silence they remembered Johann lying in his soldier's grave.

The food was good and to their surprise they ate freely. Toasting frequently with the berry wine they deliberately talked of a happier past, savoring the memories of former good times when they were surrounded by family and friends.

Finally Friedrich produced the green vial. He held it up to the light and examined it briefly. The liquid did not seem as clear as he imagined it should be. He was tempted to say, "Did that fool make a mistake again?" but he suppressed the urge. Anyway, the gas would do the job; it was flowing normally tonight. Deliberately and with great precision he poured equal amounts of the liquid into the small goblets, the vial tinkling against the glasses as his hands shook slightly, a trembling that had not left him since his nervous collapse a year ago. With an almost ceremonious flourish he added a little of the berry wine to each goblet.

Maria and Anton gazed with macabre fascination at the crystal glasses glistening in rainbow colors as they captured the light of the chandelier—they cradled their deadly contents with beautiful effect. Once more Friedrich proposed a toast with the last of the pure berry wine. The potent home-made beverage was beginning to have its effect on everyone.

Friedrich's face lost its taut expression, replaced by a serenity that bespoke his anticipation of ultimate freedom. Despite the doubts and fears remaining in her heart, Maria allowed herself to give in to the soothing lure of the wine. Anton was both fascinated and afraid, imagining how they would shortly walk to the bedroom carrying those small, glittering goblets. Being unaccustomed to alcohol he became giddy and his fears eased. A faint note of humor crept in as they toasted their past happiness and their future reunion with Johann. Setting down his glass Friedrich said a brief prayer and recited the twenty-third psalm, which always had a special meaning for the family. Maria and Anton sat hushed in reverent silence. "The Lord is my shepherd, I shall not want. He maketh me to lie down in green pastures, He leadeth me besides the still waters, He restoreth my soul. He leadeth me onto the path of righteousness for His name's sake. Yea, though I walk through the valley of the shadow... "

Suddenly the doorbell shrilled with stubborn insistence—twice, three times. Friedrich leaped from his chair. "Who in heaven's name could that be?" His face was ashen. The strident ringing resumed with more impatient bursts. Maria stirred slowly, roused from an almost hypnotic state. Anton thought his heart would jump out of his chest. He had acquiesced to the suicide plan, more numb than knowing, but now he realized in a flash that this was a last-minute reprieve. His mother's features showed a mixture of shock, curiosity, and relief.

Friedrich grimly left the room to go downstairs and answer the door. Shuffling slowly, he moved like a broken man. He sensed that the incredibly timed interruption shattered the chance to escape the coming turmoil in his own way. Dazed, Maria and Anton remained in their chairs.

After what seemed an eternity they heard footsteps approach the room. The door opened and behind the downcast Friedrich emerged the figure of a robust man of about twenty, smartly dressed, with close-cropped dark hair, his cold face set in arrogant self-assurance. He stopped and surveyed the scene without a greeting.

"Franz!" Maria shrilled, "what on earth are you doing here?" She instantly recognized the younger son of her sister Gretl who lived in Prague and was married to a Czech national of mixed Czech and Austrian parentage. "How is Gretl, how is Karel, and how is your brother?" Maria thrust out her arms and embraced the young man.

Franz's hard expression did not change. He nudged his aunt aside without returning her welcome. Still standing in the doorway, hands thrust in his pockets, he looked coolly around the room.

Anton jumped up from his chair, gaping in disbelief at his cousin. The Wildert and Pancraz brothers often saw each other, even during the war years when travel was restricted and difficult. The elder Pancraz's senior position with the railroad ministry entitled the family to free priority passes, of which they made good use. This also explained Franz's ability to travel in the current turbulent conditions. Completely fluent in Czech and German, the Pancraz family had managed to adapt well to the transition from Czech to German rule in 1938 and now back to Czech rule by shifting their allegiance each time. The elder Pancraz's civil service position was never affected, and his mixed parentage and Czech name was an obvious advantage now.

Franz finally spoke up with cool detachment. "What's going on here?" He could not have missed the tension in the room.

"Had you come just a few minutes later," Maria said dramatically, "we would have been no more—things are so bad."

"We-ell, that is something you should not do, for Johann's and Anton's sake," Franz blandly replied. His high-pitched voice rasped in the disagreeable manner so familiar to Anton. The boy did not care much for his cousin. Memories of times they played together came back to him. How often had the older boy bullied and even beaten him, taunting him in his ugly voice!

Franz affected an officious tone. "My mother sent me here to look after the house. This villa must be saved, as all German property will be taken over by our new republic for its own citizens." He paused for a moment, then continued with an overbearing air of finality. "You must sign over all your claims to my mother and father, who as Czech citizens will take ownership at the proper time. As you know my mother has a ten percent property interest, as have Aunt Martha, Uncle Herbert, and Uncle Walter. You two own the largest portion, sixty percent, and you must sign it over to us. I have the papers right here." The steady ticking of the hall clock broke through the stunned silence while the Wilderts stared incredulously at their young relative, now a swaggering intruder.

Maria almost choked on her words. "Do you realize that Johann is dead, and that the three of us are facing evacuation, deportation to Siberia, or worse?" The scorching heat of anger burned in her and she wanted to scream. Yet she forced herself to remain civil. "I ask you, Franz, what does the house matter when we are facing death?"

"It's too bad about Johann; I'm sorry to hear that. But as far as you Germans are concerned, I can't help you, although I am Czech!"

Maria shrieked at the stone-faced young man. "For God's sake, don't you realize that with your Austrian mother and part-Austrian father you also have German blood in your veins? Why do you behave like a stranger all of a sudden?"

Blood rushed into Franz's contorted features as he hissed furiously, "How dare you! I don't recognize a single drop of German blood in me! You Germans lost the war and your Nazi empire! Now the glory of our Slavic nations will begin. Together with our Russian brothers we will build a new epoch . . ."

"Shut up, you idiot, do you hear me? Get out of here this minute!" Friedrich finally shook off his lethargy and pulled himself up to his once imposing stature. He stared fiercely into his nephew's eyes with disgust and disbelief.

Franz was taken aback but quickly recovered his arrogance. His voice's pitch rose even higher. "I am not leaving here until you sign these papers. While I am in this house I have to be your protector. But I won't be staying long, my mother made me promise to return to Prague as soon as possible. She sends you her good wishes, but she and father don't want our family to get involved with Germans, so you'll have to look out for yourselves . . . but the villa must be saved!" Franz tried to look superior.

Friedrich glared at the greedy messenger. "Do you realize that giving up our property rights could leave us even more exposed?" he growled, his tone livid with rage at Franz's offensive words and manner.

His nephew's cold, impersonal monotone had varied only briefly during his outburst of passionate nationalism. Franz persisted, "All you Germans will be thrown out anyway," he rasped, adding with a condescending shrug, "We might as well save the villa while we can. Here, sign—if you please!"

Friedrich glanced at the paper the young man thrust in front of him. It was not an official document, just a handwritten paragraph in Czech which Friedrich could not understand. He grabbed the paper and pushed it over to Maria who knew conversational Czech.

Maria studied the words for a few moments, ignoring Franz, and said dubiously, "It's a simple statement that we both sign over to Gretl and her husband our majority share in the villa and the land." Her eyes were on Friedrich, questioning.

Friedrich faced Franz once more, seething with fury. Between clenched teeth he hissed contemptuously, "If it means getting rid of you, we'll sign!" He held his breath so as not to lose his composure. Then he added, "It probably doesn't amount to a damned thing under these confused conditions!"

Friedrich and Maria sat down, pushed the sparkling goblets aside and scrawled their signatures with the gold-tipped pen Franz held ready for them. As they signed they pointedly ignored their nephew and when they were finished placed the paper beside them without looking up.

Franz, who hovered over them grabbed the paper hastily. He seemed relieved and a tight grin appeared on his stony face. "I am glad you see things my way!" The grin faded and he again assumed his cool officiousness. "I would advise you to start packing some personal things as there is talk the evacuations will begin here in a day or two. You won't be able to take much, only what you can carry or put on a small pushcart." His round face took on a look of greedy expectancy. "I'll have to stay the night—whether you like it or not. There is no train to Prague until morning. As you won't be able to take much with you anyway, I'll help myself to some of your clothes, Uncle Friedrich."

This was the first time Franz used the familiar address. Not waiting for Friedrich's reply he stalked from the dining room and went to the master bedroom. There he opened the wardrobe and started to select shirts, a hat, several ties, vests and a sweater. As he garnered these articles he tried them on, admiring himself in the mirror.

The Wilderts slumped in their chairs and looked at each other across the dining table still cluttered with the remnants of their final supper. They had been to the brink and were crudely drawn back by a relative turned enemy. Franz saved their lives, only to seal their doom.

Sparkling colors continued to dance in the lethal goblets, but the spell was broken. The moment had passed.

NINE

The Prelude to Exile

Friedrich slept little during the night that for him began on such a high note of resolve. Tossing and turning, he relived over and over his nephew's unexpected intrusion at the very moment of finality. He brooded with seething anger as he was struck again by the force of Franz's greed and hostility. The thought of the young man asleep under his own roof after the nasty confrontation tortured his sense of decency, but he was helpless to do anything about it—and that enraged him even more. Only toward morning did his feverish thoughts relent enough to let him lapse into a fitful sleep that restored some of his drained energy.

Maria slept all night overwhelmed by exhaustion; her relief that fate had intervened was greater than her disgust with Franz's raw avarice. Anton, weary from struggling with grave decisions that were far beyond his comprehension, had also drifted into a heavy sleep.

In the morning Franz emerged from the guest room, dressed and ready to leave, having already breakfasted on sandwiches he brought with him. He bade a curt good-bye to the tired Wilderts in the hall and departed hastily, carrying a large suitcase bulging with a selection of Friedrich's clothes. The signed release of the Wilderts' property rights Franz securely tucked away in his inside coat pocket.

"Good riddance!" Friedrich exclaimed once Franz disappeared through the garden gate. "I would rather have total strangers invade us than our own relatives!" Maria wiped a tear from her cheek, still unable to believe the change she witnessed in her nephew during the hostile scene last night. Was there anything left to believe in?

Soon afterwards Friedrich went through the motions of readying himself for the walk to the office, a journey he had not expected to make again. With unhappy thoughts he left to meet Dr. Fischer as usual, but he carefully avoided talking with him about the events of the previous evening. They followed the familiar route in silence, their white armbands properly in place.

At the company offices *Pan* Novak came to see Friedrich and handed him a stamped official paper which certified that his services were essential during the company's transfer period. It stated that any evacuation of himself or his family must be delayed. Food ration tickets for three persons were attached. After Novak left the room Friedrich sat at his desk, his mind unable to focus on these necessities. He was only beginning to allow himself to believe that life would continue. The document Novak just presented him granted a rare reprieve from the fearsome evacuations, a privilege that thousands of others would have moved heaven and earth to obtain—even though the certificate merely postponed the inevitable. But Friedrich felt unaffected; he was still brooding over the scenes of last evening and especially the irony of being saved from death by a nephew coldly pursuing his own interests.

How impotent he felt facing this intruder, who by mere accident of birth was immune from the upheavals now consuming the Wilderts and the whole Sudeten population. Franz could have been his own son; brought into this world by an Austrian mother and a part-Czech, part-Austrian father, this young man now zealously served the other side, reaping advantages by casting his lot with the Slavic part of his heritage.

Friedrich experienced the same sense of futility that so often plagued him under the Nazi regime. Then he had been forced to yield to superior power and to the total control which the party wrested from society, hoping all along that the monolithic system would not some day confront him with a severe challenge to his personal ethics—a test that mercifully never came.

Now a superior force again disrupted his life, and once more he could not stand up to it. Last night would have provided a way out, a move of his own choice, and he blamed himself over and over again for not having insisted on emptying the glittering glasses after all.

Novak waited impatiently for Friedrich's guidance on the day's decisions, and at last came to look for him, jarring him out of his gloomy thoughts. Friedrich listlessly informed and guided his successor for much of the day. The need to focus on business matters brought some diversion from his other worries and emotions, but as he concentrated on his tasks the pain in his left side grew worse. He did his best to conceal his illness and as the day wore on he found that he worked well with Novak, who proved a quick learner and was very proper and polite in the way he treated their relationship.

Back at the villa another unwelcome visitor arrived. Anton answered the door to encounter a middle-aged man with dark slicked-back hair and clever, lively eyes, his chubby face clean-shaven but shadowed by hard-to-repress stubble. In halting German the man asked to see Anton's parents, claiming that he knew them.

Maria joined Anton by the front door and when the man spotted her he bobbed his head eagerly and smilingly exclaimed in Czech, "You do remember me, don't you, *Pani* Wilder*tova!*" When Maria hesitated he grinned. "I was your mailman before the Nazis came. Now do you remember?"

Maria nodded warily, wondering what the man wanted. "I think I do remember, *Pane*...ah?"

"*Pan* Fenclík," the man quickly added.

Maria learned conversational Czech as a girl growing up in a small town close to the language border. This skill was handy now. She vaguely recalled Fenclík coming to the villa on his daily rounds many years ago. Then she remembered the one impression that stood out: Fenclík always ardently insisted on conversing in Czech, even though the Sudeten province was officially bilingual at the time and Fenclík, like most Czechs living in the area, spoke German reasonably well.

"Well, *Pani* Wilder*tova*, I am so glad that you remember me from the old days." Still grinning broadly, Fenclík stated his purpose in a confiding tone. "You must know, of course, that it won't be long before all of you will have to leave here. That is too bad. I did happen to recall your lovely villa and the many valuable furnishings—there must be even more of everything now." His voice became expectant. "You see, you won't be able to take much with you, particularly precious things, but perhaps we can make an arrangement that I store some of these for you, if you make it worth my while." He stared at Maria, beaming an all too eager smile. His small eyes fixed on her greedily as he instinctively rubbed his hands in anticipation.

When she remained silent he was quick to continue his pitch. "Better yet, I would be prepared to live in one of the rooms of the villa, as your protector so to speak, and you could give me some of your things as compensation."

Maria was so taken aback at this new incident of unbridled greed that she momentarily lost her composure and visibly choked. The agile man saw her dismayed expression and before she could reply he spoke, his hands upturned and gesturing in emphasis. "I understand! I do understand! I'll come back later, to give you a little more time to think about my proposition. Meanwhile don't let anyone else talk you into anything before we can make a deal! Good day, *Pani* Wilderto*va*!" He bent with the slightest hint of a servile bow, turned on his heels and walked rapidly toward the garden gate. There he paused to cast a long glance over his shoulder back to the villa.

Maria and Anton lingered by the front door and watched the man stride purposefully toward the neighboring villa where he rang the bell. Wordlessly Maria put her arm around Anton and led him back into the house. The boy witnessed the exchange but could not understand what they said. Maria explained Fenclík's proposition and added, "This was the second vulture today—this time a real stranger. I'm afraid they'll be coming in droves soon. What you see now, Anton, is the carcass of a dead society being torn apart by greedy opportunists. Before too long they'll be at each other's throats fighting over the spoils."

Friedrich returned from the office in late afternoon and shrugged resignedly when told of Fenclík's visit. "There'll be many more of these types," he said with disgust. "I understand there is a whole network of informants organized among former postal employees, most of whom, as you know, were Czech like the other civil servants when we were ruled by Prague. Of course, the mail carriers were in the best position to learn who lived well and who possessed what. Just today I heard that two houses not too far from here were confiscated by postal officials. I have no idea what happened to the owners."

He then changed the subject. "At the office Novak hinted there was a good chance our district will be evacuated very soon and he gave me this document as temporary protection against expulsion. He made it clear, however, that he can't guarantee the certificate will keep us in our house, only within the city."

Friedrich discussed with the family the many decrees and regulations that began to appear on posters in the streets. Maria and Anton had already heard some of the official announcements on the radio. Among them were prohibitions against removing property from private houses, severe penalties for hiding jewelry and precious metals, and strict regulations on converting currency and bank accounts. There was nothing they could do but comply. Friedrich's face showed grave concern as he passed on the latest news of evacuations that occurred in other parts of the city. In every case the expulsions involved surprise and armed force. The numbers of women, children and old people affected by the systematic removal of the population grew daily, mushrooming into tens of thousands.

All along, the Russian occupation authorities appeared to keep their hands off the actions of the Czech government. But Friedrich heard that the Russian general in charge of Saxony was displeased with the chaotic refugee conditions developing in his border region. Perhaps he would put a stop to the expulsions? The people Friedrich talked with during the day assured him that there was enough similarity in the rumors coming from different sources to make this credible.

When Friedrich had finished the family worried about how best to prepare for the moment when they would face the order to leave. Friedrich was not at all sure that in the turmoil of a block by block evacuation Novak's document would protect them from gun-wielding militiamen storming the house. He argued that they should be prepared to share their neighbors' fate when the time came.

Maria rechecked the bundles of clothing, utensils and other necessities assembled many days before when she had sewn the bags from the rough tent cloth. As she went through the bundles she thought how pitiful their existence would be with this meager selection of belongings, but they would have to manage somehow. Ever since the moment their lives were unexpectedly spared, Maria steeled herself determinedly to go on for Anton's sake, even though she was torn between motherly love for Anton and devotion to her weakened husband. To her, Friedrich was now like a hollow tree that could be toppled by the winds of change during the coming upheavals. But the instinct to protect the only child left to her became paramount, and she knew she must not question fate but simply do her best to survive every day. A phrase from childhood echoed in her mind, taking on a new meaning: "As the Lord wills—we hold still!"

In the early morning hours unusual sounds and movements in the neighborhood alerted them. They dressed hurriedly and took their places by the picture window where they had earlier observed the retreating and conquering armies. Soon a slow trek of people plodded up the gentle slope of their street and past the villa, joining a wider column that began moving northward on the main road to their left.

Flanked by militiamen carrying rifles, a motley assembly of women, children and old men shuffled along slowly, weighed down by their bundles. Some pulled small carts heaped with bales of belongings, while others pushed baby carriages strapped with bags of clothing and cooking utensils that hid the tiny occupants from view. Their heads bowed, the people responded dully to the armed men's impatient prodding, walking mechanically as if unaware of reality. Some of the oldest hobbled along on sticks and crutches or sat on the carts, supported by their families. It was a scene of quiet despair, of uprooted human beings adrift on their own home ground. Tears covered many of the faces, and quite a few turned around to take a last look, only to resume their painful procession toward the unknown.

The Wilderts stood mesmerized, watching the spectacle of dislocation unfold. Their hearts went out to these people, though none of them were close neighbors. The adjoining district must have been targeted last night. Would they be next?

Anton tried to picture what happened before these throngs became the stream of refugees in the street. He thought of the descriptions Friedrich gave them last night. How were they notified? Did the soldiers just break into their houses and threaten everyone? Did they kick and beat people, and did they let them have things they needed? These questions were futile, for even though the column below was within easy shouting distance it would be unwise to try and communicate because of the soldiers' presence. Anton felt helpless, as if he were watching a dramatic newsreel, unstoppable, a pre-set script condemning the audience to silent observation.

Maria, in her forced detachment, found the bewildering reality of the scene almost too much to bear. She clung tightly to Friedrich and whispered, "If it's God's will we must also go through this; but He will surely watch over us." She did not sound very convincing. Friedrich gave no response. As never before she felt burdened by responsibility—had she not been the one to argue that they must go on, come what may? Now they glimpsed their fate and she was frightened. She buried her face on Friedrich's shoulder to shut out the cruel preview of their own future.

By now several hundred people had passed by, and many more moved northward on the main street leading to the border. Then the stream of refugees diminished and melted to a trickle. *Frau* Sattler emerged from the garden gate, furtively gazing about her. When she saw no soldiers near, she darted out into the street and accosted one of the stragglers, talking rapidly with the woman for a few moments. Then she turned back and could be heard thumping up the staircase far faster than her age should have permitted.

Friedrich left the window to meet her at the top of the stairs. Between gasping breaths the old woman blurted out that she was told the evacuation had ended suddenly at the house next to the woman's, an apartment building only three blocks away. A much larger area was initially sealed off for action. There seemed to be no imminent danger for this neighborhood. Still struggling for breath *Frau* Sattler moved closer to face the whole family. She was searching for words. Finally she sobbed, "I heard this morning from the caretaker next door that Judge Carstens and his wife gassed themselves last night. They knew that the evacuation would begin near us and I suppose they just couldn't face it. What a pity, such lovely people..." Her voice left her and she turned awkwardly to labor down the staircase with heavy steps.

The Wilderts could not believe this news. Maria recalled the gallant gentleman's offer of help with the Russian pursuer and his calm philosophical reasoning in the face of grave peril. Now even he had yielded to the temptation to outwit fate—just as they had done—except that the old couple succeeded. Friedrich grimaced and pressed his aching left side. He despaired over their own lost opportunity, and all his dark thoughts returned.

Frau Sattler's voice jarred them once more, trailing up from the center of the staircase. "I really didn't want to tell you, but the saddest thing is that young *Herr* Carstens just came back from the front this morning—and it was he who found them dead." Her hesitant steps echoed in the silence.

Again the Wilderts could hardly grasp the impact of the message. They were being haunted by a steady succession of dramatic losses—the loss of Johann, the loss of friends, the loss of family trust, the loss of a future... At last Friedrich pulled himself up, swallowed hard and announced that he would go to the office as the immediate danger had passed in the neighborhood. He cautioned Maria and Anton to remain inside and left the house on his way to pick up Dr. Fischer.

When he arrived at the office he learned from Novak that the Russian commander told the Czech government to stop all evacuations until order could be restored in the adjacent German border territories. Friedrich welcomed the reprieve, yet at the same time the future dangers appeared more vivid given the frightening news about the unsettled conditions in Germany.

He was convinced that he had been right in his earlier decision to end it all. During the day he learned that two associates from the company succeeded in taking their own lives. But he also heard about instances where some family members, especially children, survived suicide attempts. The thought of abandoned children facing the plight of evacuation on their own was horrific, and he consoled himself a little when he realized that Anton might have suffered such a fate.

Meanwhile Maria and Anton spent the morning going through family documents, determined to keep the most important papers as well as a small collection of photographs as memories of happier times. They discarded a growing pile of pictures, personal letters, files and papers that must be left behind, and decided to burn these in the basement furnace. Anton shuttled back and forth laden with heavy baskets and fed the roaring flames, watching family memorabilia go up in smoke.

When he looked out the window Anton spotted flakes of sooty charred paper floating from the chimney like black snow. Anxiously he called out to Maria who winced at the sight, worried that they might attract attention. But then she shrugged and said defiantly, "I suppose everyone who can is doing the same thing, so we'll just have to risk it. I don't like the idea of personal letters and papers falling into their hands, and thank goodness we still have the chance to dispose of these things."

Telephone service was still not restored and they could not get in touch with Friedrich. They worried about this separation, for one could never be sure about events from hour to hour. What if the evacuations started up again? They would not know until evening about the Russian commander's order to stop the expulsions.

Shortly after noon a sharp, crashing explosion rattled the windows of the villa, startling Anton and Maria. After the single blast they heard the soft rustle of plaster jarred loose in the roof and walls. They huddled just as they had during the Allied bombing raids, waiting for further explosions, but none followed.

An excited babble of voices arose, punctuated by hysterical female shrieks. Anton rushed into the garden and heard from bystanders that the elderly aunt of one of his schoolmates had been walking with two friends along the main street. One of them idly kicked aside a small metal object lying on the sidewalk. It was a live shell which ignited as it struck other discarded ammunition hidden under ornamental bushes, setting off a fierce explosion.

The deadly cast-off debris had not been cleared away in the general confusion since the occupation. The woman was blown to pieces, her companions gravely injured. A Russian army vehicle stopped and the soldiers administered first aid.

Anton saw the smoldering shallow crater stained with sulfurous colors and watched the lifeless bodies being carried away. The neighboring villa faced the main street and the shattering blast of the explosion blew out many windows on that side and carried human fragments inside.

As he ran home to tell his mother, Anton passed the corner villa where the distraught witness was comforted by two neighbors. Maria listened tensely to his rushing words, saddened by the death of someone she knew. Then she found herself thinking with a tinge of envy how the woman's sudden death spared her from further miseries.

Later that afternoon the wily mailman Fenclík made another appearance. Anton could not refuse the man's energetic demands to enter. Once inside he harangued Maria at length about his various schemes to save the valuable contents of the villa. Exasperatedly she tried to explain that her husband was able to retain his position for the time being, and that there was no need to develop arrangements such as he proposed. She was careful to be patient in dealing with the insistent man, afraid to arouse vengeful feelings which he might vent on the family when given an opportunity. At last the angry Fenclík left, only to return an hour later with a colleague to continue the fruitless dialogue.

After the explosion Maria felt faint, sensing that her chronic neck and back problems were recurring. By mid-afternoon sharp pains coursed down her spine and the stabs became so intense that she had to lie down. It was in this condition that Fenclík and his companion found her. Undeterred, they hovered over the bed and bombarded her with rapid-fire arguments. She responded weakly, again and again repeating her patient response. Finally the men gave up and left, vowing to return with more authority.

Maria was still lying prone when Friedrich returned home. Relieved to see him she tried to react bravely when he anxiously inquired about her condition. "I'll be all right soon—you know I always come around again after these attacks." They exchanged news of the day. The Russian general's reprieve in the evacuation process was the only positive note. Friedrich had seen the crater in the street, heard about the explosion on his walk home and voiced his frustration about the extreme danger posed by live ammunition tossed carelessly aside. It was a prophetic remark.

From what he had been able to find out, Friedrich was reasonably certain that mass evacuations would not start again for two or three weeks—perhaps even longer. But a specific order circulated which affected German refugees from the eastern provinces who had been temporarily housed in the area. They were ordered to appear with limited belongings at a campsite in the northern part of the city for processing and evacuation. This meant that the family of Silesian refugees quartered in the first floor apartment of the villa would leave in the morning to resume their wanderings. Friedrich went downstairs and found the women well along in preparations. He invited the family to join them for a final supper, and Anton helped his father prepare the meal from the last of the food stored in the basement. The subdued talk at dinner did little to dispel the gloom hovering over the group and the Silesians soon excused themselves to resume their packing. The Wilderts offered them some utensils and necessities which they accepted gratefully.

The next morning the refugee family left the villa as bedraggled as they had come months ago, carrying their small bags and pushing the baby carriage. They had the advantage of experience which appeared to give them the strength to face new uncertainties about the future, and they walked away bravely.

The villa was emptier now, housing only the Wilderts and the Sattler couple. The Sattlers had not heard from their son, although other ex-soldiers, including young Carstens, returned to their homes from the front; by word of mouth others were understood to be in Czech custody. Normal communications were at a standstill since the collapse, and the continual uprooting further barred contacts among families and friends.

Maria worried about her younger brother Walter, who had served in the German infantry on the Russian front. Her older brother Herbert was a professor in Slovakia and she also heard no news of him. Both were bachelors and so at least they had no families to worry about. Finally there was her younger sister Martha who occupied the villa's first floor apartment for some years and now lived in Eger with her husband's family. Her two small boys were born early in the war and her daughter was still a baby. Maria knew that Martha had lost contact with her husband, last known to be serving on the Russian front during the confusion of the final months of the war. She wondered how her sister managed to care for the three children and live with the uncertainty about her husband. But at least she was in the American occupation area where conditions were known to be far better for the Sudetens.

The Wildert villa had always been a central family location where Maria and Friedrich frequently shared lively and hospitable times with the extensive group of relatives and friends, even under the growing difficulties of the war. But this was all a thing of the past, severed by the realities of collapse, occupation, and dislocation.

There was no way to get in touch with any of the family, except for what contacts the Prague relatives could make by using their privileged position. After the recent confrontation with Franz this seemed a very unrewarding possibility. The Wilderts felt isolated and estranged. They prepared themselves as well as they could for the day of evacuation, forewarned as they were by events that also granted them reprieves. Yet they could not visualize how they would manage the stress of expulsion when it came.

TEN

The Relatives

Day after day passed in meaningless succession for the Wilderts, while avaricious opportunists hovered and schemed to profit from the expropriation of the population. Characters like Fenclík surfaced repeatedly, attracted like sharks to the taste of blood. Reports of massive evacuations in other cities reached the neighborhood, and descriptions of the cruelties inflicted on refugees were reminiscent of Nazi methods. The wait for the inevitable outcome stretched on endlessly.

One morning three men appeared. Fenclík was one of them, but clearly in command was an impeccably dressed older man of medium height, stocky, of rigid bearing and wearing gold-rimmed spectacles. His pinched face and thin lips bespoke the caution and circumscribed authority of a life-long minor bureaucrat. Friedrich, who was about to leave for the office, met the group at the door and led them into the hall.

The man introduced himself in Czech as *Pan* Dvořák. When he saw Friedrich shrug, Dvořák lapsed into passable accented German and stated in a matter-of-fact tone that he understood *Pan* Wildert held a priority certificate which exempted him from evacuation, at least for the time being. He added that he was an official in the postal service and planned to requisition the Wildert villa for himself and a colleague. Dvořák paused to let the meaning of his words sink in, his face flushed with an air of superiority. When he resumed his monologue he announced blandly that in a few days he would return to claim what by then would be his property.

After yet another pause Dvořák's deliberate tone suddenly became a menacing snarl. "It will be very bad for you to try to remove or hide any valuables. If you do this you will be severely punished!" He demanded to be shown through every room to get an impression of the inventory of furnishings and personal belongings.

Friedrich showed no emotion. After the turmoil of the past weeks even such a flagrant intrusion lost its shock value. What was there to do but comply? The Wilderts walked Dvořák and his eager companions through the villa. Fenclík took notes as they went from room to room.

Back in the hall Dvořák turned to Friedrich and said with cold officiousness, "You will be assigned a small flat in the workers' district not far from your company. This should be enough for you until we no longer need you and you can be moved out to Germany." The trio departed as determined as they came.

When Friedrich arrived at his office a simply dressed man waited for him. Friedrich knew him casually. Over the years they had often exchanged words on their way to and from work. He identified himself as a long-time member of the Social Democrat Party of the Sudetenland, which had been driven underground after the Nazi takeover.

Herr Berger came right to the point. "*Herr Direktor*, we have known about you and your family for years. We understand that you had no choice but to join the Nazi party because of your position. But we also know you have always been humane in your dealings with employees, neighbors, and people of lesser standing in the community. We are aware of how badly the Nazi functionary treated you when you were forced to let him occupy part of your villa during 1944."

Berger paused and looked warmly into Friedrich's eyes. "Those Sudeten Social Democrats who actively opposed the Nazi system may possibly be granted some advantages in this current upheaval," he continued. He then added with emphasis, "If we certify that you have been as decent as we know to be true, such a statement might help you and your family. Perhaps our certificate will entitle you to stay here and keep your property. There are a few people like yourself whom we would like to help."

Berger reached into his coat pocket and handed Friedrich a typed one-page document bearing several signatures. He smiled and pointed to the paper. "This demonstrates the respect our group holds for you. It has been an honor to know you, *Herr Direktor*, and Godspeed to you and your family." He rose and shook Friedrich's hand at length. Surprised and touched, Friedrich mumbled an expression of gratitude.

After Berger left Friedrich stood silent for a long time. Images of people he dealt with over the years came to mind. He never thought of himself as especially humanitarian, but he did have a simple belief about what was fair. To him, the human being mattered far more than the position or background of a person. Glancing down at the piece of paper in his hand Friedrich pondered the twists of fate. Earlier this morning he had encountered the cold stare of the self-proclaimed new owner of his property. Now he had a possible reprieve just for having lived as he thought one should. He doubted very much that the Czech authorities would respect this new certificate, but he was grateful to have such a tangible mark of respect.

When Friedrich came home late that afternoon he found another unexpected visitor. Aunt Gretl arrived from Prague carrying two huge empty suitcases. She was with Maria in the bedroom, busily packing the most valuable parts of Maria's dowry and other goods for safekeeping or barter. Maria at first tried to dissuade her, thinking of Dvořák's stern warning only hours earlier. Gretl was determined, however, to carry away as much as possible of the contents before anyone purloined the villa.

She had at least shown Maria the courtesy to express sorrow about Johann's death, and her large dark eyes filled with tears. But soon her practical nature took over, and she plunged into Maria's closets to select what to take back with her to Prague. As she sorted linens and clothes she rambled on about various schemes to deal with the local authorities; but just like her son Franz, she appeared to give little thought to the Wildert's future.

Maria told her about Dvořák and Fenclík, and Gretl's reaction was a heightened frenzy of ideas about how to forestall them from taking over the property. Maria was struck by the secretive look in Gretl's eyes at the mention of Fenclík's name—did Gretl perhaps have dealings with him? It seemed unbelievable and Maria

tried to set aside such suspicious thoughts of her sister's devious-
ness. Her brothers and sisters regarded Gretl as stubborn, acquis-
itive and reluctant to share ever since she was in her teens, and
she often annoyed the family with her habitual clumsy efforts to
take advantage of any situation. Walter and Herbert gruffly called
her a silly goose when she was particularly tactless, and openly
wondered whether barely surviving the flu during the severe epi-
demic after the First World War left her "not quite right upstairs."
Was this another one of her schemes?

Gretl greeted Friedrich with a brief show of regret about
Johann, and soon resumed her rapid chatter. She told him of her
many efforts to have the property put in her name on the basis of
the paper the Wilderts signed during Franz's visit. Friedrich
winced when she spoke his name. Undeterred by his discomfort,
Gretl dwelt on the difficulties she must still overcome to obtain
the property and declared she would speak again to the proper
local officials to "straighten things out." She was determined that
Dvořák's takeover should not succeed.

An uneasy feeling came over the Wilderts. The prospect of a
relative, even if legally Czech, drawing the attention of local
authorities to the villa and thus to themselves was frightening.
Worse yet, Gretl seemed prepared to fight with Dvořák over the
spoils. Had she indeed been scheming with the mail carriers, and
had her mindless plans backfired?

Maria looked anxiously at Friedrich, who signaled with his
eyes for her to remain silent. Instead, he tried to point out the
family's vulnerable position in a calm and reasonable tone, but to
no avail. Gretl was single-minded. The Wilderts realized she was
now in the driver's seat, and nothing they said or did would
deflect her from her purpose. Along with the others she succumbed to the lure of avarice.

Later in the evening Gretl raised questions about the where-
abouts of the Wildert family jewelry. Some of these valuables had
been inherited from their parents, and a few were held at the villa
in safekeeping for Maria's brothers. Even Gretl was unwilling to
take the risk of carrying the jewelry to Prague. Instead she tried to
convince Friedrich to bury the goods in a secluded area of the gar-

den. When he reminded her of the danger and the harsh prohibitions against hiding anything valuable Gretl simply shrugged. "What they don't know about they won't miss. Perhaps you can some day finance your son's studies with the jewelry!" She did not suggest how the jewels might be retrieved later. Friedrich looked at her as if she came from another world—as indeed she had, living as she did in the security of the now-dominant nationality.

They shared a meal prepared from a piece of ham Gretl brought with her. While they ate Friedrich described the surprise visitor at the office and passed the certificate around the table. He admitted that there was no way of knowing if the document would be of any help, but Maria was pleased with the news; good news of any kind had become rare. For a while she even forgot the troubled thoughts that constantly shrouded her.

Anton tried to picture in his mind the prospect of staying, and he wondered out loud what life might be like when all of his friends and all the neighbors were gone.

Aunt Gretl became silent and withdrawn. Friedrich glanced at her and could see that she was upset. "What is it, Gretl?" he asked.

"Well, I am not sure you should take the paper seriously, and you certainly must not use it. For heaven's sake, you have never been a Social Democrat in your life. It just wouldn't be right."

Friedrich faced her, surprised. "But this paper is not suggesting that I was or am a member of their party, only a person that dealt fairly with other people!"

Gretl's dour expression remained. "Well, I suppose so, but don't you see that this will complicate my talks with the local officials to get the house transferred to me?"

Maria burst out weeping. "Are you suggesting that this house is more important than our small chance of staying on and not being driven out into some godforsaken place? What has come over you? First Franz arrives here, cold as ice, only wanting our signatures on a miserable piece of paper, and now you carry on in the same way! Don't you have any family feelings?"

Gretl sat in sullen defiance, her head lowered, and an uneasy quiet fell over the table. Friedrich rose abruptly. Not looking at

Gretl he touched Maria gently on the shoulder and walked out of the room. Anton and Maria followed him, leaving Gretl to herself.

In the morning a man and a woman came to call in the name of the Social Democrats. The woman was the wife of the caretaker in the villa across the meadow where the conquering Russians camped. The Wilderts knew her well and always enjoyed her cheerful ways. They showed the visitors into the living room and everyone sat down, Gretl included.

Frau Huber began by saying how pleased the members of the group were about Friedrich's certificate. Was there anything else they could do? Friedrich thanked her and said no, but he described the problem with Dvořák briefly. "Well, if Dvořák returns just show him the certificate," *Frau* Huber suggested.

Gretl burst out heatedly, "You must take back this certificate, you understand? It just isn't right!" She was insistent. "Take it back, please!" Visibly startled the visitors exchanged puzzled glances.

"What on earth are you saying, Gretl?" Maria's trembling voice shrilled, "You make us appear as if we did not deserve such consideration!"

Gretl looked straight at the woman, past the Wilderts' incredulous stares. "Well, I have my reasons," she persisted coldly. After a moment's pause she rose, took one step, and ripped the document out of Friedrich's hand to offer it to *Frau* Huber. "Here, please take it back!"

The visitors shifted uneasily in their seats. Friedrich had not moved; he faced his sister-in-law steadfastly. She could not withstand his open gaze, hesitated for a moment, and abruptly turned to leave. "I meant what I said," she shouted over her shoulder at the woman and stomped out of the room. Maria felt faint. Overcome with embarrassment and anger she could not speak.

Friedrich stood up and calmly addressed *Frau* Huber and her companion, who also struggled to their feet. "I don't know what you must think of this, for I cannot explain it myself. But under the circumstances it may be best if the whole matter were forgotten. I am most grateful for your confidence in me, but I believe we have no choice but to accept what fate deals us."

Unsure of how to reply *Frau* Huber managed to say, "Please let us know, *Herr Direktor*, if we can help you in some other way." In leaving she gave Maria a tearful hug.

Gretl departed soon afterward with her heavy suitcases. The sisters exchanged very few words and Gretl said nothing to Friedrich. The feeling of betrayal spread like a slow poison. The Wilderts were too upset to talk about it further and Friedrich left for the office still seething with helpless rage.

In the evening the Wilderts once more went over the necessities to take along when they were evicted from the villa. Maria sorted and resorted clothing, linen and utensils to fill the cloth bags. They also selected the most treasured family photographs and removed them from their frames. As they re-examined and discussed the bundles they wondered how other people could possibly have made the right choices when forced to leave within minutes.

Later Friedrich opened the small wall safe behind the hall clock and pulled out the drawers containing the jewelry. "We had better not tamper much with this—given our circumstances they'll be looking for a fair amount of valuables."

Maria demurred. Her mind concentrated on survival ever since the fateful evening when Franz interrupted their final act. Might there be a chance to save the valuables? Both Franz and his mother covetously suggested that the jewelry should be preserved for it might pay for Anton's education. But hiding the jewelry entailed great risk, and even if they succeeded how would they ever be able to recover it after the evacuation? If Gretl managed to get the house it might be possible, but the chances of that seemed slim. Maria's common sense told her not to risk the penalties.

Surprised at her preoccupation with the jewelry she asked herself if she, too, had been affected by the wave of greed that washed over the area. Her thoughts kept returning to the subject as she fingered the pitiful belongings they would be allowed to take into exile. At last she turned to Friedrich and said pensively, "Perhaps we should leave only the lesser things in the safe. I've been thinking that it may be worthwhile to bury the truly valuable items in the garden. It may sound silly to say this, but I think we owe it to the family to try and safeguard the heirlooms—as you know, some of these belong to my brothers. Then there are your many loving gifts to me. Who knows, there may be a future chance to retrieve them—what do you think?"

Friedrich looked surprised. "I don't see how it would make any difference whether we try to hide the stuff or not. You can be sure that once we're gone they will dig all over these grounds to look for buried valuables. And Gretl is not likely to get the house; I have real doubts about her crazy schemes." He hesitated for a few moments and added, "It'll be risky to go out and dig a hole in the garden. But if it means a lot to you I'll do it."

Friedrich felt trapped by all the bizarre happenings and was not at all certain about the wisdom of what he just agreed to do. He surprised himself by thinking that fooling the usurpers this way would be a satisfying if small retribution. He had said yes to Maria and was amazed when he discovered that he now actually wanted to do it.

After dark father and son slipped into the garden with a small steel box filled with the best of the jewelry. They had wrapped and sealed two layers of oilcloth around it. Anton was simultaneously thrilled and frightened—in his imagination he was acting out a pirate story full of suspense.

As the cool darkness enveloped them Friedrich became painfully aware of how vulnerable they were. If someone should come by and catch them red-handed, the consequences would be severe. The deceased judge's villa was already occupied and its new inhabitants might venture into the neighboring garden. For a few moments he hesitated by the rear door, but against his better judgment he resumed walking.

Anton carried a small hand spade and a partially blacked-out flashlight. They selected a spot hidden by bushes in the back of the garden and, hearts pounding with fear and exertion, dug the soil with the metal blade and their bare hands. They took great care to put aside the top layer of soil for replacement later.

The night was clear and still. The clicking and scratching of the spade seemed alarmingly loud as the tool hit small stones in the deeper layers of the rich soil. A thin flickering beam was all the weak flashlight could muster, but their eyes adjusted to the faint light from the rising moon and the stars. When the hole was about two feet deep they decided it was sufficient.

They stopped, held their breath and listened intently. Nothing stirred as they crouched by the hole which gave off the dusky fragrance of fresh soil. Aching from the unaccustomed position they hastily lowered the box to the bottom. Again they paused, peered into the night, and tried to perceive if anyone was near. But the only sound was the rustle of the tree branches swaying in the cool breeze.

The urge to finish the task and get away was obsessive now. They filled the hole speedily, pressing down the loose earth and scattering the excess soil in the adjoining flower beds. At last they smoothed the darker top layer back in place and they did their best to make the spot appear as if nothing had disturbed it. Since they could not be sure of this in the dark, Friedrich whispered that he would inspect the area in the morning.

After fussing a few moments longer with small adjustments they struggled to their feet, cramped and stiff. Hurrying out of the garden they reached the safety of the house, heaving great sighs of relief. Friedrich patted Anton on the shoulder. "Well done, my son," he said, his face serious, "but we really should have thought twice about whether the jewelry was worth the risk we've just taken. Can you imagine what would have happened if we were caught? Now I wouldn't care to think about that. Well, whatever, it's done."

Anton couldn't sleep for a long time that night, tossing and turning until the prickling excitement of the dangerous exploit diminished.

In the morning Friedrich walked through the garden, hoping they managed to cover their traces well. The spot looked normal. He knew that over time the soil was likely to settle, leaving a telltale depression in the earth—but that was not something they could worry about now.

In the afternoon Anton uneasily took the same path and when he passed the spot with the hidden treasure he remembered reading stories about murderers who returned to the scene of their crime as if drawn by magic. He had the odd feeling of being a criminal until he reminded himself that they buried their own family property.

The waiting resumed. Dvořák's advance warning was useful to the Wilderts in preparing themselves for the loss of the villa. In another way it was added punishment, however, as the repeated reprieves and invasions of eager profiteers took a great toll on their nerves and made them wish they could face the inevitable and get it over with.

During her brief visit Gretl told Maria that their younger brother Walter had returned unhurt from the Russian front, but was intercepted by Czech militia in the nearby industrial town of Brüx. Forced to work as a laborer in a steel mill, he was held in a detention camp with many other ex-soldiers under difficult conditions. Gretl made it plain that neither she nor her family had any intention of involving themselves to help bring about his release, even though Walter had never been an officer in the *Wehrmacht.* The knowledge of her brother's detention plagued Maria; in her mind she pictured Johann in the same circumstances, and she began to plead with Friedrich to see if there was any possible way to help Walter.

Friedrich heard that they could approach the Russian high command in the city to review genuine cases of hardship, even though the results of such petitions were unknown. It also became quite plain that a gradual shift in attitudes toward the Sudeten population was occurring. While the new Czech authorities grew ever more hostile, the Russian officers began to show traces of humanity—which Friedrich considered a surprising paradox in view of the years of suffering inflicted on the Russian people by the Germans.

He could not solve this riddle except to speculate that the Russians achieved the satisfaction of victory in the war, while their Czech neighbors were occupied without resistance, chafed under Nazi rule, and had to be liberated by the Allies. Perhaps now they felt free to indulge in a chauvinistic rage of retribution, rooted in many slights to their national pride, suffered over generations of living side by side with Austrians and Germans under different regimes, and culminating in the Nazi excesses during their occupation.

Maria and Friedrich deliberated for a day or two and finally decided that they would make a petition on Walter's behalf before the Russian commander. To this end they would attempt to see the highest ranking officer who might receive them. The Russian headquarters was the former mansion of a local industrialist, situated in a tree-lined boulevard about fifteen minutes' walk from the villa.

It was the first time Maria ventured outside the immediate neighborhood since the collapse, and walking arm in arm with Friedrich in the street she felt vulnerable and exposed. Instinctively she shuddered at the sight of an armed Russian patrol, but they did not stop the couple, nor did any of the other uniformed men they encountered along the way. There were a few other civilians with white armbands whose faces looked frightened. The vehicles passing them occasionally were Russian army trucks and horse-drawn wagons clattering along the cobbled expanse of the road.

They arrived at the ornamental gate of the mansion, one of several once magnificent residences surrounded by large formal gardens. Two Red Army sentries armed with submachine guns guarded the huge wrought iron gate. With trepidation the Wilderts showed their I. D. cards and were waved on after a cursory examination of their papers. They continued along the wide curving driveway, the gravel crunching under their feet, feeling sadly moved by the unkempt look of formerly manicured greenery.

Russian officers and men crowded the large central hall of the mansion. A handsome young officer inquired about their business in fluent German. Maria explained that she wished to petition for her soldier brother's release from captivity. The officer motioned her to take a seat on one of the carved benches lining the wall and asked that her husband wait outside in the neglected garden. Friedrich withdrew reluctantly, his face reflecting his disquiet.

Soon the young officer returned and ushered Maria through an empty anteroom into the office of the commanding general.

Clutching her handkerchief Maria followed the soldier into the large room, feeling nervous and out of place. Her heart beat wildly, but summoning all her courage she walked across the huge worn oriental carpet. The high-ceilinged room was ornately paneled, and a row of tall windows on the opposite wall opened onto the garden. Near the windows, behind an immense carved desk, sat a corpulent, gray-haired man in his sixties writing on a sheaf of papers before him.

Crossing the floor seemed to take an eternity. Maria was grateful the young officer came with her. When she stopped a few feet from the desk the general lifted his head. His round Russian face, slightly flushed and marked with deep lines, bespoke authority but did not lack warmth. The tailored uniform with the huge red shoulder boards and wide red lapels gave him a distinguished air, heightened by the triple row of glittering stars and medals on his broad chest. Maria seemed impressive in her black embroidered mourning dress; the general looked at her intently, sizing up the figure and appearance of the attractive petitioner.

To her surprise the general rose briefly and gestured to offer her a seat opposite the desk. Perched on the edge of her chair Maria anxiously stated her case in German to the young officer who translated in rapid guttural bursts. The general watched her closely with his steady, clear blue eyes, weighing her words.

With a regal gesture the general stopped the flow and in a resonant basso voice asked a question. The young officer translated, "Was your brother taken by our troops or by those of our Czech comrades?"

Maria replied that as far as she knew it was the Czech militia. The general shrugged with obvious regret and explained that he had no jurisdiction over the actions of the Czech national forces. He would, however, direct his aide to take down the particulars of the case and see what they could do. Maria sensed that he was trying to be kind but that most likely very little would or could be done. She stood and thanked the general for his time, whereupon the much older man got up and gave her a slight bow from the waist, the intensity of his gaze unchanged. Maria was distressed by the way the Russian looked at her.

She turned and walked out of the office, feeling the general's eyes still on her. Her head ached with the strain and futility of her mission. Once outside the officer took down the information on Walter, but she was sure it was merely a courtesy. Nevertheless, she felt relieved that she had at least tried to help her brother.

Maria hurried into the garden looking for Friedrich and spotted him sitting on one of the rusting wrought iron benches. He jumped up when he saw her emerge from the columned portal and she rushed over to him. Exhausted, she needed to rest and they sat down together. She described the interview and both concluded regretfully that the effort had been in vain.

While she talked they saw a stocky, broad-shouldered figure in uniform emerge from the main entrance of the mansion. Maria recognized the general who ambled casually toward them, a white lace handkerchief dangling from his right hand. The Wilderts stood up as the general approached. With a broad smile that broke like sunshine over a craggy landscape, the officer bowed to the speechless Maria and handed her the handkerchief which in her nervousness she'd dropped during the interview. Then he stared into Maria's eyes with a searching look. The resplendent general stood pensively for a few more seconds, cast a glance at Friedrich, nodded almost imperceptibly and turned to walk back to the mansion.

Early the next morning the evacuations resumed. This time the target was the Wilderts' own neighborhood. Dozens of armed militiamen swarmed through the quiet streets and pounded on doors, bluntly telling the startled inhabitants that they had fifteen minutes to get ready.

When two of the militiamen appeared at the Wilderts' front door, Friedrich showed them the paper that Novak had given him. After a long and distrustful examination the soldiers shrugged, turned, and stomped down the garden path without uttering a word. The Wilderts had one more reprieve.

They stood riveted by their picture window and watched, this time recognizing neighbors and friends passing by in the street below. Like blood trickling from a mortally wounded body the flow of people drained the essence of life from the neighborhood. The slowly moving column of women, children and old people emptied the pleasant suburb until only deserted homes and gardens remained.

Instinct told the Wilderts to be cautious as they waved with their handkerchiefs whenever friends passed. Some waved back, subdued and furtive; others were cowed by the armed patrols beside them. Upturned faces glistened with tears. Anton spotted several schoolmates with whom he shared many happy days. He admired the unhesitating way in which these boys walked beside their elders and carried their share of the burdens.

The Fischer family was among the evacuees. So the chemist had decided against poisoning himself and his family! Now he gave the Wilderts an uncertain wave, pulled his shoulders straight under the weight of his bundle and walked on with his wife and daughter.

Anton felt forlorn and frightened at the sight of the throng of neighbors trudging into exile. Just like the day the Russians arrived he seemed to have a reserved theater seat from which to observe the scenes unfolding on a real stage. For the first time he began to worry how long it would be before he became part of this drama. He tried to imagine how his friends felt as they passed on the street below him, but all he could do was stare at the spectacle that went far beyond his capacity to understand.

The family was jolted to see the Sattlers struggle along the garden path toward the gate, weighed down with their sacks. They heard the old woman angrily shouting to the militiaman, "How about those people up there, when will they have to go?" The soldier ignored the question and pushed her by the shoulder to get moving. *Herr* Sattler shakily trudged on behind his wife, crying openly and biting his lip. The Wilderts tried to wave but the old couple never looked back. Now they remained all alone in the villa until Dvořák returned to claim it for himself.

When the flow of refugees finally ebbed to a trickle, then vanished, the sunlit scene seemed bleak and forlorn even though nothing had changed in the outward appearance of the houses and gardens. But like a plaintive aura a remnant of protest, fear, and resignation hovered in the air. At last the Wilderts turned away from the window.

"What will happen to us?" Maria sobbed as she clung to Friedrich. He stood with closed eyes, unable to respond except to hold his wife and son even more tightly.

Dvořák and his men would answer Maria's question the following day.

ELEVEN

The Explosion

Friedrich was badly shaken when Dvořák and his men arrived to expel them from the villa two weeks earlier and he could not get used to his new surroundings. Again and again he relived the hostile encounter with Dvořák, the greedy search of the bundles, the slow trek with Maria and Anton through empty streets, the clatter of the blue wagon, the gruff guard, and the depressing arrival in the shabby neighborhood. One evening when he returned to the worker's flat from his office he looked worse than ever. In his weakened condition a bleak depression set in, and his eyes reflected apathy and dejection. Subdued and quiet he frequently pressed his left side; it was obvious he suffered from constant pain.

Friedrich witnessed a steady erosion of his values, his position, and his physical condition. The world he had built and enjoyed gradually disintegrated and finally crumbled into ruin. The lonely trek from the villa to the simple flat convinced him that the situation was hopeless. The gentle firmness that brought him success in the past drained away in his now powerless position. He had no fighting spirit left and felt old beyond his years.

Maria and Anton tried to make him as comfortable as possible and gratefully he drank a cup of warm milk that soothed his burning stomach. They pleaded with him to seek medical help. At first he did not respond, shrugging listlessly as if to say, "what's the use?" Gradually he relented and they discussed at length how they might find medical care for him under the present conditions.

"I heard that Dr. Stieglitz was evacuated in the last roundup," Friedrich said pensively. The family physician used to practice from an office in his home a few streets from the Wildert villa. "I would have liked to get his opinion. The medicine he gave me is no longer doing the job. I'm sure he could have found something stronger for me. But I wonder if we can even locate a doctor any-more."

"I know it is difficult, but you must have professional treat-ment." Maria was insistent, but also careful not to upset him more by emotional arguments. Her face brightened, "Perhaps Novak at the company may be able to arrange something for you. They need you now—so it would be in their interest to help you. What do you think?"

"I am never quite sure how far I can trust him. Our relation-ship is correct but cool. Then again, he did volunteer to give me the certificate stating that I was needed during the transfer. When I told him about the loss of the villa he seemed embarrassed, although he tried not to show it." Friedrich paused and thought hard for a few moments. "Perhaps you are right. What have we got to lose? If he says no, I am no worse off than now. They hold all the cards, and if any medical care is available they'll know how to get it." The thought of doing something constructive made him feel better, and a touch of color returned to his face.

Maria allowed herself a moment's relief. Friedrich was willing to take a positive step—perhaps there was hope that he might also rally in spirit. Ever since the suicide attempt she watched him closely for stronger signs of the will to live. Was this a faint ray of hope in the dark dejection that shrouded him?

Maria worried about the circumstances under which medical care might be given to a Sudeten. Would Czech doctors care enough, and could they even be trusted in an atmosphere of expropriation and mass expulsion? Fear of the new authority was deeply ingrained by now, whatever the form in which it touched their lives. She was unable to shake her nagging concern about her husband having to turn to these people for help. It was her suggestion, based on a distinct feeling that his illness was far worse than he admitted. Yet the urge to find help clashed with the insistent ringing of a subconscious alarm. She tried to suppress the warning by telling herself over and over again that Friedrich had no alternative but to try, for all their sakes.

After a night of fitful, shallow sleep interrupted several times by Friedrich's need to take painkillers, Maria and Anton watched him leave the house and walk across the barren courtyard. He looked back once to wave to the upstairs window where they stood. In a few minutes he descended the hill to the company buildings and entered the Czech overseer's office next to his own.

"*Pane* Novak, I urgently need medical assistance for my stomach problem. Can you help me?"

Novak studied the appearance of his predecessor standing before him. He saw the mark of pain in the ashen face, the vested suit hanging loosely on a once impressive frame. Friedrich was most cooperative in the past weeks, introducing him and the other Czech staff to the affairs of the chemical company he no longer ran. Friedrich had been honest and forthcoming, easing the overseer's task of assuming control of the confiscated enterprise.

Novak had learned of the respect the employees and the business community held for this man who treated everyone fairly, regardless of their importance. He also talked with former Allied prisoners of war, detailed to Friedrich's company as a supplement to the indigenous manpower drafted into the *Wehrmacht,* and heard of Friedrich's insistence that they be treated with decency while under his supervision. For this Friedrich even encountered official Nazi displeasure, but his attitude remained firm. Novak realized this man had natural leadership qualities, and felt growing sympathy for him now that the task of turning over the company was nearly complete and Friedrich would soon have to face the fate of the remaining Sudetens.

Novak rose from his chair, his eyes revealing some change in his attitude, even though outwardly he maintained his official bearing. "*Herr* Wildert," he said in fluent German, "I'll get in touch with the hospital right away and set up a consultation for you. I'll call you when I've made the arrangements. I understand the hospital is functioning, and they should be able to help you."

Friedrich thanked him, and once back in his spacious office slumped into his comfortable old leather chair, shifting several times until he found the position which gave the least offense to his aching left side. He closed his eyes, trying to doze, but piercing pain pulsated like stabbing knives. As he sat there he mused about his life-long desire to be a surgeon, but could no longer muster the curiosity that always consumed him when there was a reason to be in the hospital. He was going to face the surgeon's knife in a hostile environment, weakened by poor nourishment and the recent turmoil. During his appendix operation many years ago he asked the attending physician—half in jest—whether he might watch the operation in a mirror. Apprehension and fatigue overtook him as he wondered what awaited him and he drifted into shallow sleep.

Meanwhile Novak called the hospital, but the telephone conversation took longer than expected. When he mentioned Friedrich's Sudeten nationality he was switched to another administrator who questioned him about Friedrich's position and background. Novak told him what he knew, and was instructed to wait for a few minutes while the man checked "the list," as he put it. Then he transferred Novak back to the admissions clerk who made an appointment for Friedrich to be examined in the emergency room. Novak put down the receiver with a frown. A businessman by training, he was puzzled by the hospital's insistence on finding out background data that had nothing to do with Friedrich's illness. After mulling over the strange procedure for a while he put it aside as overzealous behavior by the "new brooms" now running the hospital.

Novak had been contacted late in the war by the underground network preparing the takeover of the Sudetenland and its wealth, and was asked to hold himself ready to step into the management of one of the Sudeten companies when the time came. While pleased about being considered for such a boost to his career, he had little patience for engaging in conspiratorial games—he preferred to perform in what he knew best—business management. He only glimpsed the network of political and material opportunists who worked obscurely, often seething with greedy conflict, as they prepared for the day the Sudeten properties could be seized. He chose to remain at the fringes, feeling he had little in common with these people.

Novak rose and walked to Friedrich's office. He knocked and when there was no response he entered to find Friedrich asleep, his head leaning heavily to one side. He touched his shoulder.

Friedrich awoke with a start to see Novak towering over him, a faint smile gracing the impassive face. "I've made arrangements for you to go to the emergency room at the hospital right away, *Herr* Wildert. Of course you know the way—it'll take you only a few minutes to walk there." Novak, still standing, gazed at the gaunt executive who had hastily pulled himself together in his wide armchair, once the symbol of his authority. The quiet Czech now felt warmth and concern for the man he was replacing.

Novak still mulled over his conversation with the hospital personnel, which left him with a feeling of vague disquiet. There were so many odd things going on; the takeover of the Sudeten province turned out to be far more chaotic than he imagined. Although officially forced to consider Friedrich an enemy, he developed growing respect for what the older man represented.

Friedrich grasped Novak's hand and pressed it for a moment, feeling Novak's firm responding grip. Then he rose and bade him good-bye. As he left his office he turned around briefly to see his successor standing by his desk, the dark eyes following him with a mixture of sympathy and concern.

Walking slowly down the hallway past the glass partitions he glimpsed a few familiar faces amidst the many new employees Novak had already brought in. Several of his long-time associates looked up and gave him a polite greeting. Friedrich felt distant and light-headed, overcome by a powerful vision—he knew he was leaving this place for the last time. He had devoted the past twenty years of his life to the company and it prospered under his leadership. Everything he saw and touched on his way was familiar and yet remote. He passed the gate house, returned the doorkeeper's respectful "good morning" and broke into his usual rapid stride.

At the emergency room he waited for two painful hours before a young Czech doctor examined him. The impersonal physician used no German, but with the assistance of a bilingual nurse arrived at his diagnosis of an acute bleeding stomach ulcer, a condition that could worsen at any time. He considered an operation necessary as soon as it could be arranged. He would admit Friedrich in the late afternoon, and scheduled the operation for the following morning.

When Friedrich appeared at the flat shortly before noon, Maria and Anton were pleased with the news that Friedrich would receive such speedy medical attention amid the confusion gripping the city. But Maria's concerns about the operation persisted and she wondered out loud if adequate care for his recovery would be made available. With food in such short supply she worried how Friedrich might regain even part of his strength unless a proper diet were granted him after the operation.

Another ever-present fear was evacuation. What if the roundups started again while Friedrich was still recovering in the hospital? Previous mass displacements occurred without advance warning; the soldiers showed up at any time of the day or night to corral and march off the people of the neighborhood they surrounded. Friedrich attempted to reassure her, saying that he was in no condition to face an evacuation now. They must take the chance that they could move to Germany together after he was relieved of his ulcers. As he spoke, he lacked real conviction but tried not to let his doubts show.

With the decision made to undergo the operation, Friedrich's outward mood shifted to one of anticipation. Maria packed the few essentials he needed to take to the hospital. She wanted to accompany him on the walk, but he insisted that she stay at the flat with Anton. There was no need to run unnecessary risks being seen in the streets with white armbands. Moreover, she would have to return alone.

In the late afternoon Friedrich said good-bye. For a while he held his wife in his arms, comforting her quietly. Maria put up a brave front, suppressing her urge to cry openly. Anton clung to his father and walked out into the street with him, wanting to watch him as long as he could. He felt sad and forlorn and he stood staring at the spot where the tall man faded from view without looking back again.

The hospital staff assigned Friedrich a double room; the second bed was empty. He was overjoyed when he saw the jolly face of a Catholic sister, her small, ample body draped with the black habit and her full red cheeks squeezed by the severe white and black of the starched headdress.

"Annerl, Annerl!" he exclaimed, lapsing into the soft dialect of his home town in the western Sudetenland.

With outstretched arms the nun hurried toward him. "Fritzl, my Fritzl!" They instantly recognized each other as childhood friends who grew up together in the small-town atmosphere of what was then provincial Austria.

Sister Anna stepped back to take a long look at Friedrich. Her practiced eye saw the havoc wrought by pain, internal bleeding and stress. She wanted to warn him that conditions had changed at the hospital, that many patients did not survive operations, and that the medical staff was new. The most respected physicians and surgeons had been evacuated or even placed into the Czech concentration camps. But she held back. She could plainly see that Friedrich must run this risk in order to have a chance to live. He would not survive for long if he did nothing.

Chatting happily about old times while avoiding any mention of the gruesome happenings of the present, Sister Anna helped Friedrich to settle in. She had insisted on coming to see him as soon as she could when she spotted his name on the admissions list, and she explained that tomorrow she would attend the operation. Then she inquired about his family—and instantly regretted having done so—for a desperate heaviness clouded Friedrich's face when he told her about Johann. Sister Anna crossed herself and sat by his bed, stroking his hand. "He is with God, Fritzl, he is with God. Believe me, hard as it is for you and your family, he is better off. God rest his soul, I will pray for him."

The nun stayed with him until she sensed Friedrich was calmer. He was suffused with leaden weariness and soon became drowsy, yielding to the lure of sleep. Sister Anna checked on the food arrangements and assured herself that he would receive proper supplements to strengthen him for tomorrow's ordeal. Then she returned to her station in the operating wing of the hospital.

At the flat Maria and Anton tried to carry on their daily routine as best they could. Maria yearned for human contact and decided to visit the Sudeten women in the house at the corner of the courtyard. She and Anton had met the three young mothers during their first days in the flat. The women's husbands had not yet returned from the disbanded *Wehrmacht,* and both Maria and Anton found them to be positive and disarming in their simple ways. Maria felt drawn to the warm nurturing energy which they expended on their small children. She ventured into the streets on errands with one or the other of the women, especially with *Frau* Winkler, a jolly, positive and practical person, and always felt buoyed by their spirit and occasional banter. She was not yet able to distance herself from grief and loss to rekindle much emotional strength of her own.

The women welcomed them and showered Maria and Anton with the bustle and clatter of three adults, three infants and an eleven-year-old girl in the small living quarters of the bungalow. While they tried to cheer Maria, suggesting that all would go well at the hospital, they pursued the chores of keeping the children comfortable and fed. Anton asked if he could help and they immediately put him to work in the kitchen.

After an hour in this vigorous environment Maria and Anton returned to their flat somewhat strengthened in spirit. They prepared a simple meal for themselves and spent the early evening hours listening to the Swiss national radio. Several times Maria was tempted to turn off the concert music which churned her emotions, but she decided that the nostalgic distraction was better than giving in to her gloomy thoughts.

The next morning passed quickly. Anton went to the nearby grocery shop to purchase staples with ration tickets. Meanwhile Maria cooked a midday meal of potatoes and margarine.

In late morning orderlies wheeled Friedrich into the operating room where a team of three doctors and two nurses waited, one of them Sister Anna. Friedrich was sedated but quite conscious of the burly arms lifting him onto the operating table. He looked up at the doctors' white masks and noted a cold stare from a pair of eyes fixed on him. The man whispered something to his colleague, then placed an anesthetic mask over Friedrich's face. In the dark closeness of the mask Friedrich felt clammy and claustrophobic. Something did not seem right but he could not grasp what it was. He struggled vainly against his dark fears that grew with every moment.

The odor of the mask was different from what he remembered when his appendix was removed years ago. How he longed for the pleasant sensation of floating out of consciousness, for the languid, relaxed feeling of the anesthetic gas taking hold. He knew its effect should be soothing him by now, but he could not detect anything. What was wrong? He felt nauseated and drowsy, yet fully aware.

A burning, slashing, unbearable pain tore through his body as the surgeon's scalpel sliced deeply into his exposed abdomen. Flashes of blinding color—blood red, fiery white, and poisonous green—assaulted his tortured mind. Agonized screams gushed wildly from his mouth, muffled by the mask. He tumbled eerily through space, floating, turning over and over, a searing shaft of fire scorching his lower body. He saw his own mouth contorted, gaping, gasping, screaming, screaming, screaming . . .

Sister Anna's pulse raced madly as she tried to comprehend the enormity of an operation being performed on a conscious patient. She barely knew the two surgeons and had never met the third man who administered the anesthetic. The surgeon kept cutting on the writhing Friedrich—was it possible? She noticed that the third man repeatedly nodded to the surgeon, ordering him to proceed. At first the surgeon hesitated, but then went ahead. Oh dear God, why?

Mercifully Friedrich lost consciousness. His vital signs fluttered weakly; his heart beat in irregular spasms. Still the surgeon persisted. He opened the stomach, uncovering the ulcerated area. The wound bled profusely, and the doctors made only cursory attempts to stem the flow. Sister Anna tried to touch Friedrich but she was ordered aside harshly.

Her experienced eye followed the remaining steps of what should have been a routine operation. To her horror she noted that the ulcerated area was not repaired, and that the wounds were closed perfunctorily, without proper cauterization. Was this sheer incompetence, or was it—dear God!—was she witnessing a deliberate act?

The icy stare of the third man fixed on her. He had watched

her reactions intermittently; now his eyes were piercing, conveying a threatening message. Cold shivers ran down her spine. Numb with fear and disbelief Sister Anna lowered her gaze and appeared to busy herself with her duties. Her mind was in a whirl of frenzy. She wanted to scream but realized she was helpless. Who was this third man? Was his presence the reason that many patients did not survive? Was there a pattern?

Sister Anna took refuge in desperate prayer, praying for Friedrich, barely alive when the orderlies lifted him from the operating table, praying for herself, and praying that God put an end to the cruelty and suffering. When she looked up she met the fierce stare again.

The doctors, led by the third man, left the operating room without a word while the nurses collected the implements and cleared the equipment. Sister Anna crossed herself, not daring to say anything to the Czech nurse beside her. She knew she must keep the full truth to herself.

In the afternoon Maria left for the hospital to visit Friedrich, presuming the scheduled operation completed. It was not possible to telephone the hospital as there were no phones in the neighborhood. She asked Anton not to come. Her instincts told her that Friedrich needed to be as quiet as possible, and she did not wish Anton to witness the suffering evident in the hospital.

After Maria departed Anton decided to visit his friend Rainer who still lived in a townhouse near the villa. He rode his bicycle there, deliberately choosing a route that did not take him past his former home. As he came near the familiar street he had the strong sensation of being shut out, of being blocked by an invisible barrier that forever prevented his return to the house where he spent his childhood. It was good to see his friend again, to talk about past times, about the worries of the present, and to speculate in the simplistic way of adolescents about what the future might hold. As they chatted, Anton's mind strayed to the oddity of coming to his friend's home which remained unchanged, and then of his own neighborhood, empty of its former residents, and of being forbidden to enter the family house again.

Rainer tried to understand Anton's situation but could not

comprehend the experiences his friend had gone through. His own father was detained by the Nazis in the last year of the war for having kept secret his mother's fractional Jewish background, but he returned, shaken yet unharmed. He proved active Nazi persecution to the Czech authorities who issued him papers that entitled him to a delayed evacuation and to keep part of his personal property.

The boys decided to venture out on their bicycles. With white armbands pinned in place they pedaled to a wooded height and a small park overlooking the broad Elbe valley. It was a clear, sunny July afternoon and a pleasant breeze caressed their faces. Anton and Rainer enjoyed the sweeping view of the curving river, the bridges, the softly rolling hills quilted with fields, orchards and forests, the city, the suburbs, and the picturesque villages near and far. It was an idyllic scene, peaceful and gentle. The grim war damage was softened by the distance of the view, and the many shadings of sunlit color, of greens, reds, and bluish tints would have excited an artist.

The boys admired the splendid setting which, like a romantic painting, had at its center a steep, towering crag rising from the river, crowned with an ancient ruined castle. This fortress, called the "Rock of Horrors," served generations of knights bent on robbery to extort tribute from boats plying the river narrows below by blocking the treacherous waters with chains of iron. In the twentieth century a modern concrete power dam and barge locks tamed the narrows. These inviting targets miraculously escaped the Allied bombers.

Anton and Rainer rested on a bench, letting their eyes sweep over the vista. It could have been like any sunny summer day of their childhood except for the white armbands on their sleeves. They watched idly as a small plane hummed along high above the river. This time there was no need to duck out of sight, as they had done so often during the waning weeks of the war when Russian fighter bombers strafed the streets at will.

Without warning a huge fireball erupted on the far river bank in the industrial area, below where the plane passed. Like an evil phantom a vast black mushroom cloud began to roll and ooze skyward on an ugly stem, unfolding in unearthly silence. Wide-eyed and speechless the boys gaped at the apparition. Moments later the shock wave and roar of a thunderous explosion rocked the ground beneath them. Crashing echoes reverberated from the hillsides. More massive explosions erupted, each belching towering flames and thick, swirling smoke.

Anton and Rainer leaped from their bench and stood staring at the blazing inferno on the distant bank of the Elbe. Immediately they both knew that they must get home the fastest way possible. Their peaceful outing had been an unreal interlude in the maelstrom of disruption. Seized by a primal sense of danger and foreboding they jumped on their bicycles and raced toward the residential district only a few minutes away. It seemed to take forever. When they reached the streets from the hillside park they heard shouting and saw throngs of people running and gesturing in confusion.

Rainer veered off to hasten the remaining quarter mile to his house and Anton headed down the hill in the direction of the flat. There was screaming, running, and commotion all around. In the distance Anton noticed how those wearing white armbands were set upon, knocked down, and beaten by others. Frantic, he redoubled his speed, breathing hard and aiming straight ahead to get past the turmoil that surrounded him.

Miraculously he managed to weave his way through the frenzied crowd, nearly ramming a man who made threatening gestures and screamed at him at the top of his lungs. Holding his head low and hunching over the handle bars Anton pedaled madly, not reducing his speed even though he nearly lost control when his front wheel was momentarily caught in the groove of the street car tracks. He forced the shuddering bicycle free and shot downhill to the intersection where the unpaved street led to the flat.

The side street was a quiet haven. No one was there. Still he raced and skidded with undiminished haste over the gravel surface and the deep ruts. Trembling and exhausted he screeched to a stop in the front yard of the apartment building, slammed the bicycle into the storage shed and bounded up the stairs as fast as he could.

Alone in the flat Anton locked the door behind him with panicky haste. He collapsed on the sofa and tried to stop shaking while he stared at the ceiling, helpless and afraid. Heaving rapid breaths the boy thought his pounding heart might jump out his chest. His legs ached badly—but he had escaped. As he lay there, gradually coming to his senses, he worried about his mother who had not yet returned from her visit to Friedrich at the hospital. What had become of her?

The explosion was obviously a severe accident—or could the plane he and Rainer observed have dropped a bomb? But what was worse, the catastrophe appeared to have triggered a spontaneous upheaval where Czech mobs set upon the Sudeten population, clearly identifiable by their white armbands. The incidents he witnessed on his way home were real enough—but they took place miles from the actual site. He wondered what was happening in the city and in the industrial district, the site of the explosion. He couldn't telephone the hospital or anyone else for facts or reassurance. All he could do was lie low and wait.

He grew increasingly worried and hoped that his mother had the foresight to stay safely at the hospital instead of venturing out into the dangerous streets. Then again, he wished she would come home to him right away. The minutes crept like hours. Anton buried his face in the pillow and cried convulsively.

A door slammed downstairs. Startled out of his anxious misery he got up and tiptoed warily to the stairwell. Through the opening in the staircase he saw the old gossip neighbor returning, out of breath, her face white with fear. He called to her and when she spotted the boy she cried out, between gasping breaths, "It's terrible out there, they're beating and killing our people just because an ammunition dump blew up!"

The woman had been on an errand in the city when the massive explosion ripped through several riverside warehouses filled with discarded ammunition gathered there after the collapse of the *Wehrmacht*. Thrown together carelessly, the huge store of shells, grenades, bombs and bazookas ignited, the detonation causing catastrophic damage to the surrounding area, killing and injuring many people in the immediate vicinity.

More ominous still, the fiery eruption became the signal for an outbreak of mass hysteria and murder directed against anyone wearing a white armband in all parts of the city. The armed Czech militia took the lead, joined by roving bands of civilians and young toughs who arrived in the territory during recent weeks. Anton, standing on the stairs above listened to the terrified woman stuttering and blurting out her tale. Being fluent in Czech, she risked removing her armband and bluffed her way home.

She experienced naked terror and was in shock. Her body shook as she described the mob falling upon men, women and children, beating them mercilessly with sticks, fence pickets, and any available weapons. In the heart of the city there were large concrete ponds built during the war by civil defense teams to store water for fire fighting. Frenzied thugs dragged scores of people there and drowned them by holding their heads under water. Blood and bodies were everywhere.

"Thank God I was able to get away; I thought for sure this was the end!" Bursting into uncontrollable sobs the woman fled into her apartment and slammed the door. Her key turned noisily in the lock.

Anton dared not leave the house although no sounds came from the street. He was becoming desperately worried about his mother, but there was nothing he could do. After another agonizing hour he went as far as the house at the corner where he found the three women subdued and frightened. One of them also witnessed the horrors in the city.

Like the old gossip, *Frau* Sedlaček had quickly removed her armband while hiding in a doorway. Her ability to speak Czech fluently saved her when she was accosted by a band of young marauders. Lapsing into blunt and coarse language she gave them a piece of her mind, shouting that she was minding her own business and so should they. With her expressive face she acted like a shrew and the mob withdrew, laughing at her choice of colorful curses. In retrospect the young mother trembled at the thought of their fury if the mob had realized that she was without her armband and dared mock them. With moist eyes she described the many people she saw beaten to the ground, some lifeless, others bleeding and moaning helplessly.

Frau Winkler insisted that Anton stay with them until Maria returned. Everyone hoped that she had the good sense to wait for the turmoil to die down. It was early evening now, and Anton kept looking through the front window in the direction his mother should return. He felt alone, abandoned, and more frightened than he had ever been. The deep sense of terror that choked him back in the villa returned, but now it was worse. He was tense like a coiled spring despite the women's well-meant attempts to allay his fears.

After two hours of anxious waiting two black-clad figures appeared in the darkening street. It was Maria and a Catholic sister, one in mourning, the other in her dark habit. Neither wore a white armband. Anton raced outside to fling himself at his mother, laughing and crying at the same time. Then he bowed to Sister Anna.

The boy could see that Maria's face was distorted with anguish. Puzzled, he turned to the sister whose expression of deep concern was just as disturbing. Before Anton could ask anything, Sister Anna said quietly she must hurry back. When the explosion rocked the city, the nun asked Maria to stay with her until the end of her shift, and offered to walk her home. By that time the turmoil had passed and they were able to make their way unmolested.

The women pulled Maria and Anton into the house and Maria broke into heaving sobs. Minutes later she calmed down enough to describe Friedrich's poor condition after the operation earlier in the day. With great difficulty she related the nun's account of the surgery. Sister Anna spared her the full knowledge of Friedrich's agony under the surgeon's scalpel, hinting instead that the procedure was marred by incompetence. When Maria was allowed to see Friedrich in the afternoon he lay dazed, barely alive. Maria was certain he did not recognize her.

Stunned, the women tried to give Maria some warmth and comfort. Anton wept quietly to himself, oblivious of the others around him. *Frau* Winkler offered to go with Maria to the hospital the next morning, a courageous thing to do. She insisted on this even when Maria tried to dissuade her, reminding the kind woman how dangerous it was for her to leave her children.

The evening and night passed slowly. Anton decided not to tell his mother about his outing with Rainer and his narrow escape, afraid that knowledge of the danger he faced would add to her troubled state. They talked little, but before going to sleep they prayed together for Friedrich's recovery.

In the morning Maria and *Frau* Winkler made their way warily to the hospital through quiet streets. They encountered an old acquaintance of *Frau* Winkler's, who burst forth with more descriptions of yesterday's horrors.

The explosion had occurred in mid-afternoon, shortly before the shift change in the huge chemical works on the eastern river bank. The woman witnessed violent scenes on the graceful arch bridge that spanned the Elbe. As groups of working men and women walked across, the mob fell upon them and flung many into the water, including mothers and their baby carriages. The militia began firing at the victims in the river and arrested many of the men, marching them off to concentration camps.

Maria only half heard the account, gripped with impatience to press on to the hospital. When they arrived there, *Frau* Winkler offered to wait for her in the glass-enclosed lobby. Maria hurried to the wing where she left Friedrich the evening before.

The room was empty. A fierce jab of panic jolted her and she hurried out to the nurses' desk. No one was there. She rang the buzzer urgently. After a few seconds of agitated waiting Maria saw the gentle face of Sister Anna appear in the hallway. The nun hesitated for a moment, then rushed toward her with outstretched arms, unable to restrain her tears. "My dear Maria, I am so sorry to have to tell you that Friedrich passed away during the night. He was not strong enough to overcome the stresses of the operation. May God rest his soul."

Maria stared at her, paralyzed with shock and disbelief. Sister Anna hugged Maria and whispered, "He is better off with the Good Lord. Friedrich was tired of struggling. If only he had been granted a more dignified end." The white-faced Maria stood rigid.

"I am so sorry, Maria. Friedrich was a truly good man. But you must go on for your son's sake. I'll take you to the lobby, my dear, there you can sit down and rest a while—I'll stay with you if you wish."

In the lobby *Frau* Winkler jumped to her feet when she saw the tearful Maria and Sister Anna enter. She gave Maria a silent, understanding embrace and they sat wordless for a few minutes while Maria sobbed quietly. Sister Anna warmly hugged the women as they set off toward home. From time to time both wept openly as they hurried along. A Russian patrol gazed at the pair with idle curiosity. No one accosted them; the fury of the day before had run its course and left behind an air of dull exhaustion.

When they rounded the curve of the main street near the gravel road they encountered Anton on his way to the grocery store. The boy took one look at his mother's face and understood what had happened. Maria managed to whisper, "We're all alone now," and she hugged him tightly.

Anton nodded mechanically, his young mind unable to absorb the loss of another family member so soon after Johann. He looked at his mother and felt both compassion and fear. What could he say to her? At last the boy stuttered, "I . . I will try to take care of you, *Mutti*," and his tears started to flow.

Slowly the three walked, huddled together, along the dreary street to the apartment house which now looked bleaker than ever.

TWELVE

The Bakery

Life in the tiny flat was lonely and passive for the gaunt widow and her son. Maria kept herself occupied with the few daily chores that made their spartan life more tolerable. Conversation with Anton was mostly about daily necessities; details of their makeshift existence were subconsciously magnified to blank out the deep feelings of despair. Their emotional wounds were still too raw to allow them to talk about the torrent of events of the past weeks without bursting into tears and sobbing. Maria found it difficult in such moments to be a steadying influence on Anton while her own soul cried out for consolation. Avoiding these topics was the easier option, but she often cried to herself, especially at night, alone in the unfamiliar bed. She was careful not to display her weak moments to Anton and she nearly always managed to act with strength where he was involved. Yet this brave front—and it was only that—seemed to rally her own will to survive.

Anton ventured out very little except on necessary errands. He listened to the radio and drew sketches on a supply of paper he found. He missed his books and his model trains, and especially the pieces of laboratory equipment and supplies of chemicals which Johann had collected, and with which the two boys conducted a variety of chemical experiments—some of them noisy, smoky, and not without risk. It hurt to think of his dead brother, of the closeness they had, the sharing, and the respect with which he regarded him, now more than ever. But he kept these feelings to himself. With Maria's help he began to study an old primer of elementary Czech conversation he had been given, but the complex language did not hold his attention long. In early August the radio brought news of atomic bombs dropped on Japan, and shortly after that announced the surrender of the Japanese Empire. In his disoriented world such faraway events meant little to the boy.

The women in the corner house, especially the ebullient *Frau* Winkler, took the Wilderts under their wing. They often came to visit and insisted that mother and son visit them in return. The Wilderts enjoyed the crowded, boisterous togetherness of the women and children in the cozy kitchen-living room of the corner house, and they always returned to their own flat with a sense of renewal.

During this time official posters and radio bulletins decreed that all Sudetens aged fourteen and over must do useful labor to continue qualifying for minimal food rations. Maria became anxious about Anton when she learned that in the inner city many youths were forced to clear rubble and clean bricks under most difficult conditions.

Determined to find an alternative she went to Friedrich's company offices to seek out the advice of one of his remaining Sudeten associates. After expressing his condolences on Friedrich's death, he came up with the idea that Anton might find employment as an apprentice in a small bakery near the office. He knew that the owner always held Friedrich in high regard and appreciated his patronage in better days. The man promised to talk with the baker to see what could be done.

On the following day Friedrich's colleague dropped by the flat with good news. The baker would be glad to have Friedrich's son as a helper. The hours would be long; work started at half past five in the morning, the pay nominal. But being in a bakery might mean having extra scraps of food, invaluable with the subsistence diet rationed out by the authorities.

The job was to start in two days and Anton decided to visit his friend Rainer one more time. He pedaled to the familiar neighborhood, without feeling the total estrangement of the previous visit. He wondered if perhaps he was getting used to his new situation. Rainer was at home and the boys spent a few pleasant hours in make-believe normalcy. They avoided talking about the explosion and its aftermath; the horror of that day was too fresh in their minds.

Anton's job sounded like an interesting adventure to Rainer, whose father was going to give him work in the printing plant he still owned. They shared a boiled potato and some margarine, and laughed happily as they compared memories of the mischievous fun they used to have. When they said good-bye Rainer promised to try to visit his friend in return.

A few houses from Rainer's home Anton pedaled hard to ascend the slope of a quiet sun-speckled street. A figure stepped into his path, appearing from behind the trees that lined the sidewalk. The man pointed at his white armband and his bicycle and bellowed, "German pig *nix* have bicycle—is confiscated!" Glowering at the boy he grabbed the handle bar possessively.

He took Anton completely off guard. The icy fear of past encounters returned. Reluctantly he swung his leg over the saddle and let go of his bicycle. Terrified, he stood in silence, trembling from the shock of the confrontation, and watched the stranger mount the bike and pedal away. Shaken and alarmed he warily looked around the deserted street.

At last he walked up the slope, faster and faster, wanting to get away from the area that now meant danger and wanton expropriation. He could not stop the torrent of thoughts and feelings bombarding him and broke into a run for the final distance, crying as he reached the door of the apartment. Maria comforted him, saying that he could not have hoped to take his bicycle along when they were finally evacuated. And what did another loss matter now, anyway, after all that happened? Anton could see the logic but he would miss his bicycle nevertheless.

The day before the job at the bakery was to begin, Anton went on an errand with *Frau* Winkler. It was cool and damp, the fine rain misting in a gray drizzle. On their way home they passed one of the former dairy farms with its large cobbled yard, enclosed by a decaying plastered brick wall, its muddy brown color soaked in dark blotches. They walked on the opposite side of the street, talking, and paid little attention to their dreary surroundings except to avoid stepping into the abundant puddles on the soggy sidewalk.

A young Czech militiaman, his rifle slung low, came out of the gate of the dairy courtyard, crossed the street rapidly and accosted them with agitated gestures. Grabbing Anton by the arm he shouted at him in Czech. *Frau* Winkler paled. "Your white arm-band is too narrow," she whispered to the terrified boy. Anton glanced down at his arm and discovered that the rain had shriv-eled the white cloth pinned to the damp sleeve of his overcoat. It was weeks ago that Maria carefully sewed the armband to comply with the required width of fifteen centimeters.

Before Anton realized what was happening the soldier gripped him tightly by the scruff of his neck and dragged him across the street into the courtyard, bellowing, "You'll go to the camp for this!" *Frau* Winkler shrieked in terror and broke into a desperate run to alert Maria at home.

As he stumbled through the dilapidated gateway of the dairy, still pushed by the angry soldier, Anton saw a line-up of fright-ened people with white armbands huddled against the sooty wall. They stood motionless, staring ahead in hopeless despair. The sol-dier pushed and kicked him viciously to make him take his place in line. Choked with fear the boy joined the queue.

Anton was afraid to move but glanced about cautiously. He saw a uniformed officer sitting under the cover of a doorway by a makeshift desk—a wooden shipping crate—examining the papers of his prisoners. Anton's captor and two other soldiers were busy pushing their helpless quarry back and forth, cursing the cower-ing figures and confiscating their identity cards.

Anton dared not look into the determined faces of the guards. He heard the officer tell a trembling old man in broken German, "Never mind reason! You'll have plenty time to think about reason for arrest in Lerchenfeld!" The stooped, white-haired figure let out a groan of despair, shaking his head in disbelief. Anton knew that the former *Luftwaffe* barracks at Lerchenfeld, a settlement north of the city, had been converted by the new rulers into a concentration camp for Germans and Sudetens. Tales of horror abounded about the conditions; people died miserably from torture and neglect.

The boy shivered with fear. He thought of his mother at the flat; but then the memory of the macabre farewell dinner at the villa vividly came to mind, and he relived the moment when the poison in the glittering glasses was to end their horror of exile and separation.

Terror enveloped him, taking on a life of its own and choking off his breath. His thoughts blurred and only raw emotions surged through him in fierce pulses. Then came a floating sensation, lifting and detaching him from the scene. He viewed the hunched pitiful shapes from his position last in the line, shuffling one by one toward the merciless uniformed figure that would decide their fate. He felt very alone.

His mother's voice brought him back to reality. Startled, he spun around to see Maria running wildly toward him, her loose hair streaming. "Anton, Anton!" she shouted as she staggered through the gate, breathless. A guard jumped forward to block her, but she pushed him aside with a fury born of desperation.

She ran up to the officer at the makeshift desk and pleaded in Czech between shuddering breaths. "Why have you taken my son? He's only a boy! For God's sake, let him go, I beg you!"

The man looked up, irritated by the outburst. By now the soldier caught up with her again, grabbed her by the arm and, eyes bulging, hissed, "You German sow, get out of here this instant or we'll teach you to obey orders in Lerchenfeld!"

Maria spun around and fiercely faced the man young enough to be her son. "Then I'll go with my boy to the camp, even though we have done nothing to deserve this !"

The officer still looked at her, clearly bothered by the noisy interruption. The other prisoners stood frozen in suspense. At last the officer spoke up. "Which one is your son?" Before Maria could respond her furious tormentor shouted, "It's the young bastard over there, the one who thinks he can walk around without a proper armband!"

Maria, without realizing it, dropped to her knees before the officer. She lifted her arms and sobbed quietly. "Please, please, he is all I have left in the world. He is only a child, please give him back to me!"

Impassively the officer studied the kneeling woman's face, aware of the stares of dozens of eyes riveted on him. With a sudden touch of embarrassment he took a deep breath and said quietly, "Take your son and go." The audience gasped.

Maria scrambled to her feet, grabbed Anton's hand, and both

raced through the sinister gate into the street, running as fast as their legs could carry them. The misty rain suddenly felt warm and cleansing.

The women at the corner house waited anxiously and there were shrieks of delight at the sight of Anton, tears of joy and much hugging and commotion. He was still shaken and Maria numb and exhausted, but gradually their spirits revived.

One of the women opened her emergency flask of brandy, saved from a special Christmas ration a year ago, and the strong drink helped overcome the effects of the shock. Anton now began to grasp the narrowness of his escape, and in retrospect he suffered more spasms of fear. The women did their best to calm him and to comfort Maria, who trembled visibly as she described the details of the encounter.

Back in the quiet of their flat Maria sobbed as she recounted her extreme fear for Anton, and her fierce determination to risk everything to save him. "Something urged me to do what I did," she confided to him, "and I am so happy and grateful to God. He granted us a miracle." She held him close for a long time. Anton reflected on the events of the last hour—the unexpected nightmare and the miraculous reprieve—it seemed so unreal. What moved the officer to yield? They would never know.

In the afternoon Maria broke into spasms of uncontrollable weeping as she rested on the bed. Anton vainly tried to comfort her, crying himself at the sight of her distress. "How can we go on when there is one crisis after another?" she sobbed. "We were able to get out of this latest predicament, God willing, but I'm not sure how much more I can take!" It seemed that the accumulated stress finally broke through the defenses her will and determination had erected. Maria began to scream, flailing her arms, her words incoherent. Anton strained to hold her, but she pushed him aside, engulfed in her distress. When she did not calm down, Anton ran to the corner house for help. *Frau* Winkler hurried with him to the flat, soaked a towel in cold water and applied a cold compress to Maria's burning forehead. She spoke to her in a soothing but firm tone, holding her hand and stroking her cheeks. Anton stood by the bed, watching, anxiously waiting for his mother to regain her senses. Slowly the wailing and sobbing subsided as the kind woman's care took effect. *Frau* Winkler stayed for a long time, quietly holding Maria's hand, and smiling encouragement as Maria's eyes focused on her. She sent Anton to the corner house for some hot soup, and made sure that Maria took the nourishment. Calm now, Maria fell asleep and woke up an hour later to smile at Anton, who had stayed by her bedside.

Now the urgent practical question arose, could Anton be safe walking in the streets when he began work the next morning? His narrow escape from detention weighed heavily on them as they pondered how to get Anton to the bakery at five-thirty and return home unscathed in the early evening. The curfew was still in effect and the hours bordering it were dangerous for anyone with a white armband. Anton knew only a few words of Czech, most of them impolite, and thus could not risk going to the bakery without wearing the required marker. After today's incident this was out of the question.

They decided that Maria would go with him the first morning to see the route and talk with the owner of the bakery about the problem. Perhaps one of the other people working there might be willing to accompany Anton at least part of the way.

The bakery was located only a few streets from the apartment, and they discovered the next day that the walk took only five minutes. Anton could make his way through quiet side streets unlikely to be frequented by troublesome adversaries.

At Hammel's bakery the owner greeted them with a harassed expression. His own situation as a Sudeten native was tenuous. Only his long-term membership in the Social Democrat party gave him a temporary respite from the evacuations. He paid his warm respects to the late Friedrich, pressing Maria's hand. Then he took a long look at the tall boy, thin from meager rations, who was to help out in his bakery. "I hope you can pull your weight, Anton," he sighed, shaking his head. With a frown he added, "Things are pretty tough and poor *Herr* Werner back there is getting more nervous every day."

Werner was the skilled baker running the workroom, freeing Hammel to tend the store, locate and pick up supplies, and see to all the other chores. Werner fled from the east, arriving ahead of the Russian army, having abandoned his own bakery in Silesia. Hammel welcomed him gladly to his operation which had been gradually drained of most manpower as the war worsened. Two young men worked under Werner's supervision; one of them was part Czech, the other Sudeten, both apprenticed to the bakery for over a year.

Anton looked bravely at *Herr* Hammel and proclaimed, "I will do my best, whatever you want me to do." He had no concept of what the job entailed, but was determined to pull his weight, as *Herr* Hammel said.

A smile passed over Hammel's careworn face as he turned to Maria. "He sure looks like his father's son, doesn't he, *Frau Direktor*? He'll be safe here, as safe as any of us can be these days. I'll see to it that there is someone to walk with him in the evening." Hammel bowed politely to Friedrich's widow, who thanked him warmly. After giving Anton a quick hug Maria left for home. The fourteen-year-old felt an odd mixture of curiosity mixed with concern as he stepped into the large workshop behind *Herr* Hammel.

Three men bustled about the brightly lit room, while large machines clattered in the background. The bakers prepared and carried large sheets of raw pastry. Walking to and from the large electric oven in the corner, the men concentrated on their work in a brisk and businesslike way. Anton was reminded of the many times he and his brother visited the humming work floors in the factory buildings of his father's company. The main difference was that this time he had come not as a visitor, but to perform serious duties himself. Hammel expected Anton to do a man's work, which was a new responsibility altogether. It felt not unlike his first day of school eight years ago when he faced a new and unfamiliar experience.

Hammel approached Werner, who was absorbed in decorating slices of flat pastry with a nondescript foam squeezed from a cloth cone. Anton looked hungrily at the sweet layered confection, something he had not seen for a long time. While his mouth watered, he wondered whether these goods tasted any better than the poor quality *ersatz* products pastry shops sold during the war. The strong fragrances and artificial colors of the confections suggested that they were not at all like the fine baked goods he recalled from childhood. Yet, given the poor diet of the past several months the sight of such large amounts of food was nothing short of astonishing.

At last the burly, aging man looked up from his chores and eyed Anton, annoyed at being interrupted. Dressed in a patched and yellowing baker's overall and apron, a crumpled chef's hat clinging to his thin gray hair, he barked sternly at the boy, "So you're the new kid I have to put up with!"

Giving Hammel a half-glance over his shoulder he growled, "Just don't you get any ideas you can play the young gentleman around here! We've got too much work to do to bother with spoiled kids. Lord knows the other two are useless; they haven't learned a damned thing in all this time. If I don't do everything myself and do it right, our new Czech masters will throw us out even sooner. What is this damned world coming to?"

Paying no further attention to Hammel he grabbed Anton by the shoulder and led him to a huge stack of blackened and encrusted baking sheets. He pointed to a wide metal spatula and an apron hanging on a nail, and bellowed, "There, 'what's your name,' your job is to get these sheets scraped clean, and pronto!" Werner seized the top sheet and fiercely attacked the hardened, baked-on crusts, sending pieces flying. "There, that's how it is done, young feller, get going!" With a toss of the head he returned to his own work. Hammel winked at the boy and left the workroom.

Anton clumsily tried to imitate the practiced efficiency he had just seen, and found the scraping of the stubborn residues hard and boring. *Herr* Werner made it look so easy. The other two apprentices watched the exchange and now viewed Anton's awkward efforts, grinning and nudging each other. But when Werner turned towards them they hurriedly resumed their work. Anton hacked and scraped as best he could and the huge pile of baking sheets began to dwindle slowly. After a while he learned how to handle the awkward objects and managed to keep up a steady pace. As he worked he looked guardedly around him.

Herr Werner was a stern taskmaster, driven not only by professional pride but by a stark sense of survival. The nervous man kept up a steady monologue in the singing dialect of his home region, characterized by a heavy rolling "r" that sounded funny to Anton's ear. The influx of refugees in the last year of the war made him much more aware of the differences among regional dialects and he and his schoolmates often joked and teased back and forth with the newcomers, imitating their idioms and inflections.

Yet there was obvious tension in Werner's homely way of speaking which left no room for joking. Raw materials were extremely scarce and what could be obtained had to be used imaginatively and made to go a long way. The daily products turned out by the bakers were of the starchy variety, available for purchase by the public if they wanted to give up ration coupons for them.

However, Czech customers often brought their own ingredients for special orders, and the bakery in part became a job shop for the new rulers. This carried with it the responsibility of turning precious eggs, butter, cream, and fine white flour—all obtained through private barter—into dainty delicacies reminiscent of peaceful days. To spoil any of those orders meant not only a severe reprimand but the obligation to replace the materials, something an ordinary Sudeten would find impossible. Werner always insisted on performing the most difficult tasks himself.

Anton felt like an alien intruder. He brought no experience or skills other than what he had learned doing chores around his home. He was barely beginning to awaken to the startling demands of adulthood and could only fall back on his instincts to help him struggle through. Now he found himself among a group of tough older workmen who seemed very mature and sure of themselves.

After he finished cleaning the pile of baking sheets, Anton stood for a moment with his arms folded over his chest. He often saw his bachelor Uncle Herbert make this gesture; he was a studious type who spent a lot of time brooding about life's challenges.

"Quit standing around like a damned professor!" boomed Werner's angry voice. Startled, Anton dropped his arms and whirled around. "Haven't you got anything to do? For God's sake, now I've got to contend with children, on top of everything else!" Werner looked tired and flushed as he handed the boy a broom and told him to sweep the floor, growling that he had better not overlook the corners and the areas under the worktables.

Anton wanted to answer back but his better judgment told him the man meant business and could get very unpleasant. With an embarrassed glance at the other apprentices he gritted his teeth and swept the coarse concrete floor, collecting the scraps of burned crust, the splashes of flour and sugar and the dust from the far corners. He piled it all on a large metal scoop and carried the load to the waste bin. When he had tidied up the last remnants he was pleased with himself about the neat job, and grateful for the appreciative nod Werner gave him between his own hurried tasks. As the day wore on Anton was assigned small chores beyond the purely menial ones befitting the greenest member of the crew.

During the lunch break Anton withdrew into the background, listening to the others talk. Their conversation ranged from the latest rumors about evacuations to sarcastic jokes about the Russian occupiers, and culminated in raw sex talk by the two apprentices. They bragged about their prowess, all the while glancing sideways at Anton to check on the effect their explicit descriptions had on the shy boy. Anton found the subject both forbidden and intriguing. He had never heard such blunt frankness. He tried hard to keep from blushing, but he lost the struggle which elicited loud guffaws and hearty slaps on the back.

At last Werner, who sat apart preoccupied with his own thoughts, brought an end to their game. "Let's go back to work, and you two guys leave the kid alone, you hear?" Giving Anton a fatherly nudge he took him over to the dough kneading machine and showed him how to insert the beaters and set the adjustments. Soon Anton mastered the mechanism and was whipping up batches of dough in the gleaming copper kettles. He was handy with mechanical things and enjoyed working the machinery.

As he watched the whirring beaters and the spinning kettles his mind wandered back to the war years when he and Johann helped around the kitchen. The boys visualized all types of house-hold machinery that would ease their manual chores, a creative make-believe that helped overcome the drudgery.

At the end of the day Hammel asked one of the apprentices, who being part-Czech did not wear an armband, to walk with Anton to the flat. The young man used the short walk to tell more ribald stories to the fascinated Anton. He added the newest occupation joke about the Russian soldier who took a plundered pocket watch to a jeweler to make it run again. The jeweler opened the back whereupon a dead bedbug fell out. The simple Russian grinned with sudden insight, "Ah, understand now, operator has died." Anton chuckled about this story, one of many such tales of the backwardness of their conquerors and their single-minded preoccupation with "tick-tocks." It felt good to laugh, and Anton was eager to relate the story to Maria and the women in the corner house.

He walked the last hundred yards by himself and hurried into the open yard of the apartment house. In a paper bag he carried a few scraps of baked goods *Herr* Werner gave him. Anton proudly presented this gift to Maria who anxiously awaited his return. He told his mother all about his first day at the bakery and described the workroom, the machinery, and his co-workers. Carefully avoiding the subject the young men emphasized most, he reported that he was well treated and that one of the apprentices accompanied him home. Anton liked the feeling of being a provider and they munched away happily, savoring their good fortune.

Uneventful days followed. Anton enjoyed the regularity of the daily routine, although his duties were often menial and boring. *Herr* Werner soon began to involve him in more skillful tasks and he learned quickly when given such chances. Werner was good at improvising and had a knack for creating appetizing products from inferior materials. Most of the time, however, he remained nervous and short-tempered.

The young men joked and teased Anton with rough but good-natured banter, and slowly began to accept the shy and introspective boy. They saw it as their special challenge to expand his vocabulary of *risqué* terms. Their boisterousness was often a welcome relief when Anton felt melancholy. There was little serious talk, and the "live and let live" atmosphere, reinforced with occasional kindness—always disguised by gruff manners—wove a tentative bond of belonging for the boy.

Anton gradually overcame his inhibitions, adjusted to the newness of the work atmosphere and "pulled his weight," as the pleased *Herr* Hammel told him. There was the occasional jab in the ribs or cuff on the head when Anton made a mistake or was caught daydreaming, but such anger never lasted long despite Werner's momentary agitation.

Anton would always remember a painful incident that happened when the young men prepared a delivery for an important Czech customer. The specially made delicate pastries had been arranged in large flat plywood carrying cases, with handle openings on each side. They placed three of these containers on top of each other for loading. One of them pulled the bicycle with the special transport rack into the workshop, and together with another of the apprentices Anton eased the stack of heavy cases to the edge of the work table. Grasping the handle holes in the bottom container they lifted the precious load towards the bicycle. With a loud crash the bottom panel landed on the concrete floor, the nails pulled out by the weight of the moist pastry. They stood horrified, holding on to the stack by the lowest frame, and gaped at the distorted pastry on the fallen panel by their feet.

"Jesus and Mary," Werner screamed in anguish, "what have you damned fools done! We're late already, and now you've ruined all this work! And the good materials they gave us to use!" He rushed towards them. "Put those cases down, you stupid bastards, and get out of my sight! Now!" The distraught man knelt on the floor, trying to straighten out and save the better parts of the dainty goods. All the while he wailed in his comical accent about the young dummies who didn't even know how to handle a container of pastry.

The accident shook Anton to the core. Long conditioned to reflex reactions when it came to saving any kind of food he knelt down next to Werner and tried to help. Werner pushed him roughly aside and yelled, "It's all your fault! I should've known better than to let some spoiled kid mess around my workplace!" Anton tried to defend himself, explaining that they had lifted the cases by the holes made for the purpose, but his logic was squashed. "If you idiots had any brains, you'd know this stuff is heavy and that you hold these things by the bottom. I should beat the daylights out of you for this!" The other apprentice stood by, content that Anton took the brunt of Werner's wrath. At last the angry man chased them all out.

A few weeks passed and Anton grew more confident in his work. But then came word from Hammel that the bakery would close soon. He had been notified that he would be evacuated during the next roundup, and that also applied to Werner. They would have to leave in just a few days.

Maria went to thank Hammel for his kindness. He offered to recommend Anton to a Czech-owned bakery located on the main street in the northern part of the city, not far from the Wildert villa. The Wilderts accepted eagerly, even though the new job meant the risk of a long walk through several major streets.

The following day *Herr* Hammel told Anton that *Pan* Janáček was indeed willing to employ him starting the following week. Anton thanked *Herr* Hammel warmly for recommending him, his shyness eased by a first glimmer of self-confidence. Then he said good-bye to the gruff *Herr* Werner, who shook hands formally and with a sudden awkward move gave the boy a quick hug.

The Wildert Family in 1931:
Standing: Martha's first husband; Herbert; Maria (expecting Anton); Friedrich;
Karel Pancraz; Walter.
Seated: Martha; Grandmother Rohan; Pavel Pancraz;
Grandfather Rohan; Gretl.
In front: Johann; Franz Pancraz.

Friedrich, Maria, Johann & Anton in 1932

Anton and Johann in 1935

Anton's first day of school,
September 1937 (Gift cone is
Austrian custom)

Anton (6) and Johann (9)
celebrate joint birthday—
May 29, 1937

Family outing in Skoda convertible, Spring 1936

Maria, Johann, Anton and Friedrich in 1939

Friedrich in 1939

Maria in 1939

Anton and Maria alone in
August 1945; snapshot taken by
photographer friend

Last picture of Johann (right) with
friend, just drafted into the
Wehrmacht, October 1944

Johann in 1944

Anton in 1948

Graduation class picture, Schlossberg Oberrealschule, June, 1950.
Anton in second row, fourth from the left. His Sudeten friend Peter is last in second row, his Bavarian friend Ferdinand right above Anton.

Maria, Anton and Nannerl in Schlossberg, July 1950

Maria says goodbye to Anton in Frankfurt,
en route to the U.S., August 1950

Anton arrives in New York, August 23, 1950

Elbe River Valley in 1935

Aussig on the Elbe in 1935

184

Europe today

GERMAN REICH
Dresden •
Reichenberg
Eger •
• Prague
Breslau
Troppau
RUSSIA
• Cracow
Lemberg
Znaim
AUSTRIA-HUNGARY
Vienna • • Pressburg
• Budapest
Ungvár
(Uzhorod)
Czernowitz

Up to 1918

GERMAN REICH
Dresden •
Reichenberg
• Prague
Breslau
POLAND
• Cracow
Lemberg
CZECHO-
Znaim
SLOVAKIA
Vienna • • Pressburg
AUSTRIA
• Budapest
HUNGARY
Uzhorod
Czernowitz
RUMANIA

1918 - 1938

GERMAN REICH
Dresden • Reichenberg Breslau
Eger • • Prague
Protectorate
of Bohemia-
Moravia
Troppau
General
Government
of Poland
• Cracow
Lemberg
SOVIET UNION
Znaim
SLOVAKIA
• Pressburg
Vienna
Uzhorod
Czernowitz
HUNGARY
• Budapest
RUMANIA

1939 - 1941/45

"GDR"
Dresden •
Under
Polish
Administration
Breslau
POLAND
• Prague
• Cracow
Lemberg
SOVIET UNION
FEDERAL
REPUBLIC
OF
GERMANY
CZECHOSLOVAKIA
Vienna • • Pressburg
AUSTRIA
• Budapest
HUNGARY
Uzhorod
Czernowitz
RUMANIA

After 1945

Sudetendeutscher Rat (Sudeten German Council)

The Territories of Czechoslovakia and the Sudeten Regions in Bohemia, Moravia and Silesia.

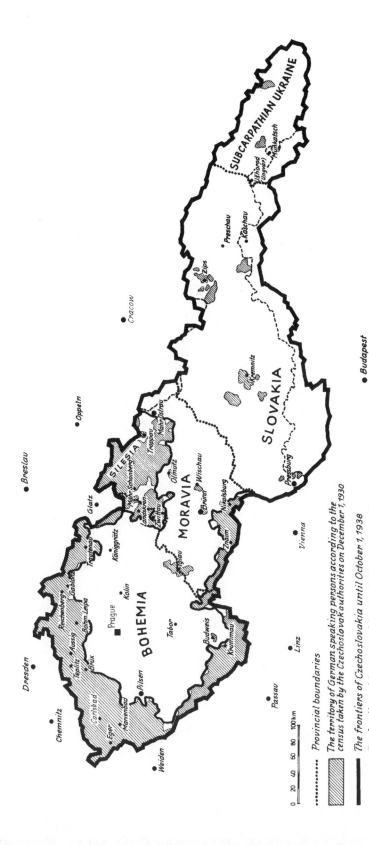

SUBCARPATHIAN UKRAINE

Munkatsch

Ushorod
(Ungvar)

Preschau

Kaschau

Zips

Krakau

Kremnitz

SLOVAKIA

Budapest

Oppeln

Breslau

Glatz

SILESIA

Troppau

Mähr. Ostrau

Königgrätz

Schönberg

Olmütz

Pressburg

Traulenau

Reichenberg

Gablonz

Brüx

Böhm. Leipa

Nachod

Landskron

Zwittau

Wischau

Brünn

Nikolsburg

Znaim

MORAVIA

Iglau

Chemnitz

Dresden

Eger

Marienbad

Carlsbad

Teplitz

Aussig

Pilsen

Kolin

Prague

Tabor

BOHEMIA

Budweis

Krummau

Weiden

Passau

Linz

Vienna

Provincial boundaries

The territory of German speaking persons according to the census taken by the Czechoslovak authorities on December 1, 1930

The frontiers of Czechoslovakia until October 1, 1938

The frontiers of Czechoslovakia after the treaty regulating the frontier with the German Reich of November 20, 1938

The frontiers of Czechoslovakia in 1938 after the annexation of territory by Poland and the cession of territory to Hungary

0 20 40 60 80 100 km

THIRTEEN

The Apprentice

The end of the week passed in the dull sameness of daily chores, lightened only by visits to the corner house and by concert music from the radio. On Monday morning the alarm clock startled Anton awake at four and he fought feebly against his drowsiness. He had no choice as he was to report for work at the new bakery at half past five. Maria readied herself to go with him, intent on exploring the route he would take every day.

They walked through the deserted dawn, wearing their white armbands and glancing warily left and right like animals in the forest, ready to run from danger. The streets were empty and silent as they came near their former neighborhood; memories stirred at the sight of familiar landmarks. At last they entered the main street heading north, the one they watched from their distant window perch on the morning of the German retreat and the Russian invasion.

Their footsteps echoed sharply against the aging facades of three-story row houses, dark and lifeless in the gray of the morning. After walking several hundred yards they found the pitted enamel sign "Z. Janáček, Cukrárna" on one of the shops lining the street. Rusty metal closures were rolled shut over the bakery display window and entrance, so they went through the unlocked side door and headed for the dimly lit stairs leading to the basement workroom.

After descending two flights of stone steps flanked by peeling walls they knocked hesitantly on the door. A slender man in his forties appeared, dressed in a baker's white overall. His face was impassive, but not unkind, and his large dark eyes sized up the two armbanded strangers.

"*Prosím?*"[1] The man's voice was cautious.

Maria lapsed into Czech, explaining that Anton was to begin work as promised by *Pan* Janáček. The baker's eyes brightened. He bowed slightly to Maria and introduced himself as Edvard Kučera, one of the senior bakers. He shook Anton's hand and motioned the Wilderts inside.

The bakery occupied most of the large basement under the row house. Small recessed windows high on the rear wall admitted feeble daylight into the work area. Bare electric bulbs dangling from the arched ceiling beneath chipped enamel reflectors provided most of the room's harsh illumination. A massive coal-fired brick oven protruded into the work area on one side, its masonry and gaping metal doors dark with age. In an alcove glistened copper kettles, cradled in the mechanism of the kneading machines or hanging from the wall.

Worktables occupied most of the space beneath the windows, and cooling racks and storage cabinets lined the wall on the left. It was a solid, well laid out place to work, and Anton recognized familiar equipment and tools. Kučera watched silently as Anton proudly pointed these out to his mother, enjoying the opportunity to show his knowledge. While they explored the workshop, the door flung open and in bounded a round-faced young man dressed in a white overall. He gave everyone a cheery greeting and introduced himself as Günther Langer. Although speaking fluent German he took pains right away to point out that he was part Czech.

The energetic Günther gave Anton a friendly slap on the shoulder. "We hear you did a good job at Hammel's bakery. We sure can use help around here! You can start by building a fire in the oven. This'll be your first duty every morning so that we can begin baking a couple of hours later."

He led Anton to the oven doors and showed him how to remove the previous day's ashes from the fire pit, and how to pile up kindling wood and coal briquettes. Soon the fire was crackling and licking through swirling smoke, and the fragrance of burning wood mixed with the sharp gaseous odor of smoldering coal.

[1] Yes, please?

Within minutes a roaring mass of flames began to heat the enormous oven structure, spreading warmth into every corner of the basement.

Günther nodded appreciatively. Then he turned to Maria and said with sincerity, "Anton will be safe with us. I know you are worried about the long walk. One of our men lives near you. If there's a problem with the curfew or any other danger we will make sure that he doesn't have to walk alone."

Kučera had quietly begun his work, but as Maria left he turned to her with a shy smile and waved, *"Dobri den, Pani* Wildert*ova."* [2] Maria walked home savoring her relief and the warmth of the encounter. Her son would be in the care of good people and she was elated with the way they again had resolved his obligation to work.

Anton put on a white cap and apron and settled down to his duties. Again there was much menial cleaning and sweeping, but he was also allowed to do some of the professional tasks he learned at Hammel's. He liked his new companions; the bouncy, vigorous Günther, the quiet but kindly Kučera, and Karl, the third of the senior men who arrived at six with Pepi, the other apprentice. All could speak German except Kučera, but he and Anton overcame that difficulty by waving and pointing. The others often interpreted.

At ten in the morning the owner, *Pan* Janáček, breezed into the bustling activity of the basement. He was a handsome, wavy-haired man in his thirties, elegantly dressed in a light gray jacket and slacks tailored in Prague fashion. Exuding vigorous cheerfulness he patted the two saleswomen familiarly and nodded to the men.

Janáček welcomed Anton with a friendly handshake and he chatted with him in accented but adequate German before bounding back upstairs to the store as briskly as he came. The serious-minded Günther ran the workshop, and Janáček did not get involved.

It took Anton a short time to become familiar with the new

[2] Good day, Mrs. Wildert

setting and he concentrated on his work. In the afternoon he climbed on a stool to get supplies from a high shelf and chanced to look out of the windows at the top of the rear wall. With a start he recognized the family villa in the distance, up on the slope, partly obscured by bushes and trees. Sadness welled up in him; he wanted to cry out but controlled himself. Vivid recollections crowded him and he again saw Dvořák's icy stare and the scenes of helplessness and humiliation that ushered in his present existence. One of these scenes was his brief and only return to the villa the day after their expulsion. After settling into the small flat Friedrich suffered severe spasms of ulcer pain. Maria looked everywhere for the metal thermos which they used to keep milk warm for him; she discovered that they left it behind. After long deliberations they decided that Anton would return to the villa to ask Dvořák for the thermos, an irreplaceable item.

Anton pedaled through the familiar streets, empty of all neighborly life, past the duplex where his friend still lived, and on to the white garden gate. The villa seemed unapproachable and he stood there for a long time before he gathered enough courage to press the bell. The front door swung open slowly and Dvořák emerged in shirt sleeves and vest. Squinting hard he recognized the boy and abruptly motioned him to enter. Anton pushed the bicycle along the path and climbed the front steps—it was like being on stage and he trembled nervously. The cold voice shot out, "What do you want?"

"I...I...would I...like to get a thermos bottle we forgot to take along. My father, ah, he...he...needs it for his illness," Anton stuttered.

Dvořák glowered at him for a few moments. The boy's throat constricted as he stood waiting for a response. With a curt nod Dvořák signaled Anton to come in. The boy made his way to the kitchen like a sleepwalker, aware of Dvořák's stare boring into his back. On the surface nothing seemed to have changed in the hall and kitchen, but he had the strong sensation of other peoples' presence.

He opened the cupboard and took out the thermos, still in its familiar place, then hesitantly turned to Dvořák whose face bore the same dour and annoyed expression. Good manners seemed to call for a "thank you"—but here he was in his own home to fetch an item belonging to the family! He swallowed hard and murmured, "This is what we forgot," and turned to leave.

"Don't get the idea you can keep coming back as you please!" Dvořák's tone was razor sharp. "I make exception only once!"

Every fiber in his body made Anton want to flee the oppressive atmosphere. He nodded in Dvořák's direction and hurried through the hall and out of the front door, looking neither left nor right. Clutching the thermos under his arm he grabbed his bicycle and left through the garden gate for the last time, hearing the distinctive metallic snap as the lock fell shut. Without looking back he raced down the slope as if pursued by the malevolent spirit of the new master of the house.

Reliving the memories from his perch by the basement window Anton sensed that the odd feeling of detachment was returning. Determined not to succumb to it this time, he tore himself away from the window, away from this unexpected view of the past, and instead resumed his present tasks, giving them all of his attention.

There was an easy camaraderie among the men, and a more positive atmosphere than at Hammel's bakery, where Werner's distraught manner often made life difficult for everyone. The pressures here were similar but the members of Janáček's crew had more energy to deal with them. Anton did what was expected of him and over the next several days he gradually gained the older men's acceptance. They saw the boy always tried to do his best and rarely repeated his mistakes. Anton appreciated being treated fairly after his initiation in the frantic atmosphere at Hammel's; there were no cuffs on the head or jabs in the ribs from any of the senior bakers.

As the days and weeks passed, a faint sense of belonging arose, a tentative feeling that grew steadily in the friendly atmosphere. Karl walked with him to and from work on most days. A convinced socialist, he bore arms grudgingly for the Nazis and returned from the *Wehrmacht* in the last year of the war with enough serious injuries to be released from duty. Anton felt safe when walking with the squat and rigid man whose physical courage stemmed from the trials of combat and an uncomplicated view of life. Once a drill sergeant, he had mellowed with age and hardship, but as far as Karl was concerned he had seen it all.

Anton struck up a solid friendship with the quiet Kučera. The two learned to communicate in a makeshift but effective way, each picking up a few words and phrases of the other's language, helped along by signs and gestures. They laughed heartily when their expressions and hand-waving became exaggerated and ludicrous.

On the lapel of his carefully brushed suit Kučera sported a crimson and gold Communist party button. He was proud to belong to the party although he never talked politics. Kučera apparently viewed his membership as symbolizing the status of a proud worker rather than revolutionary fervor.

Kučera inquired about Anton's family and home. He showed sympathy when Anton explained that both his father and brother were dead, and that the villa up on the hill had been taken from the family. He shrugged with a touch of embarrassment and tried to make Anton understand that although Czech he had no hatred toward his Sudeten neighbors, only against Hitler and the Nazi regime. "Hitler dirrt!" was his favorite expression.

With great pride he often made it clear that he rejoiced in the rebirth of the Czech state and was grateful for the assistance given by their Russian comrades. Animatedly he predicted that there would be "*nix* school, *nix* university" ever again for Germans, and that the boy should prepare himself to face a life of hard labor. He did allow that Anton would be all right if he continued to do "gutt vork." As time passed Kučera began to speculate with growing interest about the boy's future and one day declared that Anton would indeed be better off making a fresh start across the border in Germany and that he wished him well.

One day a Russian colonel came to visit the bakery, resplendent in fur cap, high boots, and an elegant greatcoat with wide shoulder boards and bright red lapels. *Pan* Janáček showed him around the workroom with polite deference, and the stocky officer nodded and grinned in approval, his gold teeth glittering. A handsome man with sparkling eyes set deep in a red-cheeked, round face, the colonel shook hands firmly with everyone, smiling and booming out *"tavarishch"* at every turn.

Günther had a hospitable idea. "Anton, why don't you make the colonel a jug of your pineapple fizz; he'll appreciate it!" Some weeks before the boy had discovered several bottles of artificial fruit flavoring on the window shelf and remembered from his home chemistry experiments that a combination of baking powder, fruit flavoring and sugar dissolved in water made a tasty fizzing lemonade. He tested all the flavors in the shop and the men liked his concoctions.

Apprehensively Anton measured the proportions and wondered about the correct mixture at this important moment. With a great deal of fuss he produced a foaming vessel of the effervescent delight. He proffered the jug to the colonel who sniffed it cautiously, then took a long, deep draft. When he set the jug down he beamed, half suppressing a loud, satisfied burp. *"Kharosho, tavarishch,*[3] kvite gutt!" Laughing in creamy basso tones he slapped his knee and again shook hands with Anton who by this time felt quite pleased with his success. He warmed to the friendly way in which the important man in uniform treated him, momentarily relaxing his firm conditioning of associating fear and danger with uniforms of any kind.

The Russian officer returned on several occasions during the following months and every time Anton was asked to prepare the "Kvite Gutt" concoction for Comrade Colonel. He always replayed the brief ritual of pleasure, sometimes shared by a fellow officer or two. Janáček and the others were glad that Anton contributed so effectively to the hospitality for their Russian comrades, and Anton in turn continued to experiment with his essences and powders to improve the quality of the liquid refreshment.

The weeks passed without serious incident and Anton settled into a comfortable work routine. He received a weekly pay envelope with crisp new Czech money, a fresh source of pride to him, but more important, he became entitled to a worker's supplementary ration card. The extra rations, together with scraps of food

[3] Excellent, comrade

he brought home from the bakery, allowed mother and son to live a notch or two above the official subsistence diet that Sudetens sarcastically characterized as "too little to live, and too much to die."

Occasionally work hours extended into the early evening, perilously close to or even exceeding the curfew. Günther tried to alert Anton the day before so that he could inform his mother, and Karl accompanied him to the apartment building in the evenings. On those walks Karl shared a few glimpses of his world. He still maintained the rigidity of his past military rank, but when he let down his guard he revealed more of himself and the conversation invariably turned to food, black market dealings, women and sex.

Anton's education in these matters was making rapid strides, if only from the graphic and exaggerated tales of Karl and the others. On one occasion the men showed him crude pornographic pictures, teasing him with robust laughter as they delighted in his red-faced embarrassment. Kučera finally cut off the boisterous joking and backslapping by urging everyone back to work. Talk of sex came naturally to the group. Though interested and intrigued, Anton was too timid to allow himself to enter a man's world that was still mysterious to him. At times he wondered quietly whether there were any other subjects he could talk about with these mature men. He was naturally curious and he tried to raise topics that interested him, but without fail the conversations returned to the men's favorite preoccupation.

In the flat there were many lonely evenings, and Maria and Anton tried to comfort each other when their grief for Friedrich and Johann surfaced. During the weeks when one dramatic event after another assailed them, powerful survival instincts deadened their pain. Now they lived through an interval of bearable conditions, and their sense of loss and abandonment often surged forth with full force and threatened to overwhelm them. When the radio carried familiar concert music Maria's emotions stirred to such levels that she begged Anton to turn it off, but the ensuing silence was just as poignant.

During this relatively quiet period Maria's health became a

problem. There was more time to reflect on the pains in her neck and back, a chronic condition that periodically immobilized her since autumn. But she pulled herself together after having given in to bouts of discomfort, and she said to Anton over and over, "We'll stick this out together, as the Good Lord wishes." She was trying to imprint on her son—and no less on herself—a message of faith and determination, not knowing what the next day might bring or where fate might eventually scatter them.

Sometimes Anton awoke abruptly in the early morning hours, startled to find himself in the cramped flat after dreaming of familiar settings of the past. In those dreams he saw himself in different rooms or in the garden of the villa and relived memories of happy times. The wide-eyed reality of consciousness was doubly jarring and painful after such pleasant dreams.

One particular dream became a recurring obsession. He saw Johann return, alive and well in his makeshift uniform, and Anton's whole being was suffused by immense relief and joy. He invariably awoke convinced that the events of the past months were not true, only to be jolted into painful awareness that Johann was gone forever. It took hours to regain his composure and he often wept when he could do so without being noticed. Once he told Maria about the dream, but she reacted with such outward grief that he resolved never to burden her in this way again.

Anton found it hard to deal with his experiences alone, yet he felt he could not talk about these matters with anyone at the bakery. He also had not seen Rainer again although his daily walks brought him near the street where his friend lived. He knew the other boy could not share his feelings, still living as he did in his own environment with his whole family. To visit Rainer meant moving between two worlds, something he did not care to do again. He decided to choose living in his own new reality and to avoid thinking about the fortunate continuity Rainer enjoyed.

Anton drew considerable strength from the bantering cheerfulness of the women in the corner house. *Frau* Winkler's daughter was only two years younger than himself, and she spent most of her time helping her mother take care of her baby sister. Heidi, in her early teenage childishness, was consumed with the pangs of growing up. He wished so much that he could be friends with her, as *Frau* Winkler became a special companion for his mother and was kind to Anton in a warm, motherly way. She confided to Maria how remote and difficult her daughter Heidi was, and how she longed for her soldier husband to return from Russia to provide a strong hand in bringing up the children.

One evening Anton suggested to the group that it might be a good idea to dig up some of the ripe sugar beets in a small abandoned field nearby. They could be boiled down to make sweet syrup as a supplement to their diet. The field was only fifty yards down the slope of the hill and within sight of the corner house. Everyone agreed that Anton and Heidi would carry out the pilferage at night under the watchful eyes of the adults.

Together they crept into the darkness, armed with a spatula and a bag. The first beet yielded easily to their anxious digging. Looking cautiously about them now and again, they loosened about thirty of the large roots, filling their bag to overflowing. The night was cool and still, but Heidi kept up an incessant nervous whispering until Anton angrily told her to shut up. Relieved when the bag was full they dragged their heavy treasure to the house.

To loud cheers they dumped their haul on the kitchen floor and everyone pitched in to clean and slice the reddish-white bulbs bursting with sweetness. Soon the harsh odor of the boiling beet chips filled the house, and hours later everyone had a glass jar of the sweet brown syrup. They repeated the exploit late the following evening, but on the third night the remaining beets were gone, taken by others in the same covert way.

The shared adventure didn't bring Anton and Heidi any closer. Anton loved to talk about whatever was on his mind as he had done with his brother before going to sleep on those many happy evenings in the past. Heidi did not respond to his interests. *Frau* Winkler liked to say she hoped they could start a new life after the evacuation together with Maria and Anton. The boy sensed her desire that at some future point they might become one family, but he gave up his efforts to be friends with Heidi. He put what energy he had left after a long week of work into reading any books he could find, although few were obtainable in their barren environment.

Danger was never far away. One fall evening Anton went down to the storage shed to fetch some coal briquettes and kindling wood for the kitchen stove that heated the flat. It was dark and the faint glow of a nearby street lamp yielded only feeble illumination, barely enough for Anton to grope in the blackness of the wooden enclosure. He hastily filled the battered metal bucket, anxious to return to the light of the kitchen. As he straightened up he felt a presence behind him.

He spun around to see the massive shape of a Russian soldier looming in the opening. The stench of alcohol crowded into the boy's face as the man grunted, "*Mat', siestr, doma?*" [4] By now Anton knew enough of the related Czech language to understand the Russian was asking if he had a mother or sister at home. Despite the shock of the sudden confrontation Anton's mind functioned clearly. Again he felt as if he were floating above the scene of his predicament.

Anton stared into the man's dimly lit visage, saw the high Mongol cheekbones, the squint of narrow eyes, and a stubbly face contorted by drink. Cradled in his right arm glinted the air-cooled barrel and circular magazine of a submachine gun, the muzzle pointing toward him. A long uniform greatcoat hung low over squat boots. The intruder blocked the only entrance to the shed.

Anton's body was rigid with terror but his brain raced frantically, seeking out what choices he had. While he hesitated the soldier became impatient and shoved the blunt muzzle of the submachine gun into his abdomen. Suddenly the boy realized that he must appear cooperative, yet somehow divert the man's attention from the dozen women and girls in the apartment building and the corner house. With a forced smile Anton faced the soldier and eagerly pointed with his left arm away from the buildings toward the dark, sloping street. He knew there was an empty house on the other side, and he had heard that Czech newcomers recently

[4] Mother, sister, home?

occupied the property next to it.

He heard himself saying firmly, *"Da, da, tavarishch, heský holký, tam jsou heský holký!"* [5] Somehow he stumbled onto the right Czech words to express the idea that there were pretty girls down the street. Would the Russian understand?

The man stood motionless for a moment, then broke into a monstrous grin and took two staggering steps back into the yard. Anton anxiously followed him out of the enclosure and continued to gesture at the distant houses. Nodding and smiling he repeated, *"Heský holký, tavarishch, heský holký!"*

Wobbling on his feet the hulk let out a foul-smelling belch, his submachine gun now dangling muzzle down on its shoulder strap. To Anton's amazement he raised his right hand in a sloppy half salute. *"Kharosho, tavarishch, spasiba!"* [6] he beamed gratefully, baring two rows of stubby teeth liberally clad in metal that glistened in the dim light. The soldier turned unsteadily, clasped his weapon, and shuffled off in the direction Anton pointed.

There was no time to lose. If the man were sober enough to discover that Anton sent him to an empty house, or worse, to a group of fraternal Czechs, he might come back raging and take revenge in whatever ways an alcohol-dimmed primitive might conceive. In great anxiety Anton waited until the soldier lurched about twenty paces, then he slunk back to the apartment building. Once inside he knocked on every door, and while he raced upstairs he shouted warnings for the women to hide from an armed Russian prowler. Then he hurtled downstairs again, crossed the yard as silently as he could, and knocked on the door of the corner house to warn the women there. Breathlessly he returned to the Wildert flat where Maria had already barricaded herself.

No one questioned the boy's desperate message and the two buildings were cloaked in silence. The women turned off all lights and hid in whatever makeshift ways they could devise. Anton crouched on top of the stairs by the window overlooking the yard,

[5] Yes, yes, comrade, pretty girls, there are pretty girls!
[6] Good, comrade, thank you!

listening intently for signs that the soldier was returning. A tense hour passed.

During his watch Anton became truly afraid as he relived the moment of terror over and over. But he never knew what happened after the soldier disappeared into the dark street. As the hours dragged on it became clear to everyone the diversion had worked. The Russian did not return.

In the early morning Anton left for work as usual. Maria hugged him at length, telling him how brave he had been to save her and the others. On entering the street he looked warily about him, and hurried to meet Karl at the intersection as usual. Never before had Anton been so glad to see the tough ex-sergeant as on this day. Anton did not speak of the encounter to Karl or any of the others; the experience was too close and real. He went about his work, fully absorbed in his duties, trying not to think of the previous night's terrifying experience. But the memory of the icy fear that gripped him on that dark evening remained with him for a long time.

FOURTEEN

The Camp Episode

Maria learned from Gretl that her younger sister Martha and her three small children were still largely unaffected by the upheavals and able to stay in their home for the time being. They lived near the western border of the Sudetenland in the ancient city of Eger. The region was occupied by American forces and thus escaped the brutalities of conquest and the ensuing hasty mass evacuations commonplace in the eastern sector. Martha's husband was still missing after serving on the Russian front but the family group included his aged mother and maiden sister.

Aunt Gretl described Martha's more fortunate situation on one of her visits. She mentioned it casually to Maria, while preoccupied with constant machinations to quench her greed. For Maria the news was a ray of hope, a straw to grasp in the enforced passivity of waiting for the final expulsion. The motivation to go west was compelling to the point of becoming an obsession for Maria. Evacuations from Aussig and the surrounding area always went north a short distance to Saxony in the Russian sector of Germany. The western location of Eger, a region that bordered on American-occupied Bavaria, made the chance of being transported to the west more favorable.

The frightening accounts about refugee conditions under the Russians left no doubt that even the slightest opportunity of moving west should be tried at all costs. The treatment the western Sudetens received from their new Czech rulers under the American occupation, while harsh, lacked the cruelty that even moved some Russian officers to intervene on behalf of Sudetens when they witnessed the worst incidents.

Maria determined that she would try with all her strength to find a way of joining her sister in Eger. Gretl would be of no help in this quest as she was single-mindedly pursuing her own interests. But Gretl agreed to carry the message to Eger that Maria and Anton would attempt to move there so that they could be evacuated together under the more tolerable conditions of that region. Maria believed that Martha would find this acceptable, as her sister had lived in the Wildert villa for some years as part of the family as well as receiving guidance and support from Friedrich and Maria, and the arrangement had worked well.

The challenge Maria took on was formidable. The idea of a Sudeten obtaining permission to travel by rail was unusual, to say the least. Subject to evacuation and harassment, a Sudeten would only have a meager chance to plead a compelling case before the bureaucracy, a system still prone to make its own rules. Undaunted, she chose to use her health problems as justification for the attempt to be united with her remaining family. Consumed with her desire to succeed in this endeavor, Maria found in it a sense of mission that helped occupy her mind and relieve her often gloomy thoughts.

If the Nazi bureaucrats were difficult to deal with in former years, nothing compared with the frustrating and alarming experiences that lay ahead in her search for pieces of paper that were the key for the two of them to join Martha's family. She was constantly reminded that anyone attempting such audacity embarked on a perilous journey and was open to extortion, harassment, and general official confusion. Regulations shifted constantly; Maria could take nothing for granted and at no point in the process was she allowed to forget that she was a person without legal standing or basic rights.

Her first effort was an attempt to reach Red Cross officials that might lend a sympathetic ear to the plea that her state of health required being with other family members. After several visits to the makeshift Red Cross headquarters in the city and countless hours of standing in line, Maria succeeded in wrangling a certificate from one of the reluctant papershufflers. He grilled her with hostile questions, intimating that she was faking her back problems. Maria calmly persisted, showing him the prescriptions for pain medication she saved. The man still bristled with distrust, but Maria used her improving facility with the Czech language to good advantage. Certainly she exaggerated her condition, but after all, this was a grueling contest of wills and she applied every ounce of acting talent she could muster. Necessity coached her well.

With an annoyed shrug the man scrawled his signature on the slip bearing the Red Cross insignia, noisily pounded two rubber stamps over it, and tossed the paper across the desk without looking at Maria. This first trophy in hand, the fruit of three weeks of effort, Maria had still to face several more hurdles.

One was the Registry of Persons which would have to issue a permit to transfer Maria and Anton's residence to Eger. Another was the local Transportation Office, where she needed to obtain a permit to use the train. This was the current procedure as explained to her at the Red Cross office. She soon learned during the ensuing weeks that there were many more paths to tread in the ever-shifting maze of bureaucracy. Anton accompanied his mother on one of her visits to the Registry Office, located on a tree-lined avenue of elegant mansions formerly owned by industrialists. One of these housed the Russian headquarters, teeming with brown-uniformed officers and men, the place where she and Friedrich petitioned the general on Walter's behalf.

Maria and Anton walked past the Russian sentries with a pained reflex of apprehension, the memories of the first days of occupation coming alive. Instinctively they quickened their steps until they reached the driveway of their destination several hundred feet away. Entering the spacious grounds through an arched wrought-iron gate, they passed slouching sentries of Czech militia in their adapted German uniforms of Rommel's Africa Corps.

Having left the noise of the street behind they found themselves in an atmosphere of oppressive silence. In the large foyer an officious reception clerk rudely demanded their purpose. While Maria explained her request Anton gazed about him in the dusky hall which was shabby and reflected little of its former grandeur. The man studied Maria's papers at length, then pointed to one of the three ornate doors, slightly ajar, that opened onto the hall. Sunshine filtered in through the narrow gaps and cut sharp angles of light and shadow.

Along the oak-paneled walls of the hall stood long benches and sofas. When their eyes adjusted to the somber light the Wilderts saw about a dozen men of different ages lined up against one side. They wore white armbands and sat motionless, their postures dejected and forlorn. Above them glared large posters in massive black and red lettering proclaiming the latest official announcements.

As they passed these pitiful shapes Maria whispered, "Look straight ahead, Anton; these people are detainees. We must not be drawn into their problems in any way, God help them." Anton felt a prickle of cold alarm flow down his spine. Fear sealed his throat and he grasped his mother's arm. Together they crossed the worn parquet floor, eyes averted until they reached the designated office.

The paneled enclosure was an anteroom, dominated in the center by a huge ornate oak table, and surrounded by a dozen matching chairs. Again several silent men waited, and one of them had flung his arm across the dusty surface, wearily resting his head. Others slumped in their chairs and only two of them looked up briefly at the woman in black and the boy, then lapsed back into abject waiting.

The door to the inner office was closed. Maria and Anton cautiously took a seat on the edge of a long carved bench along the wall, hardly daring to stir in the eerie quiet, a setting where time lost its meaning. After an hour or so the loud noise of the door being flung open jarred them. A middle-aged bureaucrat appeared, ignored the silent shapes around the table and looked searchingly at Maria and Anton. With a toss of his head he motioned them inside. He resumed his seat behind the cluttered desk and left them standing. Speaking rapidly and impersonally in Czech he inquired about Maria's purpose. He carefully examined the Red Cross certificate she handed him, looked again and again over the rims of his glasses at Maria, and finally shook his head with impatience. Anton's heart sank. Not understanding a word he assumed that the paper his mother spent so much effort to obtain was not acceptable.

Several heated exchanges in Czech followed. Then the man shrugged, pulled a printed form from the desk drawer and began to fill in the blanks, curtly questioning Maria about facts he wrote down. Finally he slammed a few rubber stamps on the completed certificate and scratched his signature in the lower corner. He handed it to Maria with a scornful gesture of dismissal.

Maria and Anton hurried back through the anteroom, past the men slumped around the table, and out into the dark hall lined with detainees. Afraid of being stopped, neither spoke a word as they passed through the succession of nightmarish scenes. They were almost running when they finally emerged into the daylight, and once on the graveled driveway that led to the ornate gate they dared to breathe again.

"What was the matter when the man questioned you, *Mutti*?" Anton inquired.

"It was a close call, Anton. He considered the Red Cross paper unacceptable, since he couldn't see that I was ill. He insisted that a separate doctor's certificate was needed. I told him that the family doctor was evacuated months ago. He changed the subject and wanted to see my other papers. Then he claimed that two of them—one from the police and one from the Housing Office— were not the correct ones."

Maria had to stop for a moment to catch her breath. She continued, "I explained that I've been going from office to office over the past six weeks and was told each time that they issued me the correct papers. He didn't take this very well and wanted to confiscate my Red Cross certificate. Thank God I was able to talk him out of it."

She heaved a deep sigh, glad that another confrontation was over, adding wearily, "The new form he gave me has to be taken back to the other offices for more approvals and signatures." She shook her head and added, "I just hope he was telling me the truth!" Maria stood still once more and sighed with a pained expression. "I'm not sure if I can face much more of this!" They left behind the ornamental gate and the surly sentries, walking rapidly to put as much distance as possible between themselves and the depressing scenes.

"It was like going through purgatory!" Maria shivered as she recalled the silent desperation of the detainees. "Did you see the hopeless expressions on those faces? They must have been there for days, not knowing what will happen to them. Thank God we got out of that place unharmed!" Drawing closer together they continued their long walk to the flat.

Many more visits to offices, bureaus, and agencies followed. Maria ventured out almost daily in search of additional papers and stamps required to make the rail trip to Eger possible, a distance of about one hundred miles. She stood in line for hours, only to find the office closed for the day before her turn came. Sometimes officials told her the regulations had changed, that the papers she held were not valid for one reason or another. Then she started all over again.

The desperate hope of escaping to the west steeled her determination. Maria suffered bouts of pain which on many days kept her from continuing to run the hostile maze. When she was well enough she resumed her frustrating quest, sometimes accompanied by *Frau* Winkler who fought her own lesser battles with officialdom.

A week before Christmas Maria and *Frau* Winkler were walking in one of the narrow angled streets of the inner city on their way to obtain yet another stamp and signature. They passed a row of bombed-out buildings where crazily twisted steel skeletons groped out of mounds of shattered brick. A group of prisoners, mostly young men in tattered *Wehrmacht* uniforms and rags cleared the rubble under the watchful eyes of two heavily armed Czech militiamen. The women felt pangs of sadness when they saw the bent figures laboring in makeshift foot wrappings, their pale faces emaciated from lack of food. It was bitterly cold, and tiny plumes of breath rose from the prisoners' mouths as they struggled with their heavy tasks.

It was dangerous to show any reaction, particularly when wearing a white armband. The two women pretended to keep up a quiet flow of conversation as they walked past the scene at a steady pace. An old woman appeared beside them, huddled in a large black shawl. She sidled up to Maria, carrying a small paper bag. Waving the bag toward her she asked, "Would you kindly throw this into the refuse bin over there?" It was a strange request, but the effort of make-believe conversation with *Frau* Winkler distracted Maria. Without thinking she took the bag from the woman and tossed it toward the bin. It missed its target and fell to the pavement near the group of prisoners.

One of the guards saw them and quickly stepped over to retrieve the bag. Tearing it open he found several pieces of bread—strictly forbidden to pass to prisoners. The old woman broke into a shuffling run, while clutching the shawl that partly hid her white armband. The guard caught up with her effortlessly and dragged her back to where Maria and *Frau* Winkler stood thunderstruck.

"What do you think you are doing, you German sows!" the angry soldier bellowed at the top of his voice. "How dare you throw bread to those Nazi pigs!" The old woman whimpered and struggled under his iron grip. "My son is in that group, God help him and me!"

Maria was unable to utter a word, too terrified at having been drawn unwittingly into such danger. The guard turned to her and shouted, "And you are in league with the old bitch, aren't you— and don't play innocent, I saw what you did—you Germans are all swine!" Not waiting for a reply he demanded their identity cards. He examined them cursorily, then unbuttoned the top of his heavy overcoat and shoved the cards into an inside pocket. With a leer the man spat and announced, "You bitches can pick up these cards at the office of the camp commandant in Lerchenfeld!"

The old woman let out an agonized scream. Maria was still too shaken to speak when she heard the guard growl, "And you better show up by five in the afternoon!" He cursed obscenely and turned away. *Frau* Winkler reached out for Maria and clung to her, knowing full well that her friend had no chance to escape the capricious sentence. Confiscation of the identity card removed the last pretense of legal standing. There was no alternative but to comply.

All color left Maria's face. She began to shake uncontrollably, the tumbling visions in her mind spiraling into a wild hallucinatory spin as she passed out. *Frau* Winkler tried to cushion her fall, but could not prevent Maria's forehead from striking one of the bricks littering the pavement. The woman knelt on the icy ground, cradling Maria's head in her lap, trying to still a thin trickle of blood oozing from a cut on her left temple. By massaging the lifeless face *Frau* Winkler managed to coax her back to consciousness. After a while Maria was able to struggle to her feet. The guard ignored the collapse, keeping his back turned. Passers-by hurried on, eyes averted, avoiding trouble.

Frau Winkler supported Maria as they managed to walk a few yards at a time, often stopping to gather strength. At last Maria faced her companion. "*Frau* Winkler, this is the end for me. No one can survive the winter in that death camp. My only thoughts are for Anton. His life must go on." She fought back her tears. "Please don't tell him the truth, just tell him that I have fallen ill and had to be put in the hospital."

Frau Winkler almost choked on her words. "I will do that, *Frau* Wildert, and we'll take in Anton as one of our own. As mother to mother I give you my promise." Her voice gave out.

"God bless you, *Frau* Winkler. I don't want to go home. I'll go directly to the camp. There is no sense in prolonging the agony." Both women could no longer restrain their tears and held on to each other for a long time. It was almost noon. The trip to the camp would take about an hour on the electric trolley heading north beyond the city, passing below the Wildert villa high on the slope, and past the bakery where Anton worked.

The two women walked towards the city center, amid scenes of destruction, piles of debris, and bizarre ruins reaching for the wintry sky. Light snow drifted in the icy air, dusting the cobbled streets and laying white shadings on the tangled shapes and patterns of the rubble. The gloomy desolation heightened the emptiness—it seemed a fitting backdrop for Maria's sentence.

They reached the main street and the plaza of the badly damaged civic theater, a place dear to Maria in a past era of cultural pursuits. Huddled against the cold wind they waited for half an hour until the streetcar rounded the corner, screeching on its worn tracks, sparks flashing from the overhead wire. With a final good-bye Maria boarded the red conveyance, shabby from the neglect of the war years, its metal sides torn by shrapnel. Remnants of blue air raid paint remained on the cracked windows and the dim light made the cold interior even more chilly.

The trolley groaned into rattling motion and the two women waved at each other, their faces distraught. *Frau* Winkler stood forlorn, watching the streetcar slowly disappear. She thought of Anton and how long it would be before he discovered the truth. With a heavy heart she turned to walk towards the industrial district and the quiet street that was home.

Maria sat motionless while the streetcar ground its way northward. Few passengers shared the bleak, drafty interior, sitting uncomfortably on the worn wooden benches. No one spoke; most stared glassily ahead, with a listless and passive air. The surly conductor gave Maria's white armband an icy stare as he took her money, but he did not make her stand on the open platform as often happened to Sudeten passengers.

Maria's head throbbed. She watched dully as familiar sights appeared and receded, landmarks of the past, stately mansions in the large park-like gardens, among them the Russian headquarters and the palatial office where she and Anton saw the detainees. The realization that she was now one of them struck her with a fiery jolt. Soon the noisy vehicle clattered into the northern section of the city, a place where Maria could see the villa on its slope. She glanced up, but this glimpse of past happiness was too much to bear and she turned her head away.

When the trolley passed the bakery, the desire to jump off and run inside to embrace Anton almost overwhelmed her. Her heart ached with the thought of her son being abandoned unknowingly, but she remembered *Frau* Winkler's kindness and her offer to look after him. She tried to calm herself with that hope and watched longingly as the bakery disappeared from view.

The trolley left the built-up area and rumbled further north through a broad expanse of fields and meadows sprinkled with snow. Small clusters of houses and farms dotted the landscape. The roadside still bore evidence of the hordes of armed men that had streamed past on their way to the city. Burned-out hulks of trucks and fighting vehicles littered the area, maimed reminders of past armed violence. Many of the buildings fronting the street showed war damage; the bombed-out ruins and piles of debris appeared ghostly in their snowy disguise.

Maria's thoughts were elsewhere, far away; her mind flooded with images of her childhood, marriage, the two boys, the recent crises, and myriad disjointed impressions. She swayed with the motion of the trolley, her gaze fixed in the distance. Even the occasional shuddering stops did not disturb her intense inward focus. Only once did her sense of reality struggle to the surface for a brief moment. It was when she recognized that she was now experiencing herself the condition she read about in novels, stories describing condemned people whose minds teem with vivid memories, knowing that life neared its end.

At last the trolley screeched to a halt at the Lerchenfeld stop; Maria was the only person to step off the platform. She wrapped her overcoat tightly around her body against the bitter wind sweeping in from the northern heights, and paused to watch the trolley rumble and clatter its way toward the horizon. She stood alone in the empty road under slate-gray skies laden with snow; the only sound was the whistling of the wind. Maria turned to walk along the country road that led to the barbed wire enclosure visible in the distance. Watch towers brooded on each corner of the large yard, while flat barracks stood toward the rear in crowded rows.

As she came near the main gate the armed guard took two steps toward her, looked at her white armband and sharply asked her what she wanted. Maria answered in Czech that a militiaman told her to appear before the camp commandant that afternoon. The man raised his eyebrows, whistled through his teeth and looked quizzically at the solitary woman in black that had the temerity to ask to see the chief. Maria did not flinch. The guard complied at last and pointed to a low wooden structure near the entrance gate. "The office of *Pan* commandant is in there." His eyes followed her curiously after he opened the small steel door set in the barbed wire.

Maria stepped into the enclosure, her mind still refusing to accept the reality of her plight. She looked up the towering wall of barbed wire mesh which angled inward at the top. Already sensing the debility of confinement she swallowed hard to stifle her emotions and walked mechanically the short distance to the building which the guard pointed out to her. It was an ugly gray-green color; the paint peeled with neglect.

When she climbed the three wooden steps, a young soldier blocked her in the doorway, gripping the rifle that hung from his shoulder. His eyes sparked venom. "What do you want, German sow?" he barked.

Maria spoke firmly. "I am here to see the commandant; please take me to him."

"Not so fast, Nazi sow; I must check this out first—wait here!" He disappeared and left her standing for many minutes. Maria waited, drained of feelings and emotion, her mind a blank void. When the young man finally emerged he jerked his head in the direction of the door. "In there, German pig!"

Maria walked with the soldier along a short hallway to a sparsely furnished office. Seated at the large desk in the center was an officer in his forties, his expression impersonal, eyes cold and clear. He was flanked by two militiamen, one of them the soldier who led her in. She stood for what seemed a long time, looking directly at the three men, while the commandant and his aides took their leisure to assess the woman in black mourning dress.

The officer waved his hand condescendingly. "Sit down!" Maria moved forward a step to sit on the edge of the single chair that faced the desk, now at eye level with the commandant. The two young men towered over her.

"What do you want to see me about?" The commandant spoke educated, clipped Czech in a precise monotone that matched his impassive, serious face. He always began interrogations in a civil manner but could soon change his tone as he saw fit. The thrill of absolute power bestowed by his position gave him immense pleasure. His reputation for cruelty reached far beyond the confines of the camp long ago.

Maria answered in Czech, looking straight into his notorious eyes. She was beyond fear. "A militiaman guarding prisoners in the city took my identity card. He told me to come here to pick it up in your office."

His eyebrows rose slightly when she used his language capably, and he watched her intently as she spoke. The young men exchanged quick glances, while the commandant kept his eyes fixed on her. She related the incident, emphasizing that she had been a bystander tricked by the old woman.

"Don't believe a word this German sow tells you, *Pan* commandant; they are all alike, these Nazi swine." The young soldier grinned viciously. "If the old biddy told her to jump in the river, she would have done that, too. A likely story, ha!"

The commandant motioned brusquely to the soldier to keep quiet and said in the same cool, clipped speech, "When did this happen?"

"About two hours ago, *Pan* commandant. I have come straight from the scene." The commandant pondered in silence, then faced Maria severely. "If it was in late morning, as you say, the guard who has your identity card is still on duty. He won't be back here until late afternoon." His expression unchanged, he sat awaiting her reaction.

In a voice far calmer than she thought possible, Maria heard herself reply, "In that case, *Pan* commandant, may I wait here until the guard returns?"

A fleeting look of surprise flickered on his mask-like face. He said nothing for an agonizing minute, the silence in the room as taut as Maria's nerves. Then he spoke firmly. "Go home." He had a compelling look in his eyes. Not fully comprehending what was happening she silently nodded her acknowledgment and rose to leave. As she walked out, the two young men again looked at each other in total surprise.

She retraced her steps like a sleepwalker, down the three stairs, along the barbed wire fence, to the steel door by the guard box, past the surprised guard who gaped after her, and out onto the country road to the main street. She did not feel the icy wind tearing at her clothes as she made her way. In the distance she saw a red trolley approaching from the north. She broke into a wild run, waves of relief engulfing her. The trolley stopped and she climbed on board. Collapsing on the wooden bench as the conveyance lurched forward and trying to calm her heaving breaths, she could not believe the miracle of her reprieve. She had to tell herself over and over again that indeed she was traveling back, leaving behind certain death. She was going home!

There were moments when worrisome doubts surfaced about her lost identity card. Then again, people simply did not return from this camp, everybody knew that, and yet here she was safe, after walking into the lion's den. She even faced the notorious Lion himself and he had said, "Go home!" Was it all really possible? For most of the freezing, noisy journey to the city she felt alternately elated and troubled before she began to accept that she would indeed see Anton and the women in the corner house again, and life might continue after all.

It was late afternoon when she rounded the corner toward the courtyard and the apartment building. Everywhere long shadows of wintry dusk surrounded her. She knocked at the bungalow door. *Frau* Winkler opened. For a few seconds the two women stared at each other, *Frau* Winkler wide-eyed as if seeing a ghost. Then a shout of relief rang out. "Thank God, *Frau* Wildert! Is it possible? We all have been praying and hoping for a miracle! Is it really you? Oh, I just can't believe it; it's too good to be true !"

Frau Winkler rushed Maria into the roomy kitchen where shrieks of excitement from everyone combined into a chorus of joy. Anton had come home from work early and was told a made-up story about Maria's going to the hospital. Now he knew the truth and gasped in awe at the incredible turn of events. When the noise ebbed, *Frau* Winkler, wordless, stretched out her hand to Maria. On her palm rested Maria's identity card.

Maria stared at the life-giving document incredulously. "How on earth did you get this?" she cried out, "do you know what this means? What happened?"

"What a series of incidents; it's like a suspense novel," replied *Frau* Winkler, laughing and crying at the same time. About an hour after she returned home and told the others about Maria's detention, a man called at the apartment building and was directed to the corner house. He was a middle-aged law clerk, and he explained in Czech that he was looking for *Pani* Wildert*ova*. When told that she had gone, he paled and became agitated.

After a few quick exchanges the women realized that the guard who confiscated Maria's card had contacted him. He instructed the man to call on her before she went to the camp later in the day. He did not say so directly, but it was plain to the women that his purpose was to trade the identity card for something valuable. Instead he found Maria's friends gathered in despair. Growing increasingly panicky, the caller waited around for over an hour. Apparently he was afraid that the guard arriving at the camp without the identity card would in some way implicate him in what seemed to be their private extortion scheme. The man finally lost his nerve and simply turned the card over to *Frau* Winkler. He left hurriedly, anxious to wash his hands of the whole affair.

The unhappy group grew more miserable with each passing hour, knowing they held the key to Maria's life and freedom—if by some miracle she were to return. Now their joy knew no bounds, the impossible had come true. Everyone was quiet in a moment of thankful prayer. It would be a good Christmas, after all.

FIFTEEN

The First Christmas

A few days before Christmas the mood among the few people remaining in the area was dispirited and resigned. Many worried about men who had not yet returned from a war that ended months before, or agonized about loved ones already expelled to Germany or detained in the burgeoning concentration camps.

During the prior Christmas they were haunted by anxieties about the inevitable collapse of Hitler's *Reich*. Now a greatly diminished population eked out a day-by-day existence as strangers in their own land, under the constant threat of physical harm and expulsion. There was little to celebrate, or to celebrate with, and yet the spirit of the season stirred the people to mark the special day as best they could. Families lucky enough to be together reached out to those less fortunate.

The bakery bustled late into the evenings turning out not only its regular products but also a flurry of special orders as Czech customers brought in eggs, butter, and flour to have the bakers create culinary delights. Working alongside the older men Anton admired their sure craftsmanship. They deftly transformed the precious ingredients and spoiled none of the goods entrusted to their skill. The hours flew by in heavy concentration, everyone working at full speed.

With Christmas so close Anton looked out more frequently from the rear windows toward the distant family villa. He was often drawn to the nostalgic view when in the early darkness he could see lights that in former times meant joyous Christmas scenes for Johann and himself. The season had always been a special time for the boys. A week before the wondrous day the dining room became off limits to them, and they heard all sorts of mysterious rustling in the forbidden room. Nannerl smiled knowingly, whispering it meant the Christ Child was busy with his angels, bringing toys and gifts. They must never try to peer in—if they did, all would be gone in a flash.

Every morning the brothers checked their colorful Advent Calendars, wishing they could hurry time along. St. Nicholas visited them in person on the sixth of December along with the chain-rattling devil "*Krampus.*" The white-bearded saint of wide pillow girth inquired about their behavior in a deep voice oddly similar to their father's. He always knew about their major pranks in surprising detail and summoned his masked, furry-black companion to give them a symbolic thrashing with an old broom. They soon forgot their stinging bottoms for gifts of candy and fruit, well mixed with pieces of coal and raw potatoes for their ill deeds. Growing up to grim reality did not diminish these magic memories.

On Christmas Eve the fabric covering of the arched doorway to the dining room fell to the strains of "Silent Night." Live candles blazed on an ornately decorated Christmas spruce, topped by a glittering star. The family, usually including Aunt Martha, Uncle Walter, Uncle Herbert and Nannerl, happily watched the wide-eyed children race to their respective arrays of presents in the alcove. The grownups exchanged gifts, and everyone sat around the festive table to savor the traditional meal of delicate river carp with innumerable side dishes. The children ate impatiently, anxious to play with their new toys, while Friedrich kept a wary eye on the tree's blazing candles. The fragrance of the freshly cut spruce melded with the aroma of the delicacies in an atmosphere of joy and goodwill.

The Wilderts tried to maintain a semblance of these traditions during the war, even though food and gifts became sparse. On their last Christmas Eve in the villa, with Johann away, the forlorn threesome decorated a small spruce and placed it on the coffee table in the alcove. While they wished each other blessings, the tree suddenly toppled over and flared up as the live-candles ignited its needles. They hastily smothered the blaze, but the Christmas mood was shattered by what they perceived as a bad omen.

"Hey, quit your daydreaming and help me get these baking forms ready," came Günther's urgent voice from afar. Anton needed a moment to shake off his vision before he resumed his chores. This Christmas was going to be different, all the magic gone. Yet Anton sensed that he would be able to face the special day much better now than he might have at the height of the turmoil months ago. Perhaps he was growing up, he mused; perhaps the discipline of work had been good for him. Soon his concentration again focused on the many tasks that still had to be finished.

During the morning of Christmas Eve the last-minute rush of work ebbed. Anton looked on as each of his colleagues unwrapped supplies and prepared his own *Stollen* and cookies. He had nothing for himself, but was happily surprised when shortly before closing *Pan* Janáček came into the workshop to hand Anton a large package of fragrant cakes and cookies, and wished everyone a Merry Christmas. The boy was proud and pleased to take home such an unexpected treasure.

Kučera offered to walk with him and they strode briskly through wintry streets, the drabness softened by the angled orange rays of the low afternoon sun. Kučera carried two packages and the two talked animatedly in their makeshift language. At the apartment Kučera bowed to Maria and was visibly pleased to converse with her in Czech. With a smile he held out one of his packages and in a short, polite speech announced that he wanted to bring this gift to his young colleague's mother. Maria thanked him warmly, touched by his gesture and especially grateful for the kindness he showed her son.

The women in the corner house invited Maria and Anton to spend Christmas Eve with them. The large kitchen was warm and glowing, and they pooled food and special treats hoarded for the occasion, the normal sparse diet forgotten for a day. For weeks they had saved fuel to heat enough water for everyone to take a hot bath. The single bathroom remained in non-stop operation all day. Maria and Anton were happy to be with the lively group, to be part of the excited babble of voices and the bustling preparation of a veritable feast. On this night more than ever the loneliness of their existence cried out for human contact, and they eagerly allowed themselves to be swept along by the festive mood.

Early in the evening the doorbell rang. *Frau* Winkler answered it and was startled to encounter a round-faced Russian soldier still in his teens. He was without a weapon and stood uncertainly in the deserted street, looking at her with bright eyes. The sensible woman quickly realized the young man sought some human contact. Touched by the spirit of Christmas she beckoned him into the noisy kitchen and offered him a seat at the table. A hush fell over the group and all eyes turned to look over the uniformed stranger in their midst.

He spoke only Russian which no one in the room understood. *Frau* Sedlaček was fluent in Czech, which saved her life when she used this talent to evade the mob after the explosion. She chattered away happily at the puzzled soldier, her expressive face alive with comical contortions and her hands gesticulating in emphasis—but to little avail. Moving steadily closer and raising her voice in an effort to help the young man understand, *Frau* Sedlaček ended up eye to eye with him, screeching into his face. In turn the hapless and flushed soldier became hotter and hotter in the warmth of the kitchen, and droplets of sweat formed on his brow. Seeing his distress the women tried to make him shed the heavy uniform jacket. The young man was so taken aback at the onslaught of screaming and gesturing that he clutched the lapels tightly and held onto his coat for dear life.

Anton could hardly contain his delight at the humorous twist of watching a Russian soldier frightened of a gaggle of women and children. He chuckled while exchanging glances with his mother, whose eyes were bright with merriment. Amid the general hilarity the others laughingly suggested to *Frau* Sedlaček that she leave the poor fellow alone. Finally realizing she was getting nowhere the young woman toned down her shrill linguistic attempts.

Even when calm was restored the soldier still insisted on wearing his coat, but he relaxed enough to munch the cookies offered him and to drink his tea. His ruddy peasant face was crimson by now, but the dark eyes lost their furtive look. The small children stood before him gaping with curiosity, and he smiled self-consciously at them between sips of tea. With a shy grin and awkward gestures he thanked the women, relieved to make his exit from the overheated room into the cold Christmas night.

At last their feast began after a hushed moment of saying grace. It was not long before the doorbell rang once more. Again *Frau* Winkler answered it and encountered another stranger. The man was dressed in the remnants of a *Wehrmacht* uniform and carried a bundle over his shoulder. He had a white armband pinned to his sleeve and his legs were wrapped against the cold in makeshift leggings. With a polite bow he said, "I understand my sister and nephew are with you. The people from the apartment house next door directed me here."

Overhearing these words Maria jumped up to find her brother Walter at the door. Hugging him like a long lost child she exclaimed, "How on earth did you manage to get here?" It seemed miraculous that he received permission to come from the work camp where he was detained. Anton ran to greet his uncle and the other women joined in a chorus of welcome. Walter had aged beyond his thirty-three years; his hands were gnarled from hard labor and he looked haggard and grimy.

They bundled the ex-soldier off to the bathroom where there was enough hot water left for a long soaking. A presentable Walter then told the group of his adventurous escape after the collapse of the Russian front. He had made his way through devastated Saxony, mostly on foot, attempting to reach Aussig and his home in the Wildert villa. After the turmoil of the Russian conquest quieted, the wandering soldier received an occasional ride and bits of food from Russians, who slapped him on the back, saying, "*Vojna*[1] over, *tavarishch!*"

When he had crossed the Sudeten mountains he became easy prey for the increasingly aggressive Czech militia. About thirty miles from Aussig he was arrested by a heavily armed patrol and interned in a work camp to labor in the steel manufacturing complex at Brüx. Life as a detainee was barely tolerable, but the inmates were fed regular if meager rations and were rarely subjected to brutality. The work was hard and dangerous. Walter was

[1] war

a trained engineer and tended a wire-drawing machine, wrestling red-hot snakes of metal writhing and darting between whirling stacks of rollers. The welts and bruises on his hands and arms showed stark evidence of his toil. After a month of trying he managed to wangle a three-day pass to spend Christmas in Aussig, and with skills of improvisation that had become second nature to him covered the distance of thirty miles in a few hours.

Basking in the warmth of the kitchen and the admiring glances of the young women, the attractive bachelor ate heartily, relishing the food and the festive setting. However, Walter was clearly pre-occupied and after the meal he took Maria and Anton aside and whispered, "Gretl told me that Friedrich and Anton buried the family jewelry in the garden. Do you realize what that stuff is worth now? Besides, my gold watch is in there, too. I know the quality of your diamonds and other stones—they would fetch fantastic prices!"

Maria looked at her brother aghast. "What on earth are you talking about, Walter? Certainly the jewelry is valuable. But why don't you think of the most important problem? Don't you realize that we are strictly forbidden to possess gold, jewels, and other such things? Do you understand what the penalties are?"

"Come on, Maria, you could finance Anton's education if we could get our hands on the stuff!" Walter seemed unimpressed by her logical arguments and became impatient.

Maria's annoyance flared into anger. She knew her brother only too well. He had grown up a loner, gifted in his studies, but not always practical in day-to-day affairs. He was headstrong and argumentative and had a short-fused temper, a brooding volatility apparently unchanged despite the hardships he suffered in the last few years. She wanted nothing to do with his foolish schemes.

"You are the one who does not understand," Walter hissed heatedly, "just leave the matter to me. I'll go to the villa tonight, in the dark, and dig up the box in the garden. Nobody will be watching on Christmas Eve. Then I'll bring it here, you can hide the box, and Gretl will take it to Prague later."

"You are absolutely mad, Walter, and you'll do nothing of the sort! First of all, someone has probably found the jewelry already, and so your insane adventure would be for nothing. But the more important thing is the danger to you, and through you to all of us. The risk is far too great, even if the jewelry were as valuable as you dream about!"

Maria's voice was shrill with anger. "I will not stand for your sneaking through the night and getting caught with contraband. Don't you know what they would do to you? For once in your life try to be reasonable and mindful of others! Don't drag us and these kind people here into this insanity! Stop it right now!" Their heated exchange drew attention. *Frau* Winkler came over to see what was going on. When she heard Walter's plans she protested energetically, but he ignored her words.

Not easily deflected from his purpose Walter picked up his bundle in the hall and produced a small hand spade and a sharply pointed two-foot rod with a handle. The probing iron was fashioned from the materials at the steel mill. He had brooded at length about the buried jewelry and went to a great deal of trouble to prepare the tools. Walter insisted over and over again before the incredulous women that his front-line experience taught him how to move undiscovered in the dark. He kept up a steady stream of arguments in the rapid, aggressive manner Maria and Anton knew so well. Proudly he declared that, after studying in Prague he knew Czech like a native, shrugging off his sister's argument that language ability clearly would not suffice if a suspicious militia patrol were to stop him and demand his papers.

Maria broke into tears and begged him not to go. He simply called her a silly goose, a term he was always ready to hurl at his older sister whenever he disagreed with her. All the women's arguments fell on deaf ears, and Walter turned to Anton to demand the location of the treasure. Carefully he marked an "X" on the spot the boy indicated on a rough map he drew of the garden and then he bounded out into the chilly night. Anton thought the paper looked just like the treasure maps he and his friends used when playing pirate games.

The children were in bed by now. The group's Christmas spirit deflated and Maria apologized profusely for her brother's bizarre behavior. Her friends reacted kindly but Maria knew they worried just as much as she did about the consequences of Walter's escapade. No one would be at ease until it was over.

The Wilderts returned to their cold flat to wait for Walter's return. Sleep was impossible and Maria talked at length with Anton about the foolhardiness of the scheme, expanding on her memories of her brother's quirky, stubborn moods which the family found impossible to influence. It was a relief for her to unburden her feelings even while the deed was being done.

Walter moved cat-like through the icy darkness. The distance to the villa could normally be covered in a brisk walk of about fifteen minutes but he chose a longer and more circuitous route. Gliding along protective fences and stealing through back roads he stopped frequently, listening intently for any signs of militia or passers-by. But the streets and roads were deserted. Walter encountered no one and he managed to cross the familiar terrain in half an hour.

Nearing the villa he saw light in the second floor windows, including the one that was once his room. After pausing a while he climbed the front fence where it was covered by bushes and the limp branches of a weeping willow and made his way cautiously into the back of the garden. The rear facade of the villa loomed darkly and no one stirred.

Carefully shielding his flashlight he squinted at the crumpled map in his hand and located the approximate place where Friedrich and Anton buried the box months ago. He crouched under the bushes for several minutes, shivering, until he became used to the still darkness. Apart from lighted windows in distant houses there were no signs of life in the neighboring gardens.

With great care he began probing the area with the wire rod. The soil was not yet frozen and yielded easily to the sharply pointed tool, but he felt no resistance against the plunging steel where the metal container should have been. Cursing under his steaming breath Walter hurriedly punctured the soil in an ever widening arc. Still there was no resistance.

Again he paused, tense with frustration, watching and listening for danger. He was determined not to give up. Returning to the original spot he started to dig the earth with the hand spade. He piled up the dirt neatly for later replacement and over the next half hour made a sizable hole—but to no avail.

Only then did Walter admit to himself that he had failed, that there was nothing to be found. Furious and shivering he quickly pushed and pressed the soil back into the hole, smoothed the surface as best he could and stole out of the garden. As he climbed the front fence again he looked up to the second floor windows, still aglow.

The hush of the cold Christmas night remained undisturbed as Walter picked his way back through the deserted streets. His angry thoughts churned with the futility of his quest, crowding out any feeling for this special night. He had prepared himself so well for this dangerous undertaking, and his front-line experience made exploits in the dark easy for him. Aching with frustration he discarded his tools under some bushes halfway to the flat. Why couldn't he have retrieved the prize? Walter was obsessed with the jewelry, oblivious to the risks to himself or to anyone else, and he swore crudely under his breath as he trudged along the unpaved street leading to the flat.

A shivering and dejected Walter knocked at the apartment door about two hours after he left. The Wilderts were relieved to see him return unharmed and not carrying the forbidden jewels. Still preoccupied with his mission Walter questioned the boy sharply about the accuracy of the map. After fruitless arguments he at last agreed that he had dug in the right spot and that the only explanation for the empty hole must be that others found the box before him.

Maria paid no attention to the irritating discussion. Still furious about the worry Walter caused all of them she concentrated on making hot tea for the half-frozen adventurer. She had lost all interest in her jewelry a long time ago. Her practical instincts told her that everyone was far better off now that Walter had found nothing. Had he brought the box here they would need to face the difficult problem of hiding the valuables and worry about the contraband until Aunt Gretl could carry it to Prague. In her dark mood Maria even suspected that Gretl might have put Walter up to this scheme.

But what did that matter now? Maria was glad to wash her

hands of the whole affair. She lay down on the kitchen sofa, leaving the larger bed for Walter and Anton. The tension of the evening tired everyone sufficiently to bring on the relief of sleep.

In the morning Walter continued to speculate about what might have happened to the buried valuables. Anton suggested that the new occupants of houses in every neighborhood probably carefully searched the gardens for likely hiding spots, especially where soil appeared to be settling. He said he even heard that army mine detectors were used to look for buried treasure. At any rate the jewelry was lost, along with everything else.

It was clear that Walter had yet to accept in his mind that day-to-day survival was more important than elusive material possessions. When he still persisted in carrying on about the jewelry Maria finally ordered him, in no uncertain tones, to shut up. In her own flat she asserted her role of older sister and head of the small household. Walter sensed he had better comply.

The following day Walter left to return to his camp, carrying gifts of food from Maria and the women in the corner house. He was treated to a stern lecture by *Frau* Winkler about the danger and worry he caused for them all. This finally made a far deeper impression than anything his sister said or screamed at him.

Shortly after Christmas Maria was walking alone in the main street near the flat when she heard the sharp crack of a whip. She looked up to see a young Russian soldier sitting high on the bench of a horse-drawn army wagon with rubber tires. He bobbed his head in friendly animation, grinning from ear to ear. It took a moment or two for her to recognize the young soldier who had visited the corner house on Christmas Eve.

Maria smiled back but the soldier kept gesturing and motioned her to join him on the bench. Maria instantly knew it was out of the question to accept. It would not do for a woman to ride in public with a Russian soldier. Searching for a way out that would not offend the youthful warrior Maria pointed in the direction the cart was headed and made signs to inquire if this was the way he had to go.

"*Da, da,*" the young man nodded, his red cheeks creased with an eager smile. Maria faked a display of regret and pointed in the opposite direction, making clear that she had to go that way. The soldier shrugged, gave Maria a smart salute and flicked the whip to stir his horses into resuming their trot.

The following afternoon Maria heard a hesitant knock on the apartment door and, alert as always, opened it just a crack. It took her a few moments to recognize the stooped figure clad in torn clothes, the sad-eyed face distorted by swollen red welts.

"My God, *Herr* Brunner, what on earth happened to you? Come in, come in, can I help you?" Brunner followed Maria inside, shuffling painfully, and slumped on the chair she offered him.

"I've just been released from Lerchenfeld camp." His hoarse voice was barely audible. "When I came home I found that my family was evacuated to Saxony months ago. Someone told me where you were and I wanted to ask you if you could kindly spare a little food. I'm planning to walk across the border tonight to find my family." Exhausted, Brunner fell silent. His hollowed eyes pleaded for help.

His story and appearance shook Maria to the core. Not yet forty and once a slender, fit man, Brunner was the father of Anton's friend and schoolmate Helmut who had been his frequent companion during the last few years. Brunner and his family lived a few houses from the Wildert villa, where for a decade they occupied a small ground-floor apartment in the Blum villa the Nazis later confiscated.

A skilled metal craftsman working for the large industrial enterprise on the opposite banks of the Elbe river, Brunner and his wife also served as caretakers in the Blum villa. The Wilderts knew and respected the decent couple and their two children. They were pleased that the boys often played together at each other's homes before the collapse.

"When on earth did they put you into the concentration camp, *Herr* Brunner, and why?" Maria was aghast with horror as she stared at the bruises and scars that covered the man's face and hands.

"I was walking home from work across the Elbe bridge on the day of the explosion." His tone was lifeless. "The militia grabbed me together with many others and marched us off to Lerchenfeld.

That was on July 30. The last five months were terrible, so terrible that it's very difficult to talk about." He paused to swallow painfully.

"These bruises are only a small part of what they did to me. They broke several ribs when they beat me, and then they refused medical help. I have great difficulty breathing. The ribs may have been broken again for they beat us often. We slept on bare concrete floors without blankets and had nothing to take care of our wounds."

Maria shivered as she looked at the disfigured man before her. "Of course I'll give you food, whatever we can spare, *Herr* Brunner. But first you must eat something right here. I'll heat up soup and there's bread and margarine. I also have a few baked goods Anton brought home from work." She was glad to avert her eyes from his injured face and busied herself with the preparation. "Do you know where your family is?" she inquired, stirring the soup.

"All I know is that they were evacuated into Saxony during the summer," Brunner replied softly. "I do hope they are safe. My little Erika is still so young. I pray that they find enough to eat. They don't know that I was sent to the camp; no one was notified when it happened, and they must think I'm dead." He shook his head dejectedly. "I am so anxious to find them, I must leave here as soon as possible."

Maria served him the steaming bowl and Brunner ate ravenously, visibly gaining strength from the nourishment. "I'm very embarrassed to come here asking for food, *Frau Direktor*," he stammered, "but I had nowhere else to turn. God bless you for sharing this with me."

As she sat down by him Maria fought back her tears. "There's no question that you're welcome to what little I can give you. I'll also pack something for you to take along. I'm so sorry about your terrible experiences, and hope and pray that you'll find your family soon."

Brunner looked at her with compassion. "I learned from the women in the corner house that *Herr Direktor* died in the hospital about the time I was interned. My sincere condolences to you and Anton. First your dear Johann and then your esteemed husband; you are very brave, and may God protect you."

At the mention of Friedrich and Johann she was jolted back into the sensation of shock she felt upon learning of their deaths. But Maria pushed her own unhappy thoughts aside, overwhelmed by her compassion for the emaciated man. She found it hard to believe the twist of fate which had overtaken this respectable workman.

Brunner continued, "*Herr Direktor* had his operation in the hospital, I hear." After a moment's hesitation he added, "*Herr* Dr. Schweringen was an inmate at Lerchenfeld, too." He fell silent, brooding. At the mention of the famous chief surgeon Maria thought of Sister Anna's account of the incompetence of the attending doctors, while at the same time the "man with the golden hands" languished in the concentration camp.

Brunner's voice was low, his words halting. "I must not say too much, but I saw with my own eyes how he was torn apart by dogs before all the inmates as punishment for informing the International Red Cross about the true conditions in the camp. Everything had been dressed up for the Red Cross inspection; we were even issued blankets and good food. But they warned us not to approach the commissioners."

The man paused, capturing his breath, and continued shakily. "At the end of the inspection Dr. Schweringen tore off his shirt before the visitors, pointed to the scars of his many beatings and shouted, "This is how we are really being treated here!" Once the foreigners left, the guards took away the blankets and made all of us stand in the open to witness Dr. Schweringen's execution. His torn body was left in place for a day as a warning to us."

He started to sob but quickly pulled himself together. "I've already said too much; please forgive me, *Frau Direktor*. I've been close to death. Why they let me go I don't know. So many others didn't survive." Brunner rose, wincing at the pain in his ribs, tried to regain some composure and said firmly, "I must go north and find my family."

He reached for Maria's hand and pressed it in both of his. Maria felt the welts on his palms and fingers. "We may never see each other again, *Frau Direktor*. Thank you ever so much for being so generous to me now, and thank you for the years when we were good neighbors, in better times. I can't give you anything in return, I can only ask God's blessing for you."

Maria was unable to reply. She placed a small bundle of food into Brunner's hands and closed her hands over them. After a moment of choked silence he turned to leave and soon was slowly walking across the empty courtyard. Before entering the street he looked up to the apartment window and raised his arm in a gesture of farewell.

SIXTEEN

The Train to Eger

The brief interlude of Christmas and the pleasant moments it brought soon faded before the realities of continued makeshift existence. Anton returned to his long hours at the bakery and Maria resumed her wanderings through the bureaucratic maze in pursuit of the elusive travel permit for the rail trip to Eger. January turned out to be especially cold and bleak and she often came home chilled and shivering after standing in line for hours in unheated corridors or out in the open.

Maria's dogged pursuit of the permit at last brought success, for by the end of the month she had finally gathered the right combination of certificates, stamps and signatures to allow them to leave for Eger within the next two weeks. On the day she brought home the final approval, mother and son celebrated with a meal a little less bland than their usual fare and they savored the last of the Christmas cookies.

Their excitement grew as they pictured themselves moving close to the western border with Germany. But they would only believe in their good fortune after the fact—too many things could still go wrong. They were glad to leave the dreary neighborhood which was still alien to them after six months, but they would miss the warmth of their friends in the corner house who had been so supportive.

"It'll be so nice to be with Aunt Martha and the children," Anton mused happily. His aunt always held a special place in his childhood memories, the years when she lived in the Wildert villa. Both she and Nannerl were fond of the growing boys, putting up patiently with their antics and enriching the brothers' lives with their ready affection. Later, when Martha visited the Wilderts with her own expanding family, Johann and Anton fussed over and played with their much younger cousins.

Now Anton realized he would be the oldest of the children when they joined the Eger family, almost a young man, and he proudly anticipated the new responsibility. He had saved some of his earnings from the bakery, and he and Maria set aside a few of the extra ration tickets issued him due to his status as a worker. He planned to bring the funds and the rations as gifts to his aunt. Anton was aglow. "I'm so glad I can take something special to Aunt Martha and the children."

Maria looked into his eager face and saw the youth's idealistic innocence. With a touch of weariness she said, "Remember, Anton, although your intentions are wonderful, you can't forget that Aunt Martha didn't ask us to come—we are looking for our family. It'll be quite different from the good times you remember when she lived with us and later visited us. She'll love your gifts, but they'll be small compared to the burden we are for her."

Maria paused, thinking nostalgically of her own past role as the central figure of her family in the villa, which for years had been home to her aged parents and younger brothers as well as Martha. Often complaining aloud about always being taken for granted and having her open hospitality abused, Maria secretly relished her importance.

The notion of holding the center stage role appealed to her and gave her the opportunity to act the long-suffering older sister who knew best, who was always generous but received very little gratitude for her many exertions. Friedrich tended to ignore the occasional annoyances and intrusions by his wife's family; he was an expert in tuning out trivial tensions and arguments. Being an only child he truly enjoyed the many pleasant aspects of a large and energetic family.

"When we lived in our own house," Maria continued, "we were the hosts and givers. Lord knows I've done my brothers and sisters a lifetime of service without ever being appreciated for it!" She frowned, "Now we need them—for the first time—and that changes matters completely." She paused, then added tensely, "You have no idea how difficult it is for me to ask to be taken in by Martha, but now it is the only answer. Don't expect that things will be as they used to be. When people have serious problems they first think of themselves, even more so than is normally true."

She looked at him knowingly and added, "When small children's needs are involved, a mother has to put them first. Family ties get stretched to a breaking point in a crisis. Don't forget I know my brothers and sisters well enough, far better than you. Remember Aunt Martha playing the role of the eternal sufferer when her brief marriage failed and she returned to the villa before the war? Remember Uncle Walter's foolishness at Christmas? And remember especially how Aunt Gretl and Franz behaved in recent months? I know it's hard, but you have to understand that everyone is different under pressure. We'll just have to hope for the best, but can't count on it!"

Anton understood and gazed at her with sadness and resignation. When she saw his face she brightened and said with conviction, "Let's look at the positive side. All along we've wanted to move closer to the western border. With God's help it now seems we are—that's all that matters."

Maria smiled encouragingly, pleased that Anton's disappointed look had disappeared. The boy began to admit to himself that the future would be more lonely than he had expected. But then he knew deep inside that he had already learned to be alone, and that even with Johann dead and his friends scattered he was strong enough to carry on.

The women in the corner house closely followed Maria's determined efforts over the past few months, freely giving their emotional support and advice when the ups and downs of official malevolence undermined her strength. When she was finally successful they rejoiced with her and became even more attentive while openly showing their regret that they would not be evacuated as a group. They had become close, welded together by shared dangers.

Aunt Gretl appeared at the flat a day or two after Maria obtained the completed documents, as she had done occasionally during the past months. When she learned that the move to Eger was becoming a reality she wondered aloud if some of the former residents' belongings left in the flat might not be bartered for food on the black-market.

Maria strongly objected to this idea, knowing the risk involved. Officials told her she was responsible for the flat and all its contents. Worn down with Gretl's continued insistence, Maria finally relented and allowed her to take some spare items from the modest flat.

Gretl had become a shrewd and efficient practitioner in the art of exchange on the black-market, shuttling with her rail pass between Prague, Aussig, and Eger. In the process she amassed in her home a large store of the best of Maria's and Martha's dowries. She occasionally turned some of the items into rare supplements of butter and meat which she delivered to her sisters. While Maria welcomed the food, especially for Anton's sake, she was never comfortable with the greedy commercialism of her older sister.

When Gretl left after a few hours, Maria asked her to send some food to Walter in his internment, if that was possible to arrange. She instructed her to take from her own dowry of fine linens what items were necessary for the barter. She was certain that Gretl would not short-change herself in the process and breathed a sigh of relief when her sister crossed the front yard for the last time, a heavy suitcase straining her arm as she disappeared around the corner.

On a dull, cold February day everything was ready for the journey to Eger. All the papers were in order—or so they fervently hoped—the bundles were packed and they hauled the little blue cart with the iron wheels from the shed.

Anton received a fine send-off from the bakery the day before. *Pan* Janáček gave him an extra month's pay and a large package of cakes and pastries. *Pan* Kučera's eyes were moist when they talked in their mixture of German and Czech about his imminent departure. He pulled from his pocket an autographed passport picture of himself, red star on the lapel, and a strong letter of recommendation carefully written in his own labored hand. He wished Anton Godspeed, shaking his hand firmly.

The others in the shop patted him on the back and added their own good wishes. Anton walked the familiar route for the last time with a calm sense of detachment. He even looked up toward the villa and saw the lights twinkling without feeling sad. He strode briskly on to the flat to share a final supper with his mother.

Early the next morning an official came to seal off their apartment and take the keys. He spoke little and made only a perfunctory check on the goods remaining inside. Maria quaked for a few moments as she thought of the things Gretl had taken, but the man didn't notice. He slapped an official paper seal over the door lock and frame, and left without even looking at the Wilderts who stood by the front door with their loaded cart.

Frau Winkler walked with them to the railroad station, insisting she would not have it any other way. They had a mile to cover on foot, as the trolleys were still not operating in that part of town. Again the wheels of the wagon ground and bounced noisily as they traversed the somber streets for the last time.

When they neared the railroad station the war damage was apparent all around them. The passenger terminal and freight yards had been a prime target for allied bombers during the last six months of the war, and the many bombing runs wrecked the buildings, collapsed viaducts and jumbled the tracks over a large area. Jammed between the old core of the city and the river bank, the elevated passenger station was completely gone and partial service was restored on only two tracks.

They reached the station with time to spare. But once they had negotiated the several flights of damaged stairs with the awkward cart, they discovered that the schedule had been changed and the only train to Eger was ready to pull out. Racing along the track they managed to reach the last carriage and strained to hoist the blue wagon aboard the rear steel platform amidst the protests of the conductor. While *Frau* Winkler threw the remaining bundles after them the train slowly shuddered into motion, yielding jerkily to the labored huffing of the ancient engine.

Breathing hard after their hectic exertion Maria and Anton stood on the carriage's platform by the handrail and waved goodbye to the kindly woman who was such a steadfast companion. Tears streaked the women's faces as the train gathered momentum and screeched into the curve, enveloping them in steam and acrid coal smoke. *Frau* Winkler's fluttering handkerchief disappeared.

Mother and son struggled to open the rear door to find seats in the cold interior of the rattling third class coach. One by one Anton wrestled the bags inside, leaving the blue cart on the rear platform. As they settled into a compartment, familiar views of the outskirts of the city rolled past the dirt-caked windows. The two felt very alone, adrift in uncertainty, and Maria reached over and hugged her son.

The noisy, smelly journey was tedious, often stalled by unscheduled stops and interminable crawling while the train inched cautiously over damaged rails, or maneuvered along bumpy detours and crossed swaying makeshift bridges. In the distance the wintry landscape seemed untouched, but whenever they passed through towns the war damage was startling. Railroad stations and freight yards bore the brunt of bombing and strafing, and as far as the eye could see there were blackened ruins, twisted rails, burned out coaches and boxcars, wrecked locomotives and mounds of debris. The bizarre scenes seemed locked in suspended motion, frozen in wintry desolation.

Few people moved about in the towns or countryside, and there was no traffic on the roads. Everywhere the predominant colors were mud gray and sooty black, made starker yet by the cold whiteness of sporadic patches of snow, sullied with grime.

Anton watched the dismal view while they sat in their heavy overcoats, shivering in the unheated carriage. They had an empty compartment—very few travelers were on the train—and they made themselves as comfortable as they could on the worn wooden seats. Maria was silent, caught up in the gloom of the dreary landscape and her own sense of the inevitable. The snail's pace of the creaking, rattling conveyance that stank of coal smoke and the neglect of years worsened the pain of leaving behind all that was familiar.

They both knew they were moving inexorably toward another episode of disruption. The strong sense of relief and joy both felt when the officials issued the final travel permits slowly eroded under the strain of preparation and the upsetting, scrambled start of the journey.

Anton also became quiet when his mother did not respond to

his boyish interest in pointing out the scenery. Losing himself in his thoughts he began to remember how he loved traveling by train in earlier, peaceful years. The family took extended annual summer holidays either in the alpine regions of Austria and Bavaria or in resorts by the Baltic Sea. These journeys had always been filled with excitement and anticipation for the two brothers. He remembered Maria's orderly packing of the many suitcases—they always took along far too much—and then her lingering over final details which caused the invariable last minute rush to the railroad station during which the company driver had to maneuver the route at high speed to arrive just in time.

The porters used to wrestle the heavy cases onto the overhead racks in the plush first class compartment, and as the train pulled away smoothly the family settled back into the soft cushions. Within minutes the brothers started to examine all mechanical features of the compartment, amidst constant reminders from their parents not to lean out the windows, where glowing cinders from the steam engine could burn their eyes, or not to yield to the ever-present temptation of pulling the emergency brake handle.

The excited pair sat still only when Maria unwrapped the crisp buttered rolls thickly stuffed with incredibly fragrant and tender Prague ham, its delicate aroma filling the air. Today's journey made the marvelous sights, sounds and tastes of those carefree days seem ethereal and worlds away.

He was brought back to the present when Maria asked him to reach for the small metal thermos bottle which he retrieved from the villa for Friedrich; it seemed so long ago. She poured steaming *ersatz* coffee into the aluminum cups and they warmed themselves with the bland liquid. There were no fragrant ham rolls, just some slices of coarse bread and margarine, but they did enjoy a tasty piece of cake from the package Janáček gave Anton on his last day in the bakery.

Maria attempted a brave smile. "We should be grateful to God that we're sitting in a train headed west, and both of us in reasonably good health." The relative calm of the trip and the forced inactivity set loose her pent-up store of feelings. She said no more; they were both absorbed in their own thoughts.

Reality intruded harshly when the conductor slammed open the sliding compartment door. Casting a mean glance at the white armbands he demanded identity papers, travel permits and tickets. Maria responded in Czech, which eased the tension somewhat, and after a long and critical examination the man found the papers in order. As he returned the documents to Maria the conductor complained angrily about the little blue wagon on the rear platform. Maria did her best to talk him into allowing the cart to remain, explaining that because of the sudden schedule change they had almost missed the train. The man looked her coldly in the eye and with an annoyed shrug turned and crashed the door shut.

Anton guessed that it would take another two hours to reach Eger at the rate they were going. They began to talk about the days and weeks ahead, avoiding any reference to their former home or any mention of Johann and Friedrich. Anton felt his excitement growing as he thought about revisiting the ancient city and again seeing Aunt Martha, whom he dearly loved. He wondered what living there would be like. Eger had been bombed heavily in the waning days of the war and Martha's family home was damaged, leaving only about two-thirds suitable for occupation.

Maria again cautioned Anton about his expectations. She suggested that he just be grateful to be escaping from the Russian occupation zone, where from their own experience and by all accounts the new Czech rulers were more cruel in subjugating and expelling the Sudeten population. Then she added sternly, "We can't forget that even in Eger we will still be living under constant threat from the both the Czech authorities and civilians. The only difference will be that the American army should be a restraint on them."

Invariably Maria returned to the subject of relatives and the stresses they were likely to experience living with family under abnormal and crowded conditions. She seemed obsessed with the subject, and talked at length about the strong personalities in her family that clashed even under far less strained conditions.

Even though the events of the past year had given Anton extensive lessons in human behavior, both good and bad, his youthful enthusiasm soon won the upper hand and he began to feel hope for the first time since the upheavals that began nine months earlier with the collapse of the *Reich*.

His optimism increased when the train made a lengthy stop at the demarcation line between the Russian and the American zones. A tall U.S. Military Police officer resplendent in a white steel helmet and belt, polished boots, and an impeccable olive drab jacket and pants opened the compartment door. *"Papiere bitte!* —Your papers, please!" The request was firm but polite. He examined the permits and identity cards proffered by Maria and returned them, stating, "All seems OK here!"

He grinned and winked at Anton, who could not take his eyes off him. This was the first American soldier he had seen. An unfamiliar fragrance of sweet tobacco surrounded the man, who looked well-fed, groomed and prosperous. With a nod to Maria the officer backed away, leaving behind a feeling of safety the two had not known for a long time.

The train started again after a half-hour delay and the landscape now reflected more life. War damage abounded and the drab winter grays and dirty snow still prevailed. But people were moving about freely and Anton saw many more vehicles on the roads, even though most bore the white five-point star markings of the American Army.

In the freight yards and on parallel tracks were new, over-sized boxcars painted in U.S. Army colors, equipment brought across the Atlantic by the invading forces. Anton began to think that life in this part of the region might be more bearable than in the deprived and uneasy atmosphere they left behind.

The train approached the outskirts of the city of Eger and crept cautiously into the large rail center. It moved past scenes of destruction that far exceeded what they had seen at the Aussig station. The vast rail yards were littered with deep craters, massive wounds from which twisted rails pointed in every direction like splintered bones.

Anton gaped at the wrecks of several huge steam locomotives, monster machines tossed about by the blockbuster bombs as if they had been miniature toys. They reminded him of his electric model trains, favorite playthings left behind. The train came close to one of the shattered locomotives which reared up from the maimed tracks at a crazy angle, half-buried and frozen in position, the heavy drive wheels clawing uselessly at the sky. It looked as if a giant had grown bored with his toys and hurled the huge vehicle into the earth.

Brakes screeching, the train slowed to a swaying stop beside the makeshift wooden platform constructed under the buckled remnants of the arched steel skeleton that was once a high glass dome. Only a few persons waited for the train to arrive, and as they rode in the last carriage the Wilderts were far removed from the small clump of people huddled on the platform.

Squinting forward through the open window of the narrow corridor they recognized the familiar figures of Aunt Martha and Doris, her husband's unmarried sister, both straining to see if Maria and Anton were aboard the train. Little Monika sat in a white baby carriage.

With considerable effort Anton managed to wrestle the bundles down the steep metal steps. It took much tugging and pushing to dislodge the blue wagon before he could haul it down as well. He supported Maria as she took the last high step to the ground. The two women spotted the Wilderts and came running along the tracks, pushing the baby carriage ahead of them. Wordlessly they fell into each other's arms, trying to keep their composure but not managing very well.

Maria finally sobbed, "Friedrich and Johann are gone from us," and gave in to her grief. For a few moments there was emotion-choked silence.

With great effort Martha pulled herself together, wiped away her tears and said severely, "There's one thing we must agree on right now. We can't afford to go on crying; we have to live for the children." Maria was taken aback at her brusque tone, but she covered up her hurt and nodded in agreement. Anton cast a puzzled look at his mother but Maria shook her head slightly and signaled him with her eyes to ignore the remark.

After the wagon was loaded and the bundles secured with string the small procession walked along the platform to the station. They made sure their white armbands were in place and then headed for the newer part of the city, a good mile away, to the family residence located in a quiet tree-shaded street.

Talking among themselves they trekked along, Anton all the while looking around at the varied civilian traffic in the streets, alive with ubiquitous American army vehicles and soldiers. A few of the store windows displayed a fair variety of food and supplies, often packaged in the distinctive olive green tins and cartons of U.S. Army provisions. But he saw no white-armband-ed people buying in these places.

Anton felt a sense of relief on this wintry February afternoon as he trod towards his second exile, the wheels of the blue wagon grinding and echoing in the streets. They passed scores of ruined buildings and the damage worsened when they traversed the old city center. Many of the old landmarks had disappeared, includ-ing dozens of oddly-shaped medieval houses huddled in angled whimsy, quaint links to the past that once made the sloping mar-ket square so attractive. In their place were mounds of rubble and gaping holes.

At last they reached the quiet street of multi-storied, spacious row houses where Martha and her family lived. These residences contained shops and stores on the ground floor and large apart-ments on the upper levels. Most of the stores were not in use, their windows and doors shuttered and the glass display cases bare.

Continuing on the wide sidewalk, lined with barren flower beds and trees, they came to the front door of the house. The love-ly paneled store where the family business had offered regional country fashions and accessories for sale was closed, as it had been for the last two years of the war. Martha's husband Oskar, heir and proprietor of the long-established company was still missing in Russia, and the business gradually ceased to function after his induction into the *Wehrmacht* early in the war. The women of the family tried to run the firm as best they could, but growing difficulties in obtaining restricted raw materials and lack of personnel had brought the operation to a halt.

Anton looked up at the familiar facade to see the bomb damage on the upper floors, where part of the roof and portions of the walls were missing. The adjoining house on the left had partially collapsed and stood roped-off and deserted. Stray bombs intended for the rail junction had struck the neighborhood, worsening the already significant fire damage from incendiaries dropped during the stepped-up air raids of the last year of the war.

Unlocking the ornate entrance door Martha said bravely, "We don't have as much room as we used to. The top floor is no longer livable, so we'll all have to share the main family quarters. Even there one of the back rooms is boarded up. But we'll manage somehow."

The halls and stairways were scarred and in disrepair, evidence of the continued shortage of paint and supplies. On the second floor the white, lace-curtained door set in a glass wall flew open and Martha's two young sons bounded out in high spirits to greet the arrivals. They'd grown visibly since their last visit to the Wildert villa two years earlier and looked well.

Everyone settled in with much bustle and talk. For Anton it was like a joyous homecoming after leaving behind the tiny flat in the barren neighborhood in Aussig. He was happier than he had been for many months, even though he knew this temporary way station was merely one more stage in the unfolding drama of their exile. Irresistible forces were pushing them along; the past was receding, and there was no turning back.

SEVENTEEN

The Evacuation

For three long months the Wilderts shared the quarters of the Eger family amidst the inevitable strains of close living. Food rations remained tight, and in his forced idleness Anton could no longer earn any supplementary coupons. Aunt Gretl brought occasional bartered meats and butter, while the Eger family used its shrinking network of rural contacts to obtain additional food.

As Maria had predicted, occasional spats over who owned what food, and over the rule of feeding children before adults demonstrated taut nerves and selfish instincts all around. Still, life was much more tolerable in the Eger environment, and the Wilderts thought themselves lucky to have come this far.

In early May the family received notification that they must report within the week to the collection camp for processing and train transport to Germany. The official letter specified the day and time and threatened heavy penalties for tardiness. Warnings to heed the prohibition on carrying valuables were printed in heavy black type, and the instructions stated that essential belongings taken along must not exceed thirty kilograms per person. Moreover, a severe limit was imposed on the amount of currency that they could carry.

The family spent considerable time going through their belongings, the scene reminiscent of the earlier preparations in the Wildert villa. Over and over the women pondered their choices, trying to pack the most practical and durable things for the children and themselves. It required careful thought to try to anticipate the needs of their growing children and to take along items that could later be refitted.

They also decided to include some of Uncle Oskar's clothes within their allowed weight limit, hoping fervently that he would be able to join them later when released from Russian captivity. As Maria had done in Aussig, the women made strong bags from the toughest fabrics they could find and carefully assembled bundles that could be carried without too much strain even by some of the smaller children. Maria contributed much useful advice from her own recent experience.

Aunt Gretl twice bustled into the house to cart off the most valuable excess belongings for safekeeping and future barter in Prague. Soon the once prosperous household stood depleted of its trappings like a tree in winter. Only furniture and rugs remained, as well as those utensils which lose their practicality when life is reduced to bare essentials. Friends and relatives came to call to discuss plans for meeting "over there" and perhaps to find a way to help each other in building a new life.

To Maria and Anton these preparations appeared amazingly orderly when compared to the frenetic conditions to which they had been subjected in Aussig, and they thought the calm atmosphere removed much of the suspense about the impending evacuation.

They were rudely jolted, however, when Maria found out two days before their departure that the Eger family had paid a considerable sum to intermediaries for obtaining residence permits to live in a Swabian town—for themselves only. They had arranged this jointly with distant relatives who were planning to re-establish their own manufacturing company in Germany as soon as that was feasible. Martha's casual revelation of her separate dealings struck Maria like a thunderbolt, even more so when she realized that her modest nest egg, which she had added to the Eger family's money to be sleuthed across the border by Martha's courier, had likely been used to fund these permits. Maria was too proud to react openly to her sister's apparent double-cross and decided not to raise the subject for the time being.

Later she took Anton aside, and fighting back her tears and bitterness said as calmly as she could, "We've come all this way to be able to move with them to Germany, after being the first in the family to lose everything. Now we'll have to take our own chances once we cross the border, and go wherever the officials send us." Her face hardened as she continued. "Anton, I know how much having a family means to you, but you must learn to become independent. The Lord helps those who help themselves." Anton nodded, although he was crestfallen at the thought of continuing the lonely life that had begun for him almost a year ago.

That night Maria quietly cried for a long time as she tossed and turned in her bed, alternating between self-pity and deep anger about how she was treated by Martha, Gretl and Walter. She had lost her cherished status at the center of the family, and worse, was now cast aside by her siblings. Maria felt abandoned, abused, and taken for granted, and memories of her past, proud hospitality flashed in her mind, contrasting with vivid images of her recent experiences. At long last she resorted to prayer to calm her whirling brain, and finally drifted off to sleep.

Now they had to make new plans. These were based on the hope that they might be able to make their way to southern Germany, to a small provincial town called Schlossberg. Near that town the owners of Friedrich's company, whose far-flung enterprises were situated mainly in the Russian occupation zone, owned a minor chemical operation as well as a large summer estate overlooking the verdant Danube valley. Before leaving Aussig, Maria had heard from one of Friedrich's former colleagues that the vonEckenbach family had managed to flee from Prussia to Schlossberg when the Russian advance threatened to engulf their mansions and company locations. Maria had no idea whether there was even a chance of making a living in the small town, but she hoped that Friedrich's excellent record with the company would be the basis for her to ask for help from the vonEckenbachs. This was speculation, but just thinking about the possibility was a straw to grasp.

Conversations with the Eger family became strained as the hour of departure drew near. Both Maria and Anton managed to suppress their lingering ill feelings by concentrating on last minute details.

A Czech official came to the apartment at the appointed time and watched closely as the family moved their belongings down the flight of stairs to the street. A second, larger cart joined the blue wagon and soon both were piled high with the white and gray bundles; they secured the load with heavy string. Even the baby carriage was crammed with belongings, riding low on its soft springs.

Martha returned to take one final look through her deserted home, the place where she had known happiness and raised her children. Closing the lace-curtained glass door for the last time she turned over the key to the impatient official with a hesitant gesture. The dour man turned abruptly to seal the door lock and frame with a paper strip bearing an official stamp, reading "Confiscated" in Czech. He left without uttering a word.

The family assembled in the street, four women and four children heavily dressed despite the mild day. Wearing extra clothes meant not having to carry them. Oskar's and Doris's elderly mother was supported by her daughter; walking slowly and painfully the fragile woman leaned heavily on her silver-topped cane. Doris had wrapped the silver handle with cloth and tape, hoping this bit of luxury would remain hidden during the final examination.

Anton led and hauled the heaviest cart, while Maria pulled the blue wagon, and Martha pushed the bulging baby carriage. The older boy guided the stroller with the baby girl, his young brother giving him playful assistance, not understanding the gravity of the situation. Doris was last, unable to do more than carry a bag while she supported her mother's shuffling gait. Everyone kept looking back until the house disappeared from view when they rounded the corner.

No one spoke, the only sounds being the rumble of the carts and their own echoing steps. Anton's emotions were the same as when he and his parents took their final walk from the villa ten months earlier. It was a detached sadness, a groping awareness of witnessing a scene in which events were somehow happening to others. Not able to understand his own feelings he kept quiet and plodded ahead.

In the next street they came upon other families tugging along their loads, all headed for the collection camp. Before much longer the trickle of people swelled into a steady flow which was now escorted by armed militia.

At last they arrived at the arched gate that breached a large walled courtyard nestled against a steep cliff. The city's historic medieval castle towered above the rocky precipice, its age-darkened battlements overgrown with the same ivy and vines that crisscrossed the natural rock wall. The lower courtyard was flanked by worn old buildings with steep tile roofs and massive walls pierced by narrow window slots. These structures had once been the stables of the noblemen and now served as a temporary holding camp where, over time, the tens of thousands of inhabitants of the city and its surroundings were processed for evacuation across the nearby border with Bavaria.

At the camp gate the armed soldiers directed the flow into the expanse of the first building. There the people waited for their turn at the processing desk where uniformed men demanded identity cards and the evacuation notice. Then they trudged through the courtyard to the next building for an inspection of all their belongings.

A dozen Czech civilians and militia men stood at long wooden tables in the dimly-lit interior, scrutinizing the contents of each of the bundles hoisted up and dragged across the scarred surface by the anxious refugees. Occasionally an item would catch the greedy attention of one of the searchers and he would remove it deftly, growling "not allowed" in Czech, and stare fiercely at the cowed owners, forestalling any attempt at protest.

When the family's turn came they watched apprehensively as the hostile examiners rifled through the belongings they had selected with such care. When several items of clothing in Martha's bundles fell prey to the searchers, Martha and Doris attempted hesitantly to argue their case. It was to no avail, despite Martha's ability to plead in passable Czech.

The Wildert bags had already been searched at the villa by Dvořák and his companions, and had been reduced to a bare minimum, but they were processed again. One of the civilian examiners spotted Friedrich's suit which Maria had packed to be fitted for Anton. The man pulled it out with a covetous grin, grunting

"Confiscated" and glowering at Maria.

Dismayed, she protested, trying to explain that her growing son would need some of his dead father's things later on. As she spoke the man angrily shook his head and interrupted her sharply. "This is much too good for you pigs! As I said already, Confiscated!" Dejected, Maria and Anton gathered their bundles and reloaded the blue wagon.

The family was directed to another building on the opposite side of the courtyard. Through an arched doorway they entered a large room where slender fluted stone pillars stretched to the high vaulted ceiling. Their steps echoed as they walked on the ancient stone slab floor. The semi-dark void was crowded up to eye level with row upon row of wooden two-level bunks. Some spaces had been left between the raw structures for the refugees to stack their belongings. On the beds lay lumpy sackcloth mattress bags stuffed with straw. A coarse blanket was folded at the head end of every bed.

After some hesitation the family decided on eight adjoining bunks near the center of the room as the more desirable locations along the walls were already occupied. The women did their best to make the barren quarters livable. They strung two strong cords between the beds and hung blankets and clothes, improvising a screen that allowed a modicum of privacy. Everyone settled down uneasily.

They assumed that their stay would last several days, although the officials said nothing specific. It was made clear to them that no visitors were allowed to enter the courtyard. If any friends or relatives tried to see them they would have to be met at the gate under the watchful eyes of the guards.

The clock tower in the castle high above chimed the noon hour, time to form the queue for the food ration of the day. The din of metal reverberated in the room as the people searched through their bundles for suitable pots and pans. Soon a long line formed by the door of the next building which housed the central kitchen. As they moved slowly forward, every person received a chunk of stale bread and a ladle of watery soup with a few pieces of potato and vegetables.

They carried the hot liquid back to their bunks and sat down uncomfortably to eat the meager meal. The food had to last them until the next distribution at noon the following day, and careful rationing was important. Maria suggested that some of the soup might be kept warm for the evening if the pot were nestled in a hole dug into the straw of one of the mattresses. They buried half their soup in this way; at least they would have a lukewarm supper.

During the afternoon there was nothing to do but wait. Time passed slowly, much of it consumed by idle talk which turned again and again to the experiences with the morning's search and the belongings lost to capricious larceny. The refugees consoled themselves by repeating that they retained most of what they had brought, and that family photographs and personal keepsakes were generally untouched, treasures which so many people had to leave behind in the early evacuations when they were forced to leave within minutes.

There were no books to help pass the time, since carrying them would have meant taking precious space and weight away from more essential things. With nothing else to do the adults dozed on their bunks, often interrupted by the cries or banter of young children for whom the confinement in the strange dusky hall was unsettling.

In the crowded conditions it was impossible to escape the sight, sounds and smells of neighbors on all sides. There could be no pretense at modesty or prudishness—people were too tightly packed together. Seeing women in various stages of undress was unavoidable and quietly accepted. Moments of strained camaraderie arose when women screened each other from sight with blankets as they changed clothes after washing by the cold water taps in the primitive lavatories outside.

The sparse lights suspended from the arched ceiling went out at ten in the evening. Soon the large room reverberated with the breathing and snoring of the multitude, sleep gradually mellowing the oppressive feeling of being crowded into this prison encampment. The black void of the high ceiling above magnified the sense of loss and disruption for those that could not sleep.

Anton lay awake for a long time, struggling with the host of impressions of the day. Much of the experience was familiar, only the setting was different. He had learned to accept many drastic changes during the past year—today's events were just one more link in a long chain of upheavals. To his surprise he felt no despair, only numb acquiescence. A spurt of helpless anger flared whenever he thought of the morning's search, but even that reaction faded, and sleep released him from reality.

The morning brought a noisy scene of mass awakening, washing and dressing. The foul-smelling lavatories provided only cold water, and the refugees hurried back to their bunks to finish preparing themselves for the day. But it would be simply another day of idle waiting, waiting for the meal at noon, waiting to eat the leftovers in the evening, waiting for news—any news—of the evacuation, and waiting to go to sleep. The only diversion came from strolling in the courtyard where one could take in fresh air and talk about the minutiae of camp life while trading the latest rumors. There was always an abundance of rumors: the train would leave in the morning, the train would leave the second day, or it would leave at some other time. No one knew and the authorities were not talking.

On the third day of collective camp life, which most people managed to turn into an awkward routine, the official announcement came at last. Train transport was arranged for the following morning. No destination was given, but so far all the trains had gone west into Bavaria. Surprisingly, the camp officials also announced that any serious complaints about items confiscated during the search on arrival could be taken up at the registration desk. Rumors circulated that the Czechs were on good behavior due to an impending visit by a commission from the International Red Cross.

Maria weighed at length the chances of lodging a successful complaint. Finally she pushed aside her nagging doubts about taking the risk and decided to try to recover Friedrich's suit for Anton's use. She persuaded Martha that she also had a reasonable claim to make for her own confiscated goods, and in the afternoon the two sisters joined a long queue in the registration hall.

A soldier and a civilian took turns listening to the complaints about purloined possessions. Some of the items mentioned were trivial and Maria saw signs of growing anger in the men's faces, but she stubbornly moved closer. When her turn came she summoned all her resolve and explained in halting Czech about the loss of the suit.

Before she could finish, the frustrated man turned scarlet in the face and let loose a tirade. "You miserable pigs, it is always one of this and one of that! Dammit all, can't you bastards be satisfied that you are getting out of here? The last three of you who complained will be held back with their families, and must wait for the next transport! And that is final!"

Maria pleaded with the enraged man, but her tears only infuriated him more. Swaggering and cursing he bellowed that the room must be cleared immediately. Maria began to shake, begging the man again to let the rest of her family go, even if she and her son had to stay behind. But he ignored her, shouting to his companion to take down the names of the three women before him and stormed out of the hall. Martha, standing behind her turned white in the face and glared at her sister with disbelief and scorn. Then she abruptly walked away.

Outside in the courtyard Maria had to sit down on a hard stone bench to try to regain her composure. Her head was spinning and she was crushed by an unbearable sense of guilt. She desperately blamed herself and relived the shocking scene with burning intensity.

Being held back from a scheduled transport could mean many days and even weeks in the wretched camp. Worse yet, the destination of all trains was uncertain. Strong rumors persisted that some future trains would be routed north into the Russian occupation zone of Germany. Maria had struggled so hard to avoid going there by finally arranging the trip to Eger. Now the renewed suspense would be hard to bear. She also blamed herself bitterly for causing such a dramatic change in her sister's situation.

Mustering all her strength, Maria rose and stood for a while to steady her quaking stomach. She walked stiffly toward the building and the waiting family, who stared at her in total silence. Martha had already described to them in detail everything that had taken place, and when Maria drew near the old mother eyed her coldly and said with contempt, "So this is the woman who is guilty of making us stay behind in this pigsty—Lord knows when and how we'll get out." She turned her back on Maria and no one said another word.

The tension in the cramped family quarters was insufferable. Maria took Anton by the arm and together they walked outside to sit on the stone bench. There she recounted the incident to him in her own way. "I should have realized that by the time it was my turn, the man had heard too many complaints. Not only that, he was the target of everyone's resentment." Maria sighed heavily as the impact of her rash decision sank into her consciousness. "I could plainly see he was getting furious. I should have known my complaint would be the straw that broke the camel's back!" She began to sob, her thoughts churning wildly.

Shattered by remorse she still could not believe her lack of judgment in pressing her claim. After months of experience of tangling with bureaucracy she should have known better. But here she was—at the brink of freedom—risking all for a suit of clothes! Anton gazed into his mother's distraught face, at a loss as to what to say. There had been so many shocks already, and his mind refused to accept it. The floating sensation returned, his subconscious way of coping with matters that went beyond his experience.

Maria finally wondered out loud if she should attempt to see the officer later and plead for the other family members' release, but she had to admit that it probably would do more harm than good. They stayed outside as long as they could before returning to the hall, where the family continued to ignore them. Shunned like outcasts they realized that they were truly alone now, far more so than when they had learned about the family's unilateral purchase of residence permits.

Their only choice was to make their own way while drifting with the other refugees in Germany. They silently prayed for a miracle, for any sign that the next transport would indeed still be routed westward. Meanwhile they would have to endure being ostracized by the family for the rest of the camp stay. Mother and son shuddered at the thought.

The next morning the hall echoed with noisy bustle as the

neighbors around the family bunks packed up bundles and read-ied themselves to assemble outside for the trip to the railway sta-tion. The mood of the departing refugees was an odd mixture of relief and anxiety, and they trudged off with subdued good-byes.

The detainees watched intently as the others streamed outside, and soon the last of the families had left the hall. In the far corner a small group huddled miserably, one of the other two families the officer had ordered to stay behind. Furtive glances went back and forth but no one stirred. The deserted hall was depressingly quiet after the sounds of departure had died down. Maria and Anton, finding the tension among their own family hard to bear retreat-ed to a corner, as far away as possible from the waves of hostility.

In mid-morning a guard strode into the hall and shouted that any adults left behind would have to perform useful work for the duration of their stay. He assembled the women and marched them off to their assignments. Maria, Martha and Doris were detailed to kitchen duty, which meant peeling potatoes and clean-ing vegetables for a few hours every day. Kitchen helpers could eat a few scraps of food, and the work was more tolerable than the menial cleaning of buildings and lavatories.

Maria was still shunned, but she accepted the situation and kept herself occupied with work. While she peeled potatoes with single-minded attention, Maria could not shake her suspicion that the officer's wild performance yesterday was at least in part a charade which served to recruit extra hands to keep the camp running. If this was so, her petition had been badly mistimed—yet she would never know the truth.

Several days passed. The Eger women did their allotted tasks and kept their distance from Maria. Anton whiled away the hours by exploring the camp, examining the ancient buildings and trying to imagine what the former inhabitants of the castle might have been like. He also rested at length, as the insufficient diet caused his growing body to tire easily.

The lull ended abruptly when another stream of refugees arrived to fill the hall. With much noise and confusion the new inmates went through the same awkward scenes of settling down in the close quarters.

All this time Martha's family never spoke another word to Anton or Maria. Somehow Martha had sent word outside to her friends about the detention, and visitors came to the camp gate to bring them food. On those occasions they ate heartily, audibly relishing the quality of their meals. Whenever possible Maria and Anton withdrew from these displays to a far corner or into the courtyard. Eventually they managed to be assigned two bunks some distance away from the family and settled down with great relief.

On the tenth day after their arrival, the guards announced that the transport was to leave the next morning. This time there were no signs that anyone would be detained. In the evening, with a surge of excitement, Maria and Anton gathered all their belongings in eager anticipation of their release from the dreary camp.

Anton slept very little that night, picturing in his imagination the events to come. He felt like a compressed spring about to be released, bursting its restraint. Soon he would see new cities and towns and be free from the capricious cruelties inflicted by ill-tempered men in uniform. He now understood how deeply ingrained his dread of faceless authority and the unexpected whims of those in power had become, far outweighing his vague concerns about the future across the border.

In the morning the Wilderts were indeed permitted to join the multitude gathering in the courtyard, no longer relegated to being wistful observers. Martha and her family stood far apart and gave no hint of recognition.

Harassed officials checked names against lists and ordered the crowd to move out of the arched gate and begin the fifteen minute trek to the railroad station. The roads were wet after early morning showers, the pungent smell of damp soil mixing with the sharp odor of asphalt. Some in the crowd had difficulty walking, slowing the pace of the long column to an arduous shuffle.

At the railroad station a string of dilapidated boxcars waited on a side track, large sliding doors ajar, the rough wooden floors covered with mounds of straw. The people at the head of the column discovered destination signs for western Germany, and the good news surged through the crowd in a flash. Relief was unbounded when the rumor followed that, for the time being, this was the last of the west-bound transports.

The guards began to divide the expellees, assigning groups of thirty to each of the boxcars. The people scrambled and clambered up the high metal step into the dusky interiors, heaving and throwing in bundles, suitcases and baby carriages, then arranging the piles of belongings to sit on. Children cried in the strange dark spaces, while anxious mothers tried to make sure all their things had been gathered. After much shouting and confusion everyone had finally found room and settled in uncomfortably.

Maria sat with several women in the interior of the boxcar assigned to them, her bundles neatly stacked on the straw to form a low seat. Anton and two other boys staked out the open doorway, letting their legs dangle outside.

A shrill whistle sounded. The locomotive hissed and puffed vehemently, its drive wheels suddenly spinning in place as if it, too, could not wait to leave. Clouds of smoke, steam and a shower of glowing cinders enveloped the forward cars of the train. A more deliberate, slow rhythm of the pistons followed, forcing the long chain of boxcars to shudder and clank forward. Slowly the train snaked its way out of the damage-riddled rail yards and, gathering speed, gained the open track leading west.

In the bright May morning the train throbbed and swayed on the rails, the steam whistle shrieking gaily. A peaceful landscape, greened by warm spring weather whizzed past the open doors, accompanied by the rhythmic clickety-clack of the wheels. The sun beamed a benign smile, and growing jubilation seized the occupants with every mile that brought them closer to Bavaria.

The shout rang out, "We've made it—this is the German border!"

Cries of relief filled the dark interiors of the boxcars. Suddenly there was lively chatter and good-natured bantering among the travelers. As the train thumped hollowly across the bridge Anton looked down into the rushing stream beneath his dangling feet and shared a sense of giddy freedom with the swirling waters.

The boy resolved not to look back as the train chugged steadily westward. He sensed that he would never return to his homeland. Today was his fifteenth birthday—and in his festive mood he mused happily that being able to leave behind this frontier was the best present he could have wished for.

EIGHTEEN

The Border of Hope

After the train rumbled across the bridge spanning the border it carried its load of expellees on a brief journey through the hilly farmlands of eastern Bavaria. Colorful wildflowers, blooming bushes and trees, and sparkling waters of rushing creeks formed a fitting backdrop for the celebration of a new beginning, for the joy of escape from hostility and fear.

The boxcar's interior became noisy with agitated and happy talk among the women and children lounging on their bundles. Now and again a figure would get up and peek out of the door into the sunny landscape, as if to look for some reassurance that the journey was indeed continuing westward, towards hope and survival. Anton and his young companions enjoyed their airy perch in the open doorway. Warm sunshine touched them as the swaying train snaked along its route, and Anton was filled with eager anticipation of the experiences to come.

This rail journey was so different from trips he enjoyed as a child, when he and Johann had thrust their hands out of the compartment window to feel them lifted by the cool air rushing by, as the express train whooshed and clacked towards summer holiday joys. Today's boxcar rode hard, lumbering with cumbersome clatter on worn wheels and springs. Only the hot cinders and harsh smell of the engine were the same.

Most of the time Anton was silent, idly watching the scenery and lost in meandering daydreams. Occasionally the brakes screeched and grabbed, sending clanking shudders through the long string of cars. Every time he eyed the sliding door beside him, apprehensive that the heavy panel might slam shut and run over his legs, but the boys had solidly jammed a large piece of wood under the rollers and the door stayed in place.

Finally the train slowed for the last time and puffed into the wrecked rail terminal of a small border town which had become the main processing point for the stream of evacuees from the western Sudetenland. They were shunted to a freight siding and soon there were shouts and commotion as men wearing Red Cross armbands came hurrying, accompanied by nurses and nuns. Most spoke the soft southeastern accent Anton remembered from past vacation trips.

The travelers stirred and readied themselves to climb to the ground. As Anton watched the uniformed figures walk from car to car, lending assistance, he had to convince himself that it was indeed possible to trust these officials, so entrenched was his fear of authority. But all he saw were helpful gestures and he listened gladly to the steady chatter in his own mother tongue.

He clambered to the ground and turned to lift down the many bundles Maria and others handed him, assisted by one of the men, and soon everyone's belongings were piled on the platform. The women and children were helped down from the boxcar opening high above the ground. Maria was lowered by the strong arms of a burly Bavarian, who grinned broadly and held her a little longer than was necessary. Maria returned the smile, grateful and relieved to stand on friendly ground, and she helped Anton reload the blue wagon once more.

When everyone assembled beside the train, the straw-littered interiors of the boxcars were inspected for anything that might have been left behind. The refugees were led in a long trek toward the nearby processing barracks, where papers were checked and destinations assigned. Maria and Anton entered the primitive shack with their ingrained fear of hostile bureaucracy. To their relief they found the men and women handling the tedious process harassed but sensitive to the plight of the confused people crowding around them. They were pleasantly surprised to hear some of them speaking with a Sudeten accent, refugees themselves.

The processing went slowly, as lists were laboriously searched and double-checked against identity papers. The few families who held official permits to live in specific towns were separated, while the large majority were herded into the next building to await transportation to another transit camp. From a distance the Wilderts could see the Eger family joining the small group with valid residence papers.

Maria stated her desire to go south to Schlossberg, but she could not produce any documents proving legal residence or support. With surprising tact the official patiently explained to her that such an assignment was not possible under the rules he had to follow. They would have to travel with the others to the western part of Germany, to a distribution camp near the Rhine; from there they would be sent to temporary quarters until they could find a permanent domicile.

Maria swallowed her disappointment, realizing there was no alternative. The man looked up at her understandingly, and said with a touch of sympathy, "Perhaps something will turn up for you."

It was now well past noon and the refugees were led back to the train to re-board the boxcars. Some of their former traveling companions joined the Wilderts. The wooden floors had fresh straw on them, and most cars bore markings for different destinations. On the way to the train the travelers were handed a sizable hunk of fresh rye bread and a generous piece of bologna. There was milk for the children and hot *ersatz* coffee for the adults.

Seated again on their bundles in the straw the refugees settled down to a happy picnic, comparing the long-forgotten aromas and tastes to the thin soup and stale bread in the dreary camp across the border. Anton recalled childhood memories and he found the meal at least as delicious as those crisp buttered rolls stuffed with fragrant Prague ham, almost forgotten delights of another era. While careful to save part of the treasured food for the journey they all ate heartily; for once they had portions that would satisfy even the emptiest stomach.

The train began to move again, lumbering steadily westward, putting more and more distance between the refugees and their lost homes. The weather remained clear and warm, and memories of past shocks and anxiety slowly receded, to be replaced by an easy camaraderie among the boxcar's inhabitants. The women passed the time talking about their former lives and what the uncertain future might bring, while Anton maintained his observation post by the open door.

As the train passed through villages and towns it was frequently detoured around heavily damaged sections of track, crawling over makeshift wooden bridges erected beside the twisted hulks and girders of railroad crossings that once spanned the creeks and rivers. Whenever the train traversed a city, the refugees' senses were jarred by bleak scenes of utter destruction. In peacetime the view from the tracks had always revealed ugliness and neglect as rail lines ran through the least attractive sections of most towns. But the present spectacle was an awesome, unending expanse of bizarre ruins left by heavy bombing and combat.

Anton was not prepared for the shock of utter destruction unfolding before his eyes as the train wound its way through the metropolitan areas of Nuremberg and Würzburg. Hundreds of city blocks had collapsed into desolate fields of rubble, marked only by the remnants of streets pockmarked with craters and littered with debris. Often the eerie wastelands sprouted scarred brick chimneys reaching for the sky as silent, blackened memorials. It was a no man's land, a barren desert devoid of life.

The boy saw rows upon rows of damaged and partially burned apartment buildings, whole flats grotesquely ripped open to the sky, with boarded-up sections where makeshift repairs allowed life to continue. Only when the train regained the open country was the war damage softened by the overgrowth of a lush spring. Viewing this grim spectacle Anton recalled stories his German schoolmates had told him. Transferred to the Sudetenland in the waning years of the war, these boys described the experience of almost daily bombings of their cities and the failure of essential services. The destruction he now witnessed helped him understand the import of those stories, the meaning of the struggle to survive and carry on when familiar things had collapsed into rubble and waste.

Reflecting on his own situation, where all he knew and loved had been lost to the avarice of strangers, he wondered whether it was preferable to have impersonal bombs destroy everything. The image of his father came back to him. At the height of the expro-priations in Aussig Friedrich said he truly wished the Wildert villa and its contents had not survived the air raids instead of becoming a prize for greedy scavengers and opportunists.

Whenever the worst scenes of destruction were starkly visible from the open doorway the travelers huddled in the crowded inte-rior fell silent, uneasily contemplating how they might find a new existence somewhere out there in the ghostly void left by the cat-aclysm of Hitler's "Total War." They were startled by the silent, almost unearthly remains of once bustling towns, unprepared for the shocking truth of the virtual obliteration of most large German cities from many hundreds of air raids and desperate final battles.

As the day wore on the accumulation of fatigue and tensions of the past weeks and the present discomfort of the primitive jour-ney began to take their toll on the refugees. The group fell silent. Some dozed uncomfortably, propped up by their bundles. The door was closed but for a crack to let in light and air.

Anton remained by the narrow opening to continue his watch. The hours grated by as the train rattled westward, jarring and swaying its huddled contents. Sometimes they were startled awake by sudden stops, then they jerkily moved forward again, the train clanking like an unwieldy iron chain. From time to time, individual boxcars were uncoupled and the shortened string of shabby wagons labored on, wrapped in a smelly shroud of steam and smoke.

Night had fallen when the train screeched to a halt in the war-ravaged railroad terminal at Frankfurt. Makeshift light bulbs, strung up in place of wrecked fixtures strained to penetrate the dusty gloom. Red Cross workers brought hot soup and bread to every car door and the travelers were helped down to use the decrepit wash rooms.

Leaden exhaustion now held them in its grip and even the children were too tired to cry. The bleak darkness magnified the sense of detachment, loneliness and drift. Feelings of loss and sor-row, always lurking in their tired minds began to gain the upper hand, spurred on by the lasting impressions of the dramatic scenes of ruin and by the gnawing uncertainty of what lay ahead. What little conversation sprang up here and there was soon stifled by fatigue and ebbed away; the refugees withdrew into themselves. They settled back into their awkward resting places, still shivering from the visit to the stark and dirty washrooms, quietly fighting their tears.

An hour later the train crawled out of the station, their final destination a transit camp just thirty miles away where they would be able to rest for the night. Anton yielded to the numbness that enveloped everyone like a heavy blanket, and he made a place for himself in the straw next to his mother. They exchanged a few whispered words of comfort.

"The Lord will provide somehow," Maria said with a feeble show of conviction, although at the moment there was nothing even remotely suggestive of hope, security and belonging. They dozed off uneasily, lulled by the pounding rhythm of the wheels.

It was late when the train applied its squealing brakes for the last time. A chill lingered in the night air, damp from a brief rainfall, and the desolate station with its dim lights and shabby, peeling walls was depressing. But they had reached the end of their journey, a destination of sorts. Again the refugees clumsily descended from the high door openings, but this time without the almost boisterous atmosphere of the first stop on the German side of the border. The Red Cross helpers on hand were tired and did their job grudgingly.

After much shouting and confusion the train was empty and the bundles were piled high on the carts and buggies. The several hundred new arrivals stumbled their way towards the camp, just a short distance from the railroad. Barely conscious of their surroundings they shuffled drowsily through the camp gate. They lost little time in formalities as everyone had been preassigned to this location. Straw-filled bunks similar to those in Eger were waiting, tightly jammed together in the former military barracks. Hot soup and milk were dished out after every person had been liberally dusted against vermin with sharp smelling DDT powder.

Well past midnight Maria and Anton sank wearily onto their straw mattresses which reeked of much prior use, but at this moment it was a welcome resting place. Too numb even to think about the discomforts of their surroundings the exhausted evacuees slept deeply, a sleep of oblivion serving to replenish their strength for the trials to come.

In the morning the camp stirred to life with loud noises and commotion. Soon a distribution of *ersatz* coffee, milk and bread was under way. The primitive washing facilities were crowded; people waited in long lines outside. Even though the rusty taps yielded only ice-cold water, the cleansing was eagerly sought by all.

Anton mused about how adept he had become at making do without comfort, although he still found it unpleasant and difficult to deal with unsanitary shabbiness. He badly wanted to wipe off the chipped wash basin before using it, but had nothing to do it with, so he quickly learned to wash under the running water without touching the bowl, mindful not to splash his shoes or clothing. He longingly thought of the past, of the abundance of hot water and clean warm towels, things he once took for granted.

A long line had already formed at the registration desk in one of the barracks and Maria and Anton joined the queue. Again Maria stated her wish to move to Schlossberg in southern Germany, explaining that it was the locale of her husband's former employers. The official shook his head firmly. "You must understand, *Frau* Wildert, that to move to any place of your own choice you must possess a valid permit from the local Registry of Persons. Since you have no such papers from Schlossberg you'll be given quarters in this area along with the others. Once you are settled here you can begin trying to obtain a permit from the Schlossberg officials, though I can assure you this will take quite a while."

Maria realized that she faced implacable regulations once again, and placing her arm around Anton's shoulders she listened to the official explaining that they had been assigned to a large farm not far from the famous wine village of Nierstein, close to the Rhine river. Two young women from their boxcar were also going there—one the mother of a baby and a small boy, the other a mother-to-be.

Maria and Anton were pleased to be with these companions in

their strange new surroundings and hurried back to their bunks to get ready to leave. The two women were housed several beds away in the same barracks. Maria went over to say how nice it was that they would be going together. They responded happily and Anton helped them to pile their belongings on their carts. He moved the loads close to the door, for they had been told to expect a cart and driver from the farm to pick them up before noon.

As they waited by the door, the young women kept up a lively chatter. "How wonderful that we're going to a farm; at least there should be milk and food for the children," said Lieselotte, the mother of two.

"There certainly should be, but the question will be whether the farmer will let us have any—you know how farmers are," responded Hannelore, the expectant mother.

During the war farmers everywhere gained increased importance, their power growing with the intensifying food shortages. As the conditions worsened they could command significant premiums in the barter trade for milk, butter, eggs, meat and poultry. Even though the Nazi regime officially frowned upon black-market dealings and often meted out harsh punishment to those who flagrantly abused the situation, barter trade flourished everywhere. City dwellers were willing to trade everything from family silver to oriental rugs and trekked to any village where the farmers were rumored to be ready to bargain. Bitter jokes circulated about farmers lining their dairy barns with Oriental rugs, and city folk resented the hold their rural neighbors had over them.

Maria broke into the conversation and said that she had grown up in a small provincial town that served an agricultural area. She thought she should help these city girls understand. "The farmers I knew were tough, down-to-earth people and very shrewd bargainers. But remember," she continued, "we've been forced onto this farmer who would prefer to have nothing to do with us. Now that they must take us in they'll want us to do our fair share of work—and then some! Everyone on a farm must pitch in and earn his keep, and I believe that if we do so, the food situation should resolve itself."

When she saw the women frown, Maria added, "Whatever we

may think of them, farmers do work long hours and labor hard—they'll expect us to do the same, whether we like it or not. For the moment we have nowhere else to turn. So let's see what the situation will be like. Right now we must be glad to have a roof over our heads."

While they talked, a rubber-tired platform cart drawn by a single mule pulled up outside. High on the driver's bench sat a thin young man barely out of his teens, dressed in simple work clothes, a visored cap lodged at an awkward angle on his tousled hair. He cracked his whip and when Anton came near said hesitantly, "*H-H-Herr* N-neum-mann s-sent me to p-pick you up." The young man climbed down from his perch and helped Anton to load the bundles. The women agreed that the pregnant Hannelore should ride next to the driver on the bench, which was cushioned by metal leaf springs. Maria, Lieselotte, and the children would sit on the bundles in the rear.

A loud crack of the whip rang out and the mule broke into a slow, reluctant shuffle, pulling the suddenly heavy cart with obvious resentment. As they rolled alongside the barracks toward the camp gate, the women waved good-bye to several fellow exiles. The mule stopped several times during the half-hour ride, each time grudgingly yielding to the rough prodding and forceful language hurled by the young driver in his lilting Rhenish accent. Occasional kicks and lashings were necessary to help convince the reluctant beast to perform its duty.

Anton looked with pleasure at the fertile rural landscape surrounding them. Tall poplars lined the roads, and shade trees dotted the fields; the flat land appeared well-tended and verdant with the bright green of late spring. But the houses and farmsteads had disappointing brown or gray exposed brick exteriors, which looked drab and uninviting to Anton, who had grown up in a region with stucco-covered houses washed in pastel shades. There was little to remind the boy of home.

The young driver pretended to be occupied with the stubborn mule. Shy and slow of thought, he reacted sparingly to the many questions his charges asked of him, but after a while he seemed to warm to the friendly strangers. Between interruptions caused by the willful animal and his repeated queries of "W-what d-did you s-say?" the group learned that the farm was a new place, one of several dozen model farms which the Nazi regime built on former public lands before the war. These homesteads were presented to a group of farmers resettled from eastern territories, where Hitler's territorial adjustments displaced them, having to give up their own family farms.

The driver's master was an elderly widower; a spinster, reputedly the man's distant relative, ran the house. Hans himself was an orphan and had lived with the farmer for many years, earning his keep by doing the daily chores. He was the only remaining helper on the farm; he had been too young to be inducted into the *Wehrmacht,* while the other two farm hands were drafted years earlier. All of this took much patience for the women to coax out of the slow-witted Hans, who turned out to be a good-natured young man, now and then even given to an occasional shy smile. He seemed cowed and more than respectful at the mention of his master and the woman of the house, and he resisted specific questions about them by shrugging silently.

The model farm area came into view. Vast fields stretched to distant green strips of forest, far larger and more uniform than the crazily checkered plots of most German farm holdings passed on and subdivided for generations. The cart's tires swished smoothly on the straight, well-maintained road and the mule, sensing it was nearly home, broke into a steady clip-clop. In the distance they saw several farm complexes emerging from the flat expanse. Each farmstead was dominated by a high, gabled three-story family residence, the red tile roofs shining in the sun. The houses looked suburban and only the low sheds and wooden barns neatly arranged around them suggested that the properties were working farms.

As the cart entered the gate in the low brick wall that enclosed the Neumann farm they all fell silent, wondering what kind of welcome awaited them. Anton looked around curiously. He saw a row of modern farm implements lined up against the inside of the wall, and through the open door of a barn more carts and tools were visible against the backdrop of a large mound of hay. Deep mooing sounds coming from another low shed suggested that it housed dairy cattle. The warm pungent odor of animals wafted in their direction.

Hans drove smartly to the main door of the residence, pulled back on the reins and growled at the mule to halt. While he turned the crank of the cart's brake the door opened and *Herr* Neumann appeared. A tall and spare man in his fifties, he stood in shirt sleeves, hands in pockets, his legs planted slightly apart in a defiant stance. His reddish face was craggy and deeply lined with age and weather. A cool breeze fanned his unruly gray hair which was thin and receding. He stolidly gazed at the women and children, his dour expression unchanging as he looked closely at each person in turn.

At last Neumann shrugged, turned away and barked a gruff order over his shoulder. "Might as well unload the lot, Hans, and show them to the two upstairs rooms!" Hans shrank visibly at hearing his master's command, and avoided looking at him directly. He climbed off his bench and helped the women and children down. Together he and Anton carried the bundles into the house, and stored the buggies and carts in the tool shed.

Inside the main house they entered a small, tiled hall, from which a wooden stairway led to the upper levels. The furnishings were solid and modern and gave the impression of utmost cleanliness. Through an open door they glimpsed a large, well-equipped kitchen, which easily accommodated a massive wooden table that could seat at least a dozen people—a reminder of normal times when family and farm hands took their daily meals together.

Near the tiled cooking stove stood a middle-aged woman in a blue cotton print dress and white apron, busying herself with pots and pans. She ignored the new arrivals. Her averted face was stern and surly, framed by grayish hair that was pulled back severely into a tight bun. Spare and tall as Neumann, *Fräulein* Hackel added no warmth to the welcome nor to the atmosphere of the house.

They climbed the stairs with Hans leading the way. On the first landing he motioned the two young women and their children into a small sunny room with a large window facing the fields, furnished simply with two beds and a crib, a table and four chairs, and a wardrobe of solid rural design, painted with a colorful flower motif. A toilet and wash basin were in a tiny enclosure that could be reached from the stairs. Pleased to find some normalcy the women began to settle in quickly.

Hans led Maria and Anton down the corridor and up another half flight of stairs to a room under the steep gabled roof, with two slanted walls and a wide window in a niche. Again the furnishings were simple but pleasant. The tiny room contained only one large bed, a small table with two chairs, and a gaily painted wardrobe.

"We don't have another room w-with two b-beds," stammered Hans, "so you w-will have to share the bed w-with your son." After a shy pause he added warmly, a faint warm smile on his lips, "I hope you w-will be all right here, *Frau*!"

After weeks in primitive camps, and after two days' travel in the smoke and dust of the boxcar it was pure bliss to be able to wash and clean up. The women took turns cleansing themselves in the spotless wash basin with the clear cold water, using coarse soap and fresh towels from their bundles. They scrubbed the children amidst loud protests. Anton was last to restore himself and he discovered that the simple joy of being clean and changing into fresh clothing made life seem worthwhile again.

The frosty welcome was momentarily forgotten.

NINETEEN

The Farm on the Rhine

The pleasures of fresh clothing and clean quarters soon gave way to the urgent practicality of obtaining nourishment. By early afternoon no one from the Neumann household had paid any attention to them. It was miles to the nearest town where they might purchase food supplies with the ration coupons and the few marks they had been given at the border stop. The women realized how dependent they were on their unwilling hosts; Maria, as the oldest, was delegated the unpleasant task of asking *Herr* Neumann for food.

She went downstairs reluctantly and approached *Fräulein* Hackel in the kitchen. "I am *Frau* Wildert. As you know we've been assigned to your farm. We have no alternative but to ask you if you could spare some food for the children and ourselves. We'll make it up to you however we can, but having just arrived we . . ."

"Well, we didn't figure on so many mouths to feed when only two or three of you can work," *Fräulein* Hackel grumbled, looking past Maria with a sour face. Ignoring Maria's hand extended in greeting, *Fräulein* Hackel twisted her own hands under her apron. For a while she stood, not sure what to do. Then she relented, "Well, I can let you have some boiled potatoes and cabbage, and some milk for the children. And here is a piece of bread."

She turned to the stove and spooned several warm potatoes from a large pot into a bowl, ladled steaming cabbage into another and poured milk into a small pitcher. "I hope you have your own dishes." Maria nodded and watched the woman carefully dole out the food, noting her hesitation to top off the bowls with a last spoonful. *Fräulein* Hackel again avoided looking at Maria when she handed her the bowls, and quickly turned away. Maria thanked her, balanced her load with care and carried the food upstairs. Halfway up the wooden steps *Fräulein* Hackel's thin, sharp voice followed her, "We need you people to work in the fields, and you had better be down here by six in the morning!"

The women cheered at the sight of Maria carrying provisions. They quickly readied the small table and everyone crowded around to eat the bland fare. The Wilderts then retreated to their own room and sank wearily onto the shared mattress that Maria had covered with sheets dug out of the bundles. The luxury of a clean bed was instant relief and they drifted into deep exhausted sleep.

The next morning around five o'clock the newcomers awoke to the sounds of the owners stirring about the house. During the night the baby cried a few times, but everyone else slept right through from the previous afternoon. They took turns using the tiny toilet and by six Maria, Anton and Lieselotte came down the stairway to be assigned their chores. Hannelore remained upstairs to look after her companion's baby and the little boy.

They found *Fräulein* Hackel bustling about her kitchen, and she barely responded to their chorus of good mornings. On the stove was a fragrant pot of steaming *ersatz* coffee and on the table lay slabs of coarse dark bread and large glasses of milk. Neumann and Hans joined them and they ate in frosty silence.

Anton took some food upstairs to Hannelore and the children, and Hans left to bring the mule cart to the front door. Neumann seated himself next to Hans on the driver's bench. Anton and the women climbed onto the cart's platform.

In the dewy cool of the morning they headed for one of the outlying fields about a mile away. They scrambled off the cart and Neumann instructed the new farm workers in the fine art of thinning out the young beet plants that were pushing through the sandy soil in neat green rows. He did not waste words and towered over the stooped figures, watching hawk-like as they started at the edge of the vast field, wielding small triangular blades, each one taking three rows. They were shown how to pull out the weaker plants from each clump, leaving the strongest, and then to weed and loosen the soil around the remaining shoots.

Anton had never done anything like it and was clumsy with the delicate shoots, trying to decide which ones to pull. Neumann watched him impatiently, barking that he better learn the difference between weeds and the real thing quickly, and, for God's sake, not to damage the shoots. Lieselotte, who worked next to him had similar difficulties; a city dweller like Anton, she was totally unfamiliar with the tender greenery. But once Neumann left with Hans—having growled a final admonition—Lieselotte's bubbly character resurfaced and she joked about their mistakes, making light of the dreary work.

Even this early the fine June day promised to be warm, and the moist breeze from the Rhine was more humid than refreshing. An hour went by and the progress of the fledgling farm workers was agonizingly slow. They had barely moved from the edge of the field, and when they looked ahead they could see nothing but an endless expanse of little green plants. They continued doggedly and soon their backs and knees were hurting badly from the unaccustomed stooping. As the sun arched toward midday the clammy heat became difficult to bear. They took frequent rests, gradually easing their way down the vast field.

At noon Hans appeared with his mule cart and delivered a basket containing a thermos of *ersatz* coffee, a jug of milk, and pieces of coarse bread. They ate greedily and afterwards the trio collapsed under a nearby tree. The steady exertion began to take its toll, every muscle straining for a rest. For a delicious half-hour they stretched out on a shady patch of grass, listening to the hum of bees and the rustling of leaves in the breeze. Anton daydreamed of the more carefree times in his childhood when he delighted in rolling over and over in the fragrant grass of sloping meadows in the gentle valleys of the picturesque Elbe region.

The long hot afternoon limped along. By evening the three had made considerable progress down the field, although they left numerous casualties among the young plants. They worried that this would not escape Neumann's attention when he came to inspect their work. At last Hans drove up with the cart to take them back and they stretched out flat on the hard wood platform. Despite the bumpy ride they were practically asleep when they arrived at the farm. Weary and grimy they staggered into the house and cleaned themselves as best they could. The refugee bundles contained little clothing that was suitable for the sweaty, dusty labors. The women decided that at the next opportunity they would ask Neumann to lend them some work clothes.

A simple meal was waiting for them in the kitchen, the familiar potatoes, cabbage and milk. Desperately tired, they carried the food to their rooms, ate quickly, and fell into bed. Neumann and *Fräulein* Hackel maintained their cold, resentful attitudes and the restful recuperative sleep of the first night eluded the workers. They slept fitfully, plagued by the awkwardness of their situation.

Roused again at five they repeated the tedious routine for the second day. Lieselotte chuckled wryly that at least they were learning a great deal about thinning beet plants, but even her brave attempts at humor could not suppress their growing frustration and depression. Maria's back throbbed with pulsating, jabbing pain. Gritting her teeth she tried to keep up her spirits with light-hearted chatter, but her bravery faded as the pain became worse and the sweltering heat sapped her strength.

Summery clouds billowed high in the sky, and in the early afternoon a light rain fell, cooling the air. But it also soaked the forlorn laborers in the field and brought new worries about damage to their clothes. That evening they sank into bed, even more despondent.

On the fourth day Anton felt giddy and faint when he got up, but stoically he went out into the field with the others. When the temperature began to rise in mid-morning, he became dizzy. The ground swayed and revolved around him and he slumped down in the middle of the field. Maria cried out when she saw him fall over and the two women dragged the limp boy to the grass under a shade tree. Maria damped her handkerchief from the water bottle and wiped Anton's flushed face. She poured some water over his forehead and was relieved when he came to and drank thirstily. He lay there weakly and since Hans would not be coming for another hour, the women took turns watching over him while the other worked on in the field.

When Hans arrived they lifted Anton onto the cart and Maria

rode along back to the house. A visibly angry *Fräulein* Hackel appeared at the door when the cart drew up, irritated that two of the field hands returned so early in the day. While Hans helped Anton climb the stairs, Maria insisted that a doctor be fetched to have a look at her son. Grim-faced, *Fräulein* Hackel shrugged and told Maria coldly there was a telephone in the neighboring farm house. She could walk there and call the doctor, if that was really necessary.

Two hours later the doctor arrived and examined Anton carefully. As he folded his stethoscope he looked warmly at Maria and said in a reassuring tone, "*Frau* Wildert, there is nothing organically wrong with the boy. But he is suffering from basic malnutrition and heat exhaustion. I also suspect he has a somewhat enlarged heart due to rapid growth while on a substandard diet. He must stay in bed for several days, drink plenty of warm milk and have some nourishing food. I will speak to *Fräulein* Hackel about it. Here is some medication to steady his heart." The kindly man left after promising to look in again within the week.

Maria sobbed with despair. The experience of the last few days drained what small reserves of energy she possessed and she was weary. She knew she must try every way to remove them both from their present predicament—they could not survive on the farm, even for a short time. She resolved to make the trip to Schlossberg to seek out the owners of Friedrich's company and explore the chance that they might help her to become established there.

After a restless night she readied herself to go into town; over breakfast she informed Neumann that she must look into moving to another area. He responded with a shrug and icy silence. When she asked if Hans could take her to town in the cart, he barked that Hans was too busy and she certainly looked well enough to walk for an hour. Maria left the table to tell the sleepy Anton what she had decided, taking him an extra piece of bread just in case the owners did not bother to feed the boy. She asked Hannelore to look in on him whenever she could.

She set out along the country road and, preoccupied with uncertainty and worry, she noticed little of the beauty of the fields and forests, sunlit in vibrant shades of green and alive with the songs of birds. After half an hour a horse-drawn milk wagon overtook her and stopped. The driver, a jolly craggy-faced man with a jaunty cap on his white hair offered her a seat. She accepted gladly and sat high on the bench, watching the sturdy brown beasts, their muscular backs rippling and shining in the sun. The ride reminded her of her youth and her father's sporty coach and horses she had loved so much. She relaxed and gazed at the swirling morning mists in the thickets, listening to the friendly chatter of the man, his sing-song dialect pleasant to her ears.

In the center of the town the sight of stores and row houses brought welcome relief from the isolation of the remote farmhouse. The driver helped her down near the city hall, which housed the Registry Office that dealt with residence permits. A line of people already waited; joining them Maria overheard snatches of conversation. The obvious similarity of worries and concerns comforted her in her lonely quest.

When her turn came she showed her papers to the official, explained her situation, and asked his advice on how to obtain a residence permit in another town. The graying, shriveled bureaucrat answered civilly and even with some interest. He pointed out that there was very little he could do to speed up the process other than have Maria fill out a form requesting a transfer of residence to the town of Schlossberg. He was prepared to send the form through the official mail to his colleagues in Schlossberg, but urged her strongly to follow up in person by traveling there after a few days, to state her case directly to the local officials. "You'll have to establish a valid connection to Schlossberg, *Frau* Wildert," he said, "perhaps the owners of your late husband's firm might be willing to do this for you? By the way, I must warn you that train travel will be very difficult; the few trains running are mobbed all the time."

Maria nodded appreciatively and gave him all the particulars for the form which the man promised to send to Schlossberg immediately. He gave her a signed copy, stamped liberally with official seals. He also handed her a stamped certificate, the required permit for long-distance rail travel. Buoyed by this tenuous hope Maria walked over to the railway station to inquire about connections to Schlossberg. After standing in line for an hour she was told the trip involved a change of trains at Frankfurt and also at a small southern town on the Danube. The round trip fare made a sizable dent in her cash reserves, but she purchased the ticket, handing over her travel permit.

She strolled through the town center which, though it escaped much of the war damage, looked bleak and uninviting. Most of the stores were shuttered, while the few open ones were dreary and poorly stocked. With ration coupons she bought four ounces of butter, a piece of colorless sausage, and a loaf of crusty grayish bread. Then she began her trek back to the farm, looking forward to Anton's delight at feasting on these rarities.

Again she was offered a ride, this time by a woman driving a horse-drawn wagon piled high with fragrant hay. Maria's heart leaped at the sight—in her family it was an old superstition that a load of hay going in the same direction was a sure sign of good luck. Happily she pulled out a tuft and rolled it into her handkerchief to carry home as a token of good fortune. The woman was friendly and chatty, and she took Maria to within five minutes' walk of the farm.

She arrived at the house in the early afternoon, greeted by glum stares from *Fräulein* Hackel. She climbed the stairs quickly and found Anton weak but improved; the rest had done him good. Lieselotte had managed to wangle some food for them, and they heated the soup on a small electric hotplate. Maria unwrapped her purchases and everyone enjoyed a buttered piece of bread and a slice of sausage. Anton was excited about Maria's news and savored the hope that they would be able to get away soon.

The next day was a Saturday. The morning was taken up with farm chores beginning at the regular early hour; in the afternoon the refugee women sat together, cleaning and mending clothes and discussing their situation. Maria's plans gave rise to much wistful speculation. The young women could think of no alternatives for themselves as they had neither relatives nor connections anywhere in Germany. Their main hope lay in finding their husbands who they thought were still being held in Russian prisoner of war camps. They resolved to call periodically at the local Red Cross office which provided an information exchange. Life for these young families would not have any real basis until they found their men.

The talk turned to the shabby treatment they received at the Neumann farm. Their presence was much resented, which was understandable—but after all, they were willing to work for their keep as much as they could, and the rooms they occupied had been assigned by the authorities. The continuous hostility depressed them, and so did the miserable diet.

Hannelore confided that while remaining in the house with the children she had seen and smelled the preparation of far better food *Fräulein* Hackel often cooked for Neumann, Hans and herself. They took such meals at different times. Grinning mischievously she added that she had spotted a barrel of salt pork in a lower passageway of the house. In view of the hard manual work that at least two in the group were doing, she suggested slyly it would not be unethical to appropriate a piece of the meat, given a chance. They could cook it secretly on their hotplate, taking care to dissipate the smells through the window.

At first the others hesitated, but then everyone agreed to the scheme. They hatched a plan for one of them to take a chunk of meat out of the barrel and hide it under the staircase, while another would sneak it upstairs into the room, thereby sharing the responsibility for the deed. Hannelore, the discoverer of the barrel, volunteered to get the meat, and Maria agreed to smuggle the booty upstairs. They decided to do it the following day, during Neumann's midday nap when all was quiet.

Shortly after one o'clock Maria heard a knock on her door, and Hannelore whispered from outside that the meat was ready to be picked up. Maria tiptoed downstairs, her throat dry with worry at the thought of stealing and getting caught. The house was still except for the distant lowing of the cattle, and the hall and kitchen appeared deserted. She spotted the prize under the staircase, wrapped in a piece of cloth—all too visible for comfort. For a moment she wished Hannelore had brought it all the way, but they had agreed to split the task and share the risk, hadn't they? Taking a deep breath she seized the heavy chunk and held it tightly under a towel draped over her arm.

Aching with tension she climbed the stairs as quietly as she could, but in her haste the door almost slammed shut behind her. Had she been heard? She had to lean against the inside of the door for a few moments to regain her calm. The deed was done. Happily the women prepared the meat, testing that the wind indeed carried away the cooking odors. They feasted that evening despite the tough texture of the almost tasteless pork.

During the next several days Anton regained much of his strength, while the women continued working in the fields or helped around the farmyard and with the animals. *Fräulein* Hackel guarded her kitchen jealously, allowing no one near her food stores or to assist her in the preparation of meals. One day the barrel of salt pork was gone from the passage. Had the owners found out about the Sunday caper, or did they suddenly realize the precious food was exposed?

On Friday, Maria and Anton made their way into town together to inquire at the Registry Office about the progress of their petition. The day was gray and overcast, and the low clouds heavy with rain. This time there was no one to offer a ride, and it took them well over an hour to reach the town. After queuing up they came upon the graying bureaucrat who remembered Maria. No word had yet come back from Schlossberg, but again he strongly advised her to go there herself as soon as possible. She told him she would make the trip on the following Monday, and he gave her several helpful suggestions.

They left the cramped office which was littered with musty file binders and piles of paper. When they emerged from the old city hall the dark skies released a cold drizzle. In the misty rain the town square with its raw brick houses looked even shabbier than before. They unfolded the old umbrella they brought along and picked their way around the puddles. After the hot weather of the past weeks the raw dampness chilled them to the bone. They walked forlornly, the moisture penetrating their shoes and clothes.

Suddenly they came face to face with a woman of short and ample stature, stylishly dressed in a white coat and hat, an apparition totally incongruous with the dreary setting. A shock of recognition flashed through Maria as the woman in white shrieked with disbelief. "Maria! For God's sake, what are you doing here?"

"Margot! I can't believe it, meeting you in this place, after all these years, it can't be true!" Maria stood wide-eyed, trembling with joy.

Margot stared at the boy in disbelief and shouted, "Anton, my dear little Anton, how you have grown!"

The women fell into each others' arms, clasping and hugging each other with moist, shining eyes. Pulling apart, they viewed each other again, one looking as well as ever, the other gaunt and marked by suffering. Anton merely stood by, too surprised to react. After more embraces and joyous tears Maria told Margot in rapid bursts the events that had overtaken the Wildert family. Her long-time friend listened with choked attention, shaking her head, unable to fully grasp the tale of death and upheaval.

Margot and her professor husband were close friends of the Wilderts for many years before and during the war. Margot was Hungarian, vivacious and sensual, and gifted with a quick, business-like mind. Her endearing accent and convoluted German always caused many hilarious moments for her wide circle of friends. The Wildert boys enjoyed her like a bubbly "aunt" who radiated love and excitement, and they secretly envied her only son, Karl, a little older than Johann, for his smooth and sophisticated manners, although the brothers thought him excessively polite.

During the last years of the war the Wilderts lost touch with the couple, who faded away and broke off all contact. As it turned out, they were forced to go into hiding when Nazi officials ferreted out some distant Jewish relations in Margot's family. The Wilderts often wondered what had become of their good friends, but were unable to get any news.

The chance meeting in the main street of the drab Rhenish town seemed nothing short of miraculous. Margot noticed

Maria's and Anton's pale faces and thin figures and, clucking like a mother hen, insisted that they accompany her to the small apartment nearby, where, as she put it, she lived with "her men." On the way she explained that she had spent several months in a tough Gestapo detention camp, but survived without serious harm, and that her husband and son were well. "Believe it or not," she said, "I now work for the Allied military government. My job is with a claims office to help Nazi victims register for compensation and also to give them basic support." Margot flashed her wide smile. "My English is good enough to do this, and I have many advantages from this position. Ever since the Americans came we've done well."

Maria listened while she recalled her friend's practical shrewdness with a tinge of envy—Margot would always fall on her feet!

Ferdinand and young Karl were at home and much greeting, shouting and excited babble ensued. Margot insisted the Wilderts take hot baths—a luxury they had not had since Eger—and bustled about to prepare a hearty dinner from ample food supplies that included a variety of American cans and packages. Chirping away happily Margot created the meal with quick and capable hands, and recounted the many hospitable occasions in the Wildert villa where she and "her men" had been welcomed like members of the large family.

She reminisced fondly about the long evenings of music and card games, Maria at the piano singing favorite melodies from opera and popular entertainment, accompanied by Friedrich. It was a time of warmth and friendship terminated only due to the growing stresses of war and the heavy hand of the Nazi regime.

"I still can't believe we're sitting here in this strange town, far removed from everything we loved, talking about those times," Maria exclaimed, seated in a comfortable arm chair, "what an incredible coincidence!"

"And to meet just like that on a rainy street—it was meant to be," Margot called out from the kitchenette which by now exuded the wonderful aroma of tasty food bubbling and simmering.

Seated around the dinner table they savored the splendid meal and engaged in a lively discussion about Maria's next step. "You must make the trip to Schlossberg—it's clearly the most important move you can make." Margot was emphatic. "Let me assure you—I have much experience in this—only a personal appearance can get the bureaucracy to move!" With much regret she added, "Unfortunately I can't help you in this mission because I am limited to assisting direct victims of the Nazi regime."

"You can't stay on the farm even a day longer than necessary—it is absolutely futile, and even dangerous because of your and dear Anton's delicate health," she continued. Margot and Ferdinand encouraged Maria to make the trip on Monday, leaving Anton behind on the farm with their belongings. They should move to Schlossberg as soon as the papers were in order. Margot offered to put them up for the night even though the small apartment would be heavily crowded.

"I can't put you through such trouble," Maria declined warmly, "you have already shown us so much kindness. It will be better for us to return to the farm and deal with Neumann to the end. Just knowing that you are near is wonderful for me."

The weather cleared and there was still light in the evening sky when Maria and Anton left to walk back to the farm. Margot and her family accompanied them for half the distance and the time passed quickly with talk of past memories, the joys, hurts, humor and sadness. For the first time in a year Maria was buoyed by the chance to converse and share her feelings with a kindred spirit. Fate had severed the myriad of crucial bonds that weave the social fabric and channel the ebb and flow of emotional exchange; Maria's forced isolation caused her to be cautious and restrain her emotions. Sharing thoughts with strangers undergoing similar stresses focused on matters of survival. She found that such tentative bonds were not strong enough to give her the kind of emotional sustenance that real friendship and familiarity provided. Now she was surprised by the animation she felt in the company of her old friends, and she was able to talk of the past, of shared experiences, and even of Friedrich and Johann without the choking emotions that haunted her in her lonely state. She felt refreshed and strengthened by Margot's loving, bustling energy and by her husband's calm stability and quiet understanding.

Anton also relished the hours of renewed companionship and warmth with Margot and her family. With Karl, who was four years older, he talked about the happy times when the boys had played together at the Wildert villa. The unexpected interlude temporarily blotted out his sense of feeling adrift in an alien world. He listened to the grownups recounting their experiences, while he relived his memories as sharp pictures. Yet these memories felt like someone else's recollections, lovely and desirable. They seemed to him as if he were observing a play from a distance, a happy sequence of scenes on a theater stage. These pleasant experiences, once a gentle flow of normal human interactions, had been cruelly interrupted and excised from his own life.

When they said good-bye in the dusky fields, Anton felt harsh pangs of separation from this brief reminder of a happier past. For the remaining distance to the farm the boy was subdued as he walked with his mother. He was anxious to hold back his surging feelings, for he sensed that Maria was fighting a similar battle with her own stirred emotions. It was quite dark now, and during the final minutes of their walk each felt depressed and alone, enveloped in their own thoughts. At the farmhouse they climbed the stairs without encountering either of the surly owners and settled down for the night.

In the morning both helped with the farm chores, but since it was Saturday they could rest in the afternoon. At dinner time Maria went to the kitchen to inform Neumann that she would go south to Bavaria on Monday for three or four days, and that Anton would stay behind to help with the work as best he could.

Neumann's reply was a frosty shrug.

TWENTY

The Schlossberg Connection

On the day of her trip to Schlossberg Maria awoke at an early hour, put on her clothes and wrapped up some bread and a thermos of warm milk. Food would be impossible to obtain during the train ride with the current food shortages and widespread confusion. She took the personal papers she and Anton saved from the villa, seemingly a lifetime ago, and packed them with a change of clothes in a small canvas bag that was easy to carry.

After a tearful good-bye to Anton she left the farmhouse and walked along the country road to town to catch the morning train to Frankfurt. In earlier times the rail journey would have been pleasant, even though it took the better part of a day because there were two train changes involved, but now she did not look forward to the overcrowding and likely delays.

Anton watched his mother disappear in the expanse of fields, her walk brisk and determined. She looked back a few times to wave and he had waved in return. He was haunted by the primitive terror that now gripped him whenever they were separated, even if only for hours; it was a tormenting fear of losing the last person close to him. Anton tried to shake off the gloomy foreboding by telling himself again and again that his mother would be gone for only three or four days, but then he pictured her traveling alone in the war-torn country, among the bleak scenes of disruption he had seen from the boxcar. What kind of risks would she encounter and how would she manage? He felt scared and very alone.

Maria arrived at the local railroad station in good time for her train, which pulled in only five minutes late. A large crowd awaited its arrival and shoved aggressively toward the doors, but everyone managed to struggle aboard. The train began moving while the fight over seats still raged in the compartments. Maria wound up standing with many others, hemmed in between bags, bundles, and suitcases piled high in the corridor of the filthy railway car. From time to time she had to flatten herself against the wall when someone squeezed by her in the narrow space.

The trip was mercifully brief, however, and soon she saw through the cracked, dirt-encrusted window that the train slowly snaked its way into the main terminal at Frankfurt. With much effort she wriggled and scrambled down to the platform, and after several attempts to get directions from uncaring railroad personnel she found the platform for the Munich train.

A huge crowd was gathered, laden with bundles, bags and cases of all sizes and descriptions. Many people had been there for hours and lounged on their belongings, sullen and tired. There was a sharp stench of cheap tobacco from re-rolled cigarette butts, mixed with the odor of perspiration and soiled clothes. Maria positioned herself on the far side of the multitude, hoping that she would be lucky enough to be near one of the doors when the train pulled in. The throng was silent and dispirited; people stared blankly ahead, occasionally craning their heads to see if the train was approaching. Maria knew that once it did come the crowd would turn into a mob, relentlessly fighting with elbows and feet to gain even the smallest advantage. They were like a huge spring coiled for sudden release, ready to slash and sweep aside any obstacle in its way. Years of war and the dreary aftermath hardened everyone's survival instincts and reactions. The thin veneer of human decency had worn through long ago.

Time stretched in tiresome inactivity. While she stood in the bleak and noisy ruin of the station, Maria focused her mind on the task of approaching the owners of Friedrich's company and the town officials at Schlossberg. As had become her habit, she began to compose mentally the points and statements she would make to them, and tried to prepare herself for negative reactions and obstacles that might be put in her way. Lost in her thoughts she barely noticed the arriving train, although the crowd had begun to stir.

Slowly the heavy locomotive hissed and shuddered past her, trailing steam and oily water, followed by the tender and the first cars. Everyone on the platform was poised to storm the doors. When they realized the train was moving farther than expected in Maria's direction, the solid, implacable mass of people pursued it and began shoving and pushing towards her. The crowd surrounded Maria, swept her up with the surge of bodies and lifted her off her feet. Elbows gouged her sides and the hard edges of suitcases chafed her legs. Angry shouts filled the air as she struggled vainly for a footing. Maria was jammed against the moving side of the nearest carriage and suddenly lost her balance. Trying to claw for a hold on the sliding surface, she screamed with terror when she plunged into the narrow gap between the platform and the moving train.

In falling she instinctively pulled her arms tightly against her body. Her feet struck the oily gravel and rail ties, and she tumbled sideways against the concrete wall of the pit. A single, elemental thought suffused her: she must avoid being run over. Instinctively she arched her bruised body and arms away from the steel rail beside her and flattened herself against the grimy concrete wall. Terrified, she held her breath as the huge iron wheel came toward her, inexorable, like a silent executioner, gliding within inches past her rigid body and finally her face. Then she passed out.

At the sight of Maria's plunge below the platform the crowd reared back in horror. The wall of people ebbed away with the same relentless energy that forced it to push forward only moments earlier. The area beside the carriage was suddenly abandoned—no one dared step to the edge of the platform to see the mangled body below. After a few seconds a young man dressed in the shabby remains of a soldier's uniform dashed forward and dropped to his knees to peer into the opening. He called out joyfully, "She is all right, she is all right!"

A conductor pushed his way through the crowd and together the two men jumped into the pit and lifted Maria out. Half conscious and white with shock she kept groping to touch her arms and legs, reassuring herself that she had not been run over. Her body and back throbbed with pain from the fall, and her overcoat and stockings were torn. The canvas bag sat forlorn where the retreating crowd stood before Maria's fall. A brief cheer went up.

While Maria was trying to recover with the conductor's help, the mob resumed shoving and elbowing onto the train, preoccupied with the fight for space. The conductor stayed with her, asking repeatedly if she was well enough to go on. Maria, nodding faintly, turned to board the train herself, only to find that the crowd was stuffed into every nook and cranny inside. Some latecomers still tried to wriggle into the open doors and the corridors already jammed with people and baggage.

The conductor shrugged helplessly. "It doesn't look like you will be able to get on this train—they won't budge for you or anyone else!"

A window near them slid open and the young soldier who had helped Maria stuck out his head. "*Frau, Frau,* I've got a seat for you in this compartment, come quickly!"

The conductor hesitated for a second, then said hurriedly, "The only way you'll get in is through the window! I'll lift you up so he can pull you in!" He handed Maria's bag to the soldier, then interlaced the fingers of his hands, palms up, forming a step. "Here, *Frau,* put your foot on my hands and I'll boost you up!" The burly man stooped to let Maria step into his cradled hands, then straightened up while leaning against the side of the railway car. With a strong push he lifted her high enough for the soldier to grasp her arms, then pushed her by the legs until she cleared the window. Maria half fell into the crowded compartment and was met by the unconcerned stares of people seated on both sides.

The soldier grinned happily. "Thank goodness you are all right, *Frau,* and here is a seat for you!" But when he turned around he saw that another woman had taken it. She sat stone-faced, wordlessly ignoring his pleas to give up the seat for Maria. Her set jaw bristled defiantly.

Maria and the soldier stood helpless for a moment. Then a gaunt middle-aged man with a patch over one eye and his empty sleeve carefully tucked into the pocket of his old uniform jacket slowly got to his feet. Leaning painfully on his cane he said quietly but firmly, "You may have my seat."

Maria hesitated for a moment, but then slumped gratefully into the worn cushions. She felt faint and dizzy and struggled to recover her senses, oblivious to the strangers around her. The young soldier saluted the man smartly, suspecting an ex-officer although the shabby uniform remnants gave no clue. Together they inched into the jammed corridor to find space to stand during the journey. Outside new throngs gathered to storm the next train.

Maria gradually became aware of the unpleasant sights, sounds and odors of the oppressively crowded compartment. Stoic silence prevailed in the cramped cubicle; the stale air smelled strongly of dust, smoke and perspiration. The overhead luggage racks were piled high with a melange of belongings, while bundles and cases covered the floor between the legs of the travelers. No one spoke, but a few passengers stared curiously at Maria. Repeatedly she wiped her hot face with her handkerchief.

Well past its scheduled departure time the train clanked into sudden motion with a rough forward jerk. Maria, facing the direction of travel sat bent over, her head propped up on her palms. The abrupt lurch sent a heavy piece of luggage tumbling down from the opposite rack. It struck a painful glancing blow to her head before crashing into the bundles on the floor.

Startled and hurt Maria reared back, no longer able to stem her tears. The grim-faced owner of the suitcase jumped up to place it more securely, ignoring Maria entirely.

One of the women looked at her with a touch of compassion. "Isn't it a shame, first she falls under the train and now this—some people just seem to be unlucky!" She pulled a thermos from her carrying bag and offered Maria a sip of hot tea. Another woman produced a bottle of drinking water and poured some on her handkerchief so that she could cool the swelling bruise on her forehead.

Maria wiped her face and eyes with the soothing damp cloth and then held it against her wrists to slow her pounding pulse. Her thoughts swirled in hopeless confusion now that the numbing effect of the initial shock had worn off. She closed her eyes and leaned back, trying to shut out the images bombarding her senses.

Gradually the train gathered speed, screeching and bouncing around the curves. At last Maria succumbed to the hypnotic rhythm of the wheels, swaying with the motion and drifting into an uneasy sleep. At several stations along the way the clamor of the unruly crowds reminded Maria of her close call at Frankfurt. Some of the passengers in her compartment left after much wriggling and extraction of limbs and belongings from the packed space.

The gentlemanly ex-officer returned and sat across from her, while her young rescuer departed at one of the stations. When her time to change trains neared, the man offered to hand her the bag through the window so that it would be easier to squeeze her way out of the carriage. The train began to slow and Maria twisted and pushed herself through the jammed corridor. Stepping onto the platform she gratefully gulped the fresh air. Her companion lowered the bag to her and then saluted her with his only arm.

Maria had half an hour's wait until the local train was to leave for Schlossberg. She found a place to sit on one of the dilapidated benches in the provincial depot. Mechanically she pulled the piece of bread and the thermos from her bag. She was not really hungry, but instinctively she knew she must provide some nourishment for her stressed nerves. She felt terribly alone; the pains in her bruised body compounded her unhappy emotions. The childhood phrase "As the Lord wills—I hold still," echoed in her mind like a self-hypnotic suggestion.

As she sat, images of the accident began to stalk her, circling and mocking like evil spirits. Again and again the huge wheel glided past her, steady and unstoppable. She descended repeatedly into the pit in a slow surrealistic tumble that seemed to last forever. Then she saw herself lying on the oily gravel, straining away from the cold hard steel and crushing death.

Maria covered her eyes, shaking with sobs. She thought of Friedrich and Johann and became convinced that they watched over and protected her. For a moment she yielded to the luring thought that her death would have brought the peaceful release from daily torment, the endless struggle for survival over, and she would feel the joy of being reunited with Friedrich and Johann. But then Anton's image emerged, waiting for her at the farm, and she wondered what he would do and how he could cope if she did not return. She told herself that she must go on for Anton's sake; she had survived several tragedies already, and perhaps her escape was meant as a sign for her to live.

Slowly she ate her bread and drank the warm milk from the thermos that somehow survived the buffeting and hazards of the day. The food strengthened her. After a while her practical sense returned and she examined the damage done to her clothes. She was pleased to find that she could clean the stains and repair the tears in her overcoat. She fiddled with one of the torn seams for a few minutes and rubbed out the worst of the dirt spots with her wet handkerchief. At last she rose to join the small crowd waiting for the local train to Schlossberg. It was late afternoon, the air was balmy, and Maria began to hope that her difficult journey would prove successful after all. With mounting confidence she resolved to face the local bureaucrats tomorrow and fight hard for a residence permit.

The short train pulled in half an hour late and Maria boarded without difficulty. She found a seat in a shabby carriage, an especially ancient version of the aging equipment still running on the decimated *Reichsbahn*.[1] Tired but pleased to be moving again she noticed that every compartment had doors to the outside on both sides, and stepping boards ran along the whole length of the coach. With relief she leaned back on the wooden bench.

She glimpsed the tiny, pleasant villages of the Danube valley through the dirty window, recognized the characteristic onion-shaped church steeples and the houses built in the cheerful wood and stucco architecture of southern Germany. Before long the train ground to a halt at the tiny Schlossberg station, and with immense care Maria stepped down from the running board high above the dirt pavement. Clutching her canvas bag she went to the station house and inquired about accommodations in town.

---

[1] German National Railway System

She was told the hotel *Zur Donau* might have a room available. It was only a ten minute walk from the station.

Slowly making her way toward the town's center, Maria observed only minor war damage to some of the pleasant bungalows and apartment houses along the tree-lined street. The old part of the town came into view, crowned by a Baroque castle high on a hill, surrounded by medieval houses and churches and encircled by remnants of the ancient fortified wall. She continued on to the more modern lower town, spread at the foot of the rise and flanking the Danube. The river was narrow where the hill dropped in a steep bluff, the rushing green waters foaming over the jumbled remnants of the stone bridge that once arched over the river in peaceful times.

The main street in this section of Schlossberg had a solid feeling; it was lined with shops and residential houses, and expanded into inviting green areas shaded by ancient chestnut trees. The curving side streets revealed many rural touches, including walled-in farmyards and workshops engulfed by the gradual growth of this regional trading center and former seat of minor nobility.

At last Maria stood before the hotel *Zur Donau*, a modern three-story structure next to a movie house bearing the same name. The river esplanade was only a few dozen yards away, and she could hear the roar of the water forcing its way through the ruins of the destroyed bridge. Maria rang the bell at the desk and a shrewd, wiry woman of indeterminate age responded. Maria asked her about a room for two or three nights. The woman gave the visitor an inquisitive look and requested her identification papers. Maria told her the purpose of her stay and added that her late husband had been in charge of one of the companies owned by the vonEckenbach family.

The woman's face brightened. "So you know the vonEckenbachs!" She became talkative and volunteered, "You'll find that quite a few former managers of the vonEckenbach companies have come here. I am sure you'll meet old acquaintances. Also, we have many Sudeten refugees in our town already. Some are even officials in city hall!" Maria thought she detected a tone of resentment in the woman's voice.

After a lengthy search in her tattered reservation book the owner announced Maria could have a small room for three nights, payable in advance. The woman continued her chatter while Maria signed the register and counted out the money. She mentioned that the Sudeten commissioner in charge of refugee affairs was recently made a city supervisor. His name was Kastner and he came from Aussig—did she by any chance know him?

Maria could hardly contain her surprise. Kastner had been the sales manager for Friedrich's company, a coarse, street-wise, and ambitious man with a nimble mind who had weathered the war cleverly. He was one of the few of Friedrich's associates able to stay on the job almost until the end of the hostilities before he was drafted for a brief stint with the *Wehrmacht*. Maria knew him sufficiently well; she was always wary of his energetic machinations, including his spurts of black-market dealings that were dangerous—and profitable—during the waning years of the Nazi regime. He had been a difficult man to manage because he was eager to take advantage of Friedrich's declining health and energy.

Images of the past crowded her as she stood by the desk, holding the room key in her hand and pondering the news of finding many of her husband's former associates in this small town, all trying to establish a new existence. How would they react to her coming? But then she remembered the reasons that spurred her on: Anton's precarious health, the farm by the Rhine and the hopeless situation there.

She climbed the stairs to the spartan but adequate room and washed away the grime of the long journey in the large porcelain bowl on the dresser. When she touched her bruises, the image of the pit and the iron wheel flashed in her mind, but she pushed these thoughts aside, unwilling to dwell on her narrow escape. For a while she sat up in the narrow bed and concentrated on mending her clothes by the dim light of the single bulb. Eventually fatigue overtook her and she drifted into sleep, dimly conscious of the soothing sound of the river's rushing waters.

The next morning the sky was overcast. Her window overlooked the narrow street which widened into a cobbled expanse sloping toward the river bank, a pleasant tree-lined promenade with stone benches and ornamental cast iron railings.

When she dressed the bruises still hurt and her back ached. She said a quiet prayer of thanks for her rescue and asked for guidance in the confrontations to come. After a breakfast of *ersatz* coffee and a stale rye roll—exchanged for a ration coupon—she inquired at the desk about directions to the Refugee Office and the City Registry.

Maria had considered her difficult situation at length. She was realistic enough to understand that the numerous claims and demands now placed on the owners of the once vast industrial concern would probably exceed their diminished ability to assist their former employees. She remembered Friedrich telling her that the small Schlossberg operation was an almost insignificant adjunct to the extensive vonEckenbach holdings in eastern Germany and Austria, facilities that were most likely destroyed or confiscated.

Years ago the industrialists built a lovely summer estate above the river valley which Friedrich visited occasionally on business. Maria presumed that the members of the large vonEckenbach family had come there from all directions to take refuge.

To approach the head of the family at this point was probably premature, and she thought that a first meeting with Kastner made more sense. Given his position and apparent influence in this town she would ask his advice and help, despite her instinctive dislike of the aggressive man. If he was willing to assist her with a residence permit all else could wait until she and Anton were safely in Schlossberg. She walked with resolve to the shabby baroque building which housed Kastner's Office of Refugee Affairs. Her apprehension grew with every step, but she reassured herself that at least she would be dealing with a known entity—the man's character was no mystery to her.

There was already a long queue formed in the dim hall. Maria patiently awaited her turn, summoned all her courage and knocked. Hearing an officious "come in," her heart pounded when she opened the door to the dingy office. She immediately recognized Kastner's features, though he looked older and thinner than the last time she saw him.

The commissioner jumped to his feet, unable to conceal his surprise. Maria extended her hand in greeting, trying to bridge the awkwardness of a former employee's authority over her. Kastner was quick to gather his wits and broke into the familiar wide grin that made his small eyes squint. "Well, well, *Frau* Wildert," he chuckled, choosing to address her without the formal courtesy of her husband's title, "sooner or later we all do get here, don't we? A lot of people from Aussig are here already, and we're all trying our best to get by."

His expression became somber. "I'm sorry about *Herr* Wildert," he continued, again employing the untitled form of address he would never have dared to use were Friedrich still alive. "We heard about his untimely death, and also about young Johann." He paused awkwardly. "But life must go on. I'm taking care of a lot of people who depend on me, and I'm the official head of the Aussig contingent. Everybody had better understand that!" His voice was suddenly not so welcoming and he paused again for emphasis. "If anyone tries to say anything against me or tries to put obstacles in my path, they'll regret it!" Kastner flushed, displaying the fierce temperament he always found difficult to control.

Maria stood in silence, looking firmly into the menacing eyes. An uneasy minute passed.

At last Kastner recovered enough to offer a seat to the widow of his former superior. Maria struggled to understand the meaning of his combative words; certainly she had no intention of hindering the man—or did he have some reason to think she might? She decided to ignore the outburst and calmly stated the purpose of her visit. She requested his personal assistance in obtaining residence permits for Anton and herself.

The wily man averted his eyes and began a long discourse on administrative difficulties and the overcrowded conditions in the town. Maria listened for a while, but then her patience gave out. "*Herr* Kastner, you know very well my husband's position and the distinguished service he gave to the vonEckenbachs for more than two decades. If there is anyone that can legitimately claim to come to this town it is my husband's family, at least what is left of it. With your current responsibilities you must certainly know how to cut red tape! In the name of my late husband I ask you to help me and my son! I am sure I need not remind you that he stood by you during some trying times!"

As her indignant words rushed out, she suddenly remembered how an incident of Kastner's black-market dealings came to the attention of the authorities during the last year of the war. Friedrich vouched for his subordinate despite personal misgivings and even danger to himself, sparing the man from severe consequences. An embarrassed grin spread over Kastner's coarse face. Glancing sideways at Maria he realized she was not easily fooled. But there was hostility in his eyes, resentment at having to deal with a person who knew more about him than he was comfortable admitting.

An uneasy silence ensued while Kastner played with a pencil, tapping the surface of his battered desk. Finally he spoke up, his tone reluctant, but leaning forward for emphasis. "Very well, then, *Frau* Wildert, I'll arrange to get you and your son permits to live here. But I repeat what I said earlier: everyone here must recognize the facts as they are. Do you understand me?" His voice rose aggressively as he snapped, "I have no intention of being challenged by anybody, if you know what I mean!"

Maria again ignored the renewed threatening outburst, forcing herself to look squarely in his fierce eyes. "I thank you for your assistance, *Herr* Kastner!" She was angry and puzzled at his display of raw power, but the past year taught her that only survival mattered in a chaotic world. She had grown adept at hiding her feelings; in fact, she discovered in herself an ability to be cunning. Now she was prepared to negotiate shrewdly with her adversaries to gain an advantage as long as she didn't compromise her elementary values.

Kastner rose clumsily and stretched out his hand. "I do believe we understand each other, don't we?" He chuckled again although his squinting eyes had the cold look of steel. "I'll get the papers processed through City Hall by late today. You can go to the registry official tomorrow for signatures. Once you have

moved I'll tell you more about conditions here—they're not wonderful, I can assure you. Good-bye."

Maria was glad to leave the domain of this crafty surviver; she
felt drained by the combative encounter. Her back began to hurt
unbearably and she hurried back to the hotel to rest, but she was
relieved to have achieved her main objective far sooner than she
dared hope.

As she lay on her bed her mind raced ahead to the new life in
this town, wondering how she would be able to manage the
undercurrents of hostility and jealousy rooted in the past. Fate
catapulted her out of a comfortable, sheltered existence into an
elementary fight for survival. Her accustomed social status, based
on her parents' background and on Friedrich's position was
always so important to her in better times. Now it was lost along
with everything else, and she deeply resented the cavalier treatment Kastner had given her. Again her thoughts churned in a mix
of grief and anger.

Her convent school education and upbringing in a prosperous
setting imparted very little of the practical matters necessary to
start a new life; home and family had always been her all-encom-
passing purpose. She was not trained in worldly skills, and now
she even lacked any standing in the new town she was to live in.
She realized that as a widow without anyone to protect her interests she would be outmaneuvered by men and reduced to a pawn
in the struggle.

Yet she also clung to the unshakable belief that Schlossberg was
the only place she could turn; rejoining the Eger family was
impossible after the events in the camp. The ostracism she experienced there deeply hurt her pride, even though she admitted
that the family had some reason to be angry with her—after all,
she had suggested going to the official and Martha went along.

Maria could be unbending when her pride was involved, having inherited her parents' strong will and determination. She
remembered her French Huguenot mother liked to cite the
phrase: "The pigeons fly in clusters, but the eagle soars alone."
Maria now saw herself as the wounded eagle that would not read-
ily turn into a pigeon if she could help it. She resolved to be

strong, to fight if she must, and to have faith in her destiny.

She thought of Anton stranded on the desolate farm, and as she did so the urge to hurry back to the farm and return to Schlossberg with him became overwhelming. She could hardly wait to take the first available train as soon as the signed permit was hers—the hint of stability which that piece of paper represented gave her growing confidence that she and Anton could weather the perilous times still ahead.

TWENTY-ONE

The Daily Struggle

As she sat in the overcrowded train compartment on her trip back to the farm Maria reflected on her experiences at Schlossberg. The residence permit securely tucked away in her bag, she was now eager to accomplish the move without delay. At the small, rural beer garden restaurant frequented by the Sudeten refugee community Maria encountered one more link to the past. Having finished her starchy supper, she was leaving through the dark, cobbled passage when she encountered a tall, balding man and his wife.

"*Frau* Wildert, imagine seeing you here after all the things that happened to you in Aussig!" *Herr* Bauer exclaimed. "My cousin Kastner told me today that you are planning to move here." Maria knew Friedrich's former office manager from the war days when he visited the villa to deliver urgent papers to Friedrich.

Bauer's mention of his cousin brought back to her the threatening tone Kastner used in their first meeting. Bauer increased her unease when he stressed how grateful everyone was for Kastner's efforts and, with a sideways glance, added, "After all, my cousin did have added responsibilities in Aussig during the last year or so, didn't he?"

What was the man suggesting? In a flash she remembered that the owner of the hotel used the title "*Direktor*" when she first told her about Kastner, the formal appellation normally reserved for the chief executive. Had Kastner come to Schlossberg representing himself as such, secure in the knowledge that Friedrich was dead? Kastner was certainly ambitious and pushy, but Maria knew her husband was fully in charge until the Czech overseer Novak relieved him.

Her discomfort grew when Bauer continued in his suggestive

tone, "Don't you agree, *Frau* Wildert," again using the familiar form of address, "that past titles and rank are of no importance now? Only the present counts. So much has changed that it would be silly to insist on outdated practices. The main thing is that we all find a way to get started again, isn't it?"

Maria understood. It must not have occurred to Kastner that she and Anton would be able to make their way to Schlossberg, and he had used the opportunity to elevate himself in the eyes of the community by taking on a dead man's mantle. But what was the vonEckenbachs' reaction to his intrigue? Probably acquiescence, she thought, if Kastner proved himself useful to them in their current situation—nimble manipulator that he was. To them a widow and her son would be merely a burden, and therefore expendable.

As the train continued northward she realized that her effort to gain a footing in Schlossberg would be even more difficult than she originally envisioned, since her very presence would unravel the attempted elevation of Kastner's status. He could be a dangerous adversary, and she expected that under such circumstances he would be lukewarm at best in extending to her the assistance of his office. The refugee community might take sides in the situation, but Kastner held all the cards, able to bestow important favors in the form of basic necessities. It would take immense courage to contradict him, but she was still convinced she had no other choice except to begin a new life in Schlossberg.

It was late evening when the train arrived at the Rhenish provincial town and despite the hour she called Margot from the station telephone. Her friend effusively insisted on preparing a meal and putting her up for the night. Ferdinand and Karl were away visiting a nearby relative and the two women would have the apartment to themselves.

Bedded down on the sofa in the living room Maria shared her experiences with Margot who talked with her well into the early morning hours. Her wily friend was generous with advice; she had sharpened her own survival skills during the twists and turns in her life over the past several years. Maria sensed that Margot was capable of either using power when she had it, or manipulating conditions to her advantage when she did not, and that she always knew where she stood. Maria had a great deal to learn from her.

"I would be very careful not to challenge Kastner directly," Margot said emphatically. "You must always consider how your actions will affect your basic needs. That is the key point, however much you might wish to put the man in his place!" She added shrewdly, "If you handle this right he'll have no choice but to help you—after all, he is the Refugee Commissioner." She gave Maria a few helpful suggestions of how to appeal to Kastner's sense of importance without appearing submissive.

When Maria tearfully told her the story of the family estrangement at the Eger camp she listened without comment. Finally she sighed. "I see both sides of the problem—but I also remember how stubborn Martha can be. It's really sad that this had to happen, but you must not let your hurt feelings fester!" With a compassionate smile she added, "My dear friend, difficult as it may be you must use logic to understand that you couldn't be welcome with Martha's family, unless you contributed materially to the needs of her small children. Her protective instincts as a mother are too strong now to let her share anything—regardless of how generous you were to her when she needed you before the war. It'll be better if you go your own way!" In the end Margot fully agreed that Maria's only option was to move to Schlossberg.

In the morning Maria walked to the farm where she found Anton busily helping in the yard. He yelled with excitement when he saw her and came running, having been constantly worried during her absence. Back in their room she told him of her train mishap, of the encounters with people from the past, of the pleasant small town, and proudly showed him the residence permit. She was determined to leave the Neumann farm the very same day and stay the night with Margot before they took the morning train to Schlossberg. Anton could hardly believe that the dreary existence on the farm would be ending so suddenly. He tried to be useful during Maria's absence, but he still tired easily.

Later, when Maria told Neumann that they were leaving he shrugged and mumbled that this was just as well, but he balked angrily when Maria asked that Hans drive them and their belongings into town. She decided not to press the point for the moment and went to visit Hannelore, who wished her well. The wistful young woman repressed her tears and added, "We'll have to get out, too, before we go crazy in this place. Tomorrow we'll begin to explore what can be done. You have given us the courage to think it may be possible."

No sooner had Maria returned to her room when she heard a knock at the door. Hans delivered an envelope from Neumann. It contained a detailed handwritten bill for daily room rent, food, supplies, and a charge for the mule cart pickup from the refugee camp. The sum amounted to more than half of the money she had left. She handed the paper to Anton, while she sat down to recover her senses. At the sight of the boy's worried face Maria suddenly burst out laughing. Anton joined in and neither mother nor son could stop the convulsive relief until tears came to their eyes.

Maria then took pen and paper and wrote out a bill to Neumann for her and Anton's labors on the farm. She carefully estimated the hours they worked, not counting Anton's days of illness or her own travel time. Then she applied the local minimum wage rate and calculated the total amount due her. The figure was more than sufficient to cover Neumann's ridiculous charges. She circled the difference of about 20 marks and wrote below, "I herewith cancel the net amount you owe me, considering the fact that we were forced by the authorities to live in your house."

Calling softly from the window she asked Hans to come up. When the young man arrived she instructed him, "Please take this envelope to *Herr* Neumann and tell him that I expect the mule cart to be ready to take us into town at five-thirty this afternoon." She became even firmer in her tone. "If it isn't there, my son and I will walk to town, leaving our belongings here. *Herr* Neumann will be held responsible for them. We will give a full report to the authorities about the treatment we have received here and also show them his outrageous bill." She smiled at Hans who hunched at her energetic words, and patted him on the arm reassuringly.

At five-thirty they heard Hans yelling from below. "I–I–am r–ready to t–take you into town!" Neumann and *Fräulein* Hackel were nowhere to be seen. Hans and Anton loaded the mule cart with the bundles and lifted the blue wagon onto it. Maria hugged Lieselotte and Hannelore warmly and, breathing a deep sigh of relief, walked out of the farmhouse for the last time.

Margot put them up for the night and they spent another happy evening filled with lively talk and reminiscences.

The next morning they embarked on the rail journey to Schlossberg under conditions similar to those Maria experienced days earlier. Working together mother and son were able to get their belongings on board, expending an enormous effort wrangling with the jostling crowds. At Frankfurt station Maria showed the awed Anton the place where she had fallen, and told him she believed her narrow escape was a sign that they must go on, come what may. Again they managed to fight their way into the train headed south.

During the trip Anton mostly stood or perched on the bags and bundles in the crowded corridors. He had much time to reflect on what his mother told him about the conditions in Schlossberg. The town held little promise for them, but at least they would know some of the people. He knew that Maria was adamant about him returning to public preparatory school, as she would often quote to him her father's favorite expression, "what you know no one can take from you." Even though, like all boys of his age, he had rebelled often against the heavy load of homework when school still functioned in Aussig, he now missed his studies, not having attended classes for well over a year.

He wondered whether he would be able to remember any of the subjects in which he had done well. His English had been tested to the limit with the South African protectors, and he was proud of that, while the American presence in Eger had given him exposure to English inscriptions and street signs. But other subjects like mathematics, history, literature, and natural sciences faded in his memory due to an all-consuming concentration on daily survival. Now he was eager to begin again, and already the dreary farm episode seemed far away.

At Schlossberg station they loaded their wagon and Maria led the way to the hotel. Anton liked what he saw of the town and he vaguely pictured a more normal life in the simple, provincial atmosphere. He was especially intrigued when they passed the regional headquarters of the American occupation forces and he took a long, slow look at the soldiers' uniforms and their olive drab vehicles.

They rented a tiny room with two beds at the hotel *Zur Donau* and Maria drained her funds further by paying a week in advance. She knew that the first most critical chore would be to go to the Housing Office and seek to be assigned a decent room in a private home. The second important task was to meet with the senior vonEckenbach and to argue her case for support. The next few days would bring many changes to their lives.

The Housing Office was a crowded, dingy place filled with long queues of people looking for a place to stay or trying to move from where they were now quartered. Like every village, town, and city in postwar Germany, Schlossberg overflowed with refugees; there were at least one-third more people than the prewar population crammed into the war-diminished living space. The officials operated under emergency authority, requisitioning rooms and whole sections of houses that exceeded the allowed per capita space for all residents. In turn, they distributed these piecemeal quarters to eligible refugees.

Rents paid to the owners were strictly controlled. In effect, the Housing Office wielded the power to force strangers into other people's homes against the owners' will. It was a thankless task which pitted the bureaucrats against both angry residents and dissatisfied newcomers.

When Maria and Anton reached the surly official he already showed the strain of having dealt with thoroughly unpleasant duties for most of the day. The man looked quizzically over his half-glasses, seemingly assessing the Wilderts' appearance. He reached for a questionnaire printed on grayish recycled paper containing a long list of items. "Do you have any furniture?" the man asked brusquely. "It's very difficult to get a furnished room at this point!" He went over all the other questions in detail, his pen scratching, asked Maria to sign, and pounded several rubber stamps on the finished document. "You'll have to wait your turn now, because the Housing Commission must pass on your request," he said in an officious tone, "you can check with this office in three to four days, but I can't promise anything." Maria tried to impress on the bored man that they simply could not afford the hotel for more than a few nights and grudgingly he scrawled a special notation on their file.

Back at the hotel they began to deliberate about the appropriate way to approach the vonEckenbachs. It had to be done as soon as possible, for they would need funds to cover basic needs. As a stopgap measure Maria decided to write to her sister Martha to ask for a speedy return of the modest sum she entrusted to the Eger family for transfer to the west. This nest egg would help support them over several months.

The important vonEckenbach matter required careful handling. Maria thought that a brief letter of her intentions to the head of the family was in order, including a request for a personal meeting. She began to compose the letter using a very formal tone. After three drafts, none of which was satisfactory to her, Maria felt drained and gave up. As he watched his mother struggle, Anton wished he had the experience to write such a document.

In the morning the writing became easier, and after two more drafts Maria had an acceptable letter. She talked the hotel owner into giving her some stationery, and also asked the woman how best to deliver the letter to the summer residence. She learned that an employee of the vonEckenbach company regularly picked up mail and supplies in town and that her letter would reach the estate the same day.

Maria then pondered about how to manage the sensitive relationship with Kastner. Perhaps the best way was to treat him politely and mollify his ample ego by paying due respect to his official capacity, while ignoring his machinations unless there were a direct confrontation. She decided to call on him soon and formally seek his assistance like any other refugee. Margot would approve of my approach to things, she thought.

As there was nothing more to do except wait, Maria gave in to the insistent demands of her tired body. Apart from taking basic meals, available without ration coupons, which they ate at the simple restaurant she did not leave the room, preferring to lie flat on her bed which helped to alleviate her recurring back pains. Anton went out as much as he could to explore the town with boyish enthusiasm.

On the third day, *Herr* Bauer called on her in his cousin Kastner's name. He came right to the point. "We would like you to understand the situation. There are many claims against the remainder of the vonEckenbach enterprises, and there's a limit to what they can do for any of us. The local company is overmanned already; all of their own large family have come to live here, and their properties are managed by a public trustee for as long as the formal process of investigating industrialists for Nazi involvement continues. They're probably clean on that score, but they'll not be masters of their own fate for as long as these proceedings take."

Maria listened intently. What was the man's purpose? Bauer continued, "My cousin is very important to the vonEckenbachs as a witness, and also as a town official here. So it's necessary that all of us cooperate, isn't it? Don't expect too much from the vonEckenbachs under the circumstances—but perhaps we can be helpful to you, if things go right." His face was tense, his look cunning as he studied her passive expression. Maria mused with quiet satisfaction how fast she was learning to mask her true feelings.

Bauer ended his monologue. "We understand you've written to the head of the family, and we know that he expects to see you in a day or two. My cousin will probably be there when you meet the elder vonEckenbach at the summer estate." He rose clumsily to say good-bye.

Later in the day Anton brought a letter up to the room which the company messenger left at the hotel desk. Maria took a deep breath and opened the envelope anxiously. Sitting side by side they read the note which was typed on fine stationery embossed with a family crest. The senior vonEckenbach's words were courteous and formal, extending Maria an invitation to come to see him at eleven the following day, to bring Anton along, and to plan to stay for lunch.

It was a bright, sunny morning when they passed through the new part of Schlossberg and followed the gently rising country road to the east. Rows of stately chestnut trees pleasantly shaded the street. Soon they left the built-up area to walk along a country lane that led through open meadows and fields.

At last they reached a wooded area with attractive houses nestled on one side, while the buildings of the small chemical processing company were visible on the other. They glimpsed a sweeping view of the river valley beyond the trees and followed the sun-speckled road for another fifty yards until they reached an ornamental gate. Behind the wrought iron fence large manicured lawns and formal gardens swept up to a pastel-colored mansion with a large terrace positioned to take advantage of the lovely view.

Maria remembered Friedrich's descriptions of the elegant summer estate, and she wondered how she would be received. Anton pressed the bell on the stone pillar and an electric buzzer released the small door beside the main gate. They walked along the curving driveway past the lawns and flower beds to the main house where a liveried butler received them at the portal. He ushered them into the Green Room, a large chamber exuding opulence. Precious paintings graced the walls, while brocaded upholstery and silks competed with fine oriental rugs, sparkling crystal and statuary for the visitor's attention. Was it possible that people still lived like this in the shattered postwar world?

The senior vonEckenbach strode into the room. He was a short, rotund man in his sixties with a slightly flushed face, silky white hair, and an air of shrewd vitality. Impeccably dressed in a dove-gray suit, he paused for a moment to squint at Maria through wary eyes. Then he extended his hand to greet the somber-faced woman in black. Anton jumped to his feet and bowed awkwardly when the man glanced at him with a detached look.

Without preliminaries the industrialist began to talk at length of losses he had suffered during and after the war, and complained bitterly about how a public trustee now controlled his fate. His nasal northern accent seemed out of place in this Bavarian country setting. He inquired perfunctorily about Friedrich's passing, then immediately returned to his own concerns.

Maria sat impassively until *Herr* vonEckenbach rose and suggested that she follow him to the next room where they could discuss her request with "the others." She maintained a dignified front despite the resentment welling up in her.

On the verandah, a large glass-walled room with a breathtaking view of the Danube valley, Maria shook hands with Kastner and Dr. Korn, the former managing director of an eastern operation. She had met the latter previously during his occasional visits to Aussig. Also present were Dr. Zimmermann, the managing director of the local company, and *Herr* Lippstadt, the public trustee. After the stiff introductions there was an awkward pause.

Maria sensed that the men expected her to present her case. Nervously she began by citing Friedrich's position and many years of leadership, and the innovations he had instituted in the company. She went on to describe the circumstances which had brought the loss of all property and support for the two survivors of Friedrich's family. While she spoke the five men watched her without reaction. No one made any attempt to put her at ease. Maria felt as if she were on display, and she would have been grateful for any sign of understanding in one of the impassive faces.

When she hesitated for a moment to gather her thoughts, Dr. Korn abruptly began a monologue, heatedly speaking of the losses he suffered in fleeing from the Russian advance. Maria yielded to his torrent of words, reminding herself of Margot's advice not to be hasty in her reactions. At last she found an opening to respond blandly, "But you were able to escape, all your family are well, and you can continue working here. How fortunate you are." Silence ensued.

Kastner watched her intently during her plea, but now he glanced sideways at Dr. Korn. Maria thought she saw a twinkle of satisfaction in his eyes, as if he wished to give him the same answer.

Finally *Herr* Lippstadt, the public trustee, spoke up, his voice monotonous. "Your case is certainly not without merit. But there are serious circumstances that leave us unable to provide you with any financial assistance for now. Most of the von-Eckenbachs' remaining assets are frozen and the local company is having difficulty making ends meet. As you may know, we employ a large number of former associates from different enterprises—at this point we can do no more." *Herr* vonEckenbach remained silent, merely nodding his head in emphasis.

Maria's heart sank. She now felt there was little hope for her after this frosty reception, which was certainly not in keeping with Friedrich's position and contributions to the vonEckenbach enterprises.

Kastner broke in. "We'll try to give you whatever basic assistance is available through the Refugee Office, although that is small indeed. I understand you have already applied for a room."

Dr. Zimmermann now took his turn. "The one thing we can provide for you is some coal and firewood, the type of allowance we give to our employees. This should help, especially in the winter. We'll also let you have a peck of apples once the company orchard has been harvested."

The interview seemed to be over when vonEckenbach rose abruptly and said, "Why don't you wait with your son in the Green Room. Luncheon will be served on the terrace in about half an hour."

Severely disappointed Maria stood, bravely hiding her feelings. She turned and left the verandah to join Anton. He came eagerly toward her. "They won't help us much," she said. "Somehow we'll have to manage on our own." Anton looked worried, at a loss for words. Maria smiled thinly, then added, "Up with your head, my son; always look at the positive side! If one door doesn't open, another will. We must trust in the Lord."

Anton could see that his mother was under great strain and wondered what had happened in the other room, but he did not press her for details. Maria thought to herself that her brave words were as much for her own benefit as for the boy's. She then told him about the coal and the apples and made it appear very important.

There was a knock at the door and Dr. Zimmermann peered in. "I beg your pardon, *Gnädige Frau*,[1] but if there is any assistance I

---

[1] Gracious Lady

may give you with personal papers, insurance matters, and so on I will be pleased to advise you." The slender, highly-strung man smiled pleasantly, bowed politely and raised her hand halfway to his lips. The aging bachelor and head of a large family of relatives took great pride in his formal good manners. Incongruous as his courteous address and gesture seemed at this moment, Maria was touched. "Is this your son, *Gnädige Frau?*" He extended his hand to Anton, who bowed shyly. Dr. Zimmermann said a few pleasant words to the boy, then withdrew.

At twelve o'clock the butler escorted Maria and Anton to the sun-drenched terrace, where large umbrellas shaded a long table for about twenty persons set with snowy linen, fine china, cut crystal and gleaming sterling silver. A finely lettered card marked every place.

Herr vonEckenbach introduced the Wilderts to his wife, a cool-eyed, reserved woman who said with some reluctance that she remembered meeting Maria. Maria sat next to her at the table and lunch began. Anton was placed between vonEckenbach Jr., a smooth-talking man in his twenties, and a well-dressed young woman, his cousin. The boy thought he was dreaming when the liveried butler began serving with white gloves. The meal began with a delicious soup, followed by fresh salad, a huge platter of delicately seasoned fish in a creamy sauce and garden vegetables, and ended with a rich dessert. The butler poured fine Rhine wine liberally and served real coffee as the finishing touch.

While they ate, mother and son exchanged furtive glances across the table. Had they been through hell and were they now in heaven? How was it possible to maintain such a lifestyle only one year after the collapse? Here was a family claiming to have lost most of its wealth, yet carrying on in a manner that seemed to exist only in storybooks.

Anton felt totally out of place. His perturbed mind yielded nothing intelligent to say to his table companions. They asked a question or two of him but soon turned to their other partners for conversation. Frustrated, Anton decided to concentrate only on the fragrance, texture and taste of the exquisite food. The boy sensed that his mother was struggling also. He wanted to be far away, to get up and run as fast as he could. He could find no common ground with the people around this lavish table. Anton grew increasingly embarrassed by his inept silence, but his thoughts and words remained blocked. From time to time he heard Maria's voice as if through a fog.

After coffee Maria and Anton rose with the others and hastily said their thanks and good-byes to the hosts. To everyone's relief they were soon walking back through the glen toward the open fields and meadows. Reaching the sunny country lane they hurried toward the main road, down the hill into town and back to the hotel.

While they walked, tears streaked down Maria's face as she again realized that they were alone in the world. She felt rejected and offended by the dismissive treatment of her husband's achievements and of her own needs. She knew she would be a burden to everyone unless she managed some degree of self-sufficiency. But how could she do this in a hopelessly shattered country? Anton paced quietly beside her, glad to turn his back on the mansion and the ornamental gate. He sensed his mother's despair but was at a loss to know what to say or do. The streets of Schlossberg seemed more alien than a few hours ago. There was a cold indifference in the air, and the boy became afraid.

Back in their room Maria tried to put her feelings into words. "How can they really understand what we've been through? Your father often told me that the vonEckenbachs were distant, demanding, and intent on living a grand lifestyle. He felt they always acted like they had generations of wealth instead of their relatively short span of success. I do admit they must have lost a fortune with their eastern holdings—but they still have so much! We can't expect them to understand, or even to want to understand. The women have no warmth; it's plain to me that status is all they care about—even now."

Maria shook her head and closed her eyes as she spoke, reliving her choked embarrassment at the splendid summer mansion. "Let this be a lesson to you, Anton. It's quite proper to strive, to advance, and to be successful—but everything has its cost. You take of life what you want, but sooner or later you pay for it in some form. Be careful you do not pay for your success with your own humanity!" Maria became agitated. "Have you noticed how many times simple people were kind to us, even when they could ill afford it? Think of the women in the corner house, for example, and how they cared for us. When a person is stripped of everything the true human being emerges. It's comforting to know that there are people who rise beyond themselves while thinking of others, if only in feelings and moral support." Anton shuddered as he felt again the chill of the closed world of wealth that touched him briefly.

Maria stood up suddenly, shaking her head as if to clear it, and took a deep breath. "But all this talk isn't going to help us." She sounded more vigorous, clearly wanting to break the shackles of self-pity that threatened to immobilize both of them. "We can't go anywhere else to live. This is the place where we must try to exist. First thing tomorrow, we'll go to the Housing Office to check on our application, and I will not hesitate to use Kastner's name to get their attention. Our money is running out, we can't afford this hotel much longer."

She became even more determined. "Then we must look into your schooling. There is no question in my mind that you have to continue with your education, finish preparatory school here, and even go on to university. You study easily, you were always in the top group of your class. We'll find a way to achieve all that." After a moment she added, "Somehow doors will open up. The good Lord brought us this far, and He'll help us again."

Given their present plight Anton thought his mother's words grandiose and extreme. He was becoming quite anxious about how they might scrape along even for the next few weeks. Not wishing to quench the hopeful ardor and resolve he saw in his mother's eyes, he smiled and nodded bravely. As for Maria, she felt better for having said these things. It was as if the burst of positive energy began to blow away the dark clouds enveloping them. She knew they must continue to strive for their own survival, come what may.

TWENTY-TWO

The Long Road

In driving rain, armed with a stamped slip of paper from the Housing Office, Maria and Anton walked to an address in the new section of Schlossberg near the American occupation headquarters. The single room allotted to them was in an apartment on the second floor of a modern three-story building above an empty furniture store. The building belonged to a carpenter and furniture maker living with his family in a larger structure to the rear. They could hear the distant screeching of a power saw in the workshop and smelled the aromatic scent of fresh-cut lumber stacked in neat piles in the yard.

Hurrying past the show windows covered with stained, yellowing paper, they turned into the narrow hallway and climbed a flight of stairs. Quick steps of clicking high heels responded to the ring of the bell. An attractive woman of about thirty opened the door. Rich black hair framed a pale, oval face with deep, dark eyes and a sensuous mouth glistening with scarlet lipstick. Her expression hardened at the sight of Maria, looking stately in her mournful black dress. After sizing up her visitors for a moment, the woman said in a cool, impersonal tone, "Yes?"

"I'm *Frau* Wildert and this is my son Anton. The Housing Office has assigned us a room in your apartment." Maria held out the official paper as she spoke.

The woman remained stiff and unbending. Obviously annoyed, she replied in a clipped northern accent. "Well, we've been expecting something like this. This isn't a large apartment, you know. There's my husband and myself, and our little daughter— well, we'll just have to manage somehow. Unfortunately the room they took away from us opens onto this corridor, and so do all the others. There's only one bathroom, so privacy will be difficult.

I hope you have your own furniture."

"All we have is what we could carry; everything else was lost," Maria said quietly.

The woman went on, obviously calculating as she talked. "Well, we'll leave the dining table, four chairs, a small buffet and a wooden chest in the room, since we cannot use those now, anyway. I hope you will be careful with the furniture. The rent will be forty marks per month, but without kitchen privileges. You'll have to find a hot plate and stove to put into the room—we don't want to share the kitchen *and* the bathroom."

"The document says the room will be twenty marks," Maria observed coolly.

"Yes, but that was for the unfurnished room, the furniture is extra!" The woman's voice had a hard edge.

"The document also says the room is partly furnished," Maria responded without raising her voice. The housing official instructed her to insist on the prescribed rent.

"Well, you'll have to talk with my husband about that," the woman snapped, a fierce look distorting her face. They were still standing in the hallway by the open door. After a resentful pause the woman shrugged and led them to their assigned room. Anton walked behind her and saw that she was shapely, her hips swaying over long, slender legs. The fragrance of strong perfume lingered in the air.

They entered a bright, modern room. Its windows looked out onto a bank of windows facing them across the driveway, with a smidgen of gray sky visible in one corner, past the facade of the neighboring house. Plain pale green curtains allowed for privacy. In the center stood a square dining table and chairs of light brown wood, and a matching small buffet against the back wall. The only other furniture was a large wooden armoire with drawers, and in the middle of the spotless parquet floor lay a light brown rug. But there were no beds and no stove.

Maria turned to the woman and said firmly, "This will do, although we must find beds and a stove. I'll pay you twenty marks as stated here for the first month, and you can take up the rent issue with the Housing Office." The woman shot her an angry look, her wide lips narrowing into a ruby line as she clenched her jaw. Unperturbed, Maria continued, "Would you please show us the bathroom? Also, we must ask you to let us use the kitchen for the first few days—after you have finished your cooking, of course—until we can set up our own stove."

The woman clattered ahead on her spindly heels down the passage to the small modern bathroom, and as they passed an open door on their right Maria and Anton glimpsed a comfortable sunny kitchen and breakfast nook.

Maria pulled a twenty mark bill from her purse. "May I have a receipt, please?"

"Just a moment," came the curt reply. The woman swished to the end of the hall into the living room, closing the door behind her. After a minute she emerged with a sheet of stationery bearing her printed name, Hildegard Blohmstett, on which she scrawled the receipt of twenty marks as a down payment on rent of forty marks per month.

She handed Maria a key to the apartment door. "We'll discuss other particulars, and the chores to be shared around the building, once you have moved in. My husband will be home from work after five. Good-bye."

The Wilderts left in an uplifted mood. The Blohmstetts would be difficult, that was obvious, but the room was pleasant and over time they would make it comfortable. Meanwhile they must see Kastner about beds and a stove. They went to the refugee administrator's office and he received them formally, an attitude Maria welcomed. Neither of them mentioned the strained meeting at the vonEckenbach estate.

"We can do something about the beds and the stove right away," Kastner said briskly, explaining that there was a supply of U.S. Army cots and blankets for just such a need. A small stove would be available in a few days, he went on. He described it as a flimsy brick-lined sheet metal firebox on four spindly legs, which had to be connected through the wall to a flue to expel the smoke from the wood and coal briquettes it burned. The contraption must do for both heating and cooking, and the owner of the building would be required to hook up the stovepipes for them. The total price for cots, blankets and stove was a nominal thirty marks.

In parting Kastner asked about Maria's financial situation. She replied that she still had a little cash and was expecting an amount due to her from her sister. However, unless she could draw on her blocked savings accounts—very unlikely for the foreseeable future—she would be short of funds in a few months. Kastner nodded and made a notation in her file.

Back at the apartment Maria rang the bell even though she had her key. A dark-haired man in his thirties, round-faced and chubby, opened the door. "Good evening, *Herr* Blohmstett," Maria said, "we've come to put in our cots and we'll move in with our other things tomorrow." Blohmstett smiled pleasantly, tenderly putting an arm over his three-year old daughter who peeped coyly at the strangers. He pointed to the door of their room.

Once in the room the Wilderts saw immediately that the rug was gone, as was the armoire. Only the table, chairs, and buffet were left. Blohmstett, standing in the doorway, said nothing and neither did Maria. Without the armoire they would be hard-pressed to store their few belongings properly, but then they had managed in far worse circumstances. They departed quickly to return to the hotel.

In the morning they awoke early, and after breakfast of bread and *ersatz* coffee left the Hotel *Zur Donau* with their belongings piled on the blue wagon. On the way they passed an electrical supply store, its show window barren but for a few leaflets on local happenings. Maria decided to inquire inside about buying a small hot plate, knowing full well that appliances of any sort were unavailable. The elderly store owner looked incredulous when Maria stated her need. "I haven't had one to sell for ages!"

Maria smiled knowingly. "Could you use some saccharin? Perhaps this would help to get me a hot plate?"

The woman's furrowed face brightened. "Well, you know, it's hard, but I might be able to find you one—eh, how much saccharin do you have?" Maria had a packet of 100 tablets. "Why don't you come back in a day or two, and we'll see what we can do." With a wink of understanding the woman went to the back room and Maria and Anton left the shop to continue their walk to the

Blohmstett apartment.

How typical this type of exchange became, Maria thought. It was hard to find even minor necessities, and barter was the only way to induce people to part with what merchandise they had squirreled away. She had prudently saved several packages of saccharin she found in the workers' flat in Aussig. There was nothing else she could spare for bartering, as the many "inspections" of the bundles reduced their belongings to the bare minimum.

At their new lodging they let themselves in. In the hall they encountered Hildegard Blohmstett dressed in a low-cut morning robe, inhaling an American cigarette, a sign of considerable affluence given the high black-market value of tobacco products. Trailing perfume and smoke she swept past the Wilderts and barely acknowledged their presence.

After settling in as best as they could, Maria and Anton went to look for *Frau* Blohmstett to arrange their temporary cooking needs. They found her lounging in the kitchen, reading an American magazine and sipping—by its unmistakable fragrance—real black coffee. Without offering Maria a seat the woman said in a bored and strident tone, "You realize, of course, that you're paying well below the normal rent for this room. The furniture is of very good quality and we've left you what you need. We expect you to get your own stove without delay. Until then you may use our kitchen, but *only after*—I repeat, *only after*—we've finished using it for the day. And that's just for a short while, understand? By the way, I also want my curtains back as soon as you can put something on the windows." She glared at Maria, who was battling her growing anger.

"Now, as far as the building chores are concerned, the two tenants in this house take turns each week to wash down the stairs. We'll expect you to do it every other time—and no ifs, ands, or buts!" She shifted her long legs to sit more comfortably, letting the robe open wider, while casting admiring glances at her shimmering nylon stockings and blowing a smoke ring toward the ceiling with practiced nonchalance.

Her voice took on a note of stridency. "It's an awful imposition to have strangers crowding you in your own home. We expect you to be considerate, and that goes for the young man, too. If you want to bathe you must provide your own fuel for the hot water. And you'd better keep the tub clean. Let's also avoid running into each other to use the bathroom—my husband and I have first choice, and we get up early—that is, he does." Hildegard Blohmstett completed her well-planned tirade and inhaled the last of her cigarette deeply. Her large dark eyes sparkled with aggression. She reached for the cigarette pack on the table, pulled out a fresh cigarette, tapped its ends carefully, and lit it in a swirl of smoke. Then she again faced Maria coldly while pursing her ruby lips to form another perfect smoke ring,

Maria, still standing, felt like a schoolgirl being scolded by the headmistress. She was tempted to give the younger woman a severe dressing-down, but instinct told her not to instigate any trouble now. There would be many future clashes, she was sure of that. Anton watched the strangely attractive creature with adolescent curiosity, angered by the ice-cold arrogance directed at his mother, but also intrigued by her seductive display.

Maria took a deep breath and said as evenly as she could, without giving away her seething frustration, "We didn't choose to come here, *Frau* Blohmstett. As you well know, we were officially assigned the room in your apartment. You can rest assured that we value privacy as much as you do. Good day." She nudged Anton to leave.

Frau Blohmstett met Maria's determined stare without blinking, blew another smoke ring toward the ceiling, and lavished on Anton a parting look through long, sensual eyelashes. The boy turned red in the face with embarrassment and the Wilderts withdrew to their room. There Maria cautioned Anton to stay clear of the Blohmstetts, especially the woman, who would use every excuse to make life difficult for them. "Be polite, but avoid unnecessary conversation. She's the type that thrives on aggression, and you are no match for her—just ignore her when you can. It won't be pleasant to live here, but then again, wherever we went we'd be in somebody's way."

Over the next two weeks they made the room habitable. They found the army cots adequate for sleeping, although the thin canvas surface was likely to be uncomfortably cold in the winter, with only an extra blanket as a mattress. Maria put up a spare set of bed linen in place of the Blohmstett curtains. The tiny stove had been installed by one of the landlord's workmen and the owner of the electrical shop had indeed "found" a small electric hot plate to trade for the package of saccharin. They were now independent of the Blohmstett kitchen and grateful for being able to minimize contact with the couple.

Dr. Zimmermann, as promised, arranged for delivery of two sacks of coal briquettes and some kindling wood. One day he appeared himself to see how the Wilderts were faring. When he found out that they had no place to hang their clothes, he offered to loan them an old wardrobe, brightly painted in peasant style, which arrived the next day. He also promised that he would look into finding more adequate beds for them before the cold weather set in.

The Wilderts existed from day to day, taking some of their frugal meals at the beer garden restaurant the refugee community frequented. There they met a number of acquaintances from Aussig and were introduced to refugees from many different parts of the Sudetenland. Conversations invariably centered on the losses everyone suffered, and on the daily difficulties of surviving in the shattered economy. The Wilderts repeatedly heard stories of family members lost in the evacuations, of suicides, interrupted careers, financial hardships, and the aggravating unpleasantness of living in other peoples' homes with very little to subsist on.

The sharing of common problems brought some solace with the knowledge that others were struggling, too. At the same time the Wilderts could not help but be aware that a number of refugees were a good deal better off than they, both financially and in family ties. Having connections with people of influence or links to the barter network was the key to living at a more tolerable level—but this presupposed an ability to return favors, something Maria and Anton were not in a position to do. Such connections were sarcastically referred to as "Vitamin B," short for the German word *Beziehungen* that denoted them.

There was much talk about the coming winter and how to survive all the shortages. Long queues formed whenever a store had anything to sell—one had to stand in line even for newspapers. They spent huge blocks of time waiting to obtain daily essentials. But time was the one thing they had in abundance, as work was simply not available for most. They could expect little improvement from an economy that, if anything, still declined under the debilitating effects of postwar stresses.

Maria decided that this was a time for testing her faith, for believing that doors would open up unexpectedly when things became desperate. She looked for and found small miracles, such as the money she had entrusted to her sister arriving just as her own funds ran out, or a kind soul among the refugee community sharing some windfall of food or ration tickets.

Anton's schooling was now uppermost in Maria's mind. Registration for the September classes at the Schlossberg public preparatory school was imminent. She recalled how her feelings were hurt during the meeting at the vonEckenbach mansion when Dr. Korn suggested that Anton be apprenticed to a bank or to a tradesman to be able to earn some immediate income—although it was doubtful that a place could be found for Anton even with the vonEckenbach's connections. She bristled at the idea, insisting to herself that her son must have a formal education.

Together they called on the principal of the Schlossberg *Oberrealschule*.[1] It was an institution that in its heyday enjoyed a fine reputation. Now it was a mere shell of its former prominence, run down physically, and propped up by a faculty more notable for its makeshift improvisation than its academic achievement. Conditions here were really no different from what happened to such schools everywhere as the war years took their toll. But the official certificate of graduation, the *"Reifezeugnis,"* awarded after passing a uniform and comprehensive examination lasting several days, was still the essential admission ticket to university training. Maria was determined that Anton should have

---

[1] Public preparatory school

it, whatever she had to do to bring it about.

Oberstudiendirektor [2] Niederholzer sat behind his large worn desk, looking as distinguished as he could manage. A tiny man well into his sixties, his head crowned with a mane of snowy hair, he sported a pointed goatee under his white mustache. Rimless half-glasses endowed him with a scholarly mien. Stiffly formal, he looked like a curious throwback to the turn of the century, incongruous and pitiable in his old-fashioned garb.

Maria explained that she was a widow who had just moved to Schlossberg and that she was anxious for her son to complete his education. The old man listened absent-mindedly, twisting his goatee. After a while he replied in a high-pitched voice, guaranteed to evoke student hilarity, "Well, *Frau* Wildert, surely you must know how it is, we have too many applicants and too few spaces. Your son will have to take his chances and apply along with the others next week. I know you mentioned his good grades—I shall look at his record when the time comes . . ."

"I have his certificates right here," Maria interjected.

"Fine, fine," the principal squeaked back, "we have good students here, too, and everyone must wait to take his turn." He gave his goatee a ferocious twist, straightened his back to ramrod stiffness, one hand held behind him and rose slowly, the audience over. He bowed ever so slightly to Maria as his traditional manners demanded.

The following week the newspaper carried the notice that new students could apply at the preparatory school the next Monday, bringing along documentation of their past schooling. Anton decided to go an hour early to make sure he was well positioned in the expected crowd. He walked through the musty hallway toward the principal's office, his steps resounding on the worn stone slab floor. A babble of voices reverberated from the vaulted ceiling, and he quickly submerged into a milling group of teenagers. Together they waited patiently until the appointed hour—but nothing happened.

The crowd of young students grew larger and more agitated.

[2] Senior Director of Studies

Anton shouldered his way closer to the door and recognized a tall boy from Karlsbad, Peter, who he met by the river bank on his first day in Schlossberg. Aggressive by nature, Peter wriggled forward and shouted in his distinctive accent, "What's going on here, anyhow?" The other youths eyed him expectantly. Peter grinned at Anton. "This is a real mess—I've been here for two hours already! The principal doesn't seem to know what to do, so he's hiding in his office!"

Anton recalled the frail little man with the goatee and chuckled. "I can understand that; he's a funny old clown!" Having said this, Anton looked suspiciously about him, hoping that no one overheard his disrespectful remark.

A loud, coarse voice echoed above the din, coming closer. It belonged to a bald, bullnecked man wearing a brown apron. The stocky figure pushed his way forcefully through the startled crowd. "Shut up, everybody, dammit!" he bellowed. When this had no effect, he furiously shook a large brass hand bell above the students' heads. In the congested space the sharp metallic din hurt the ears.

The movement and talking abated. "I am the *Pedell*," [3] the man announced grandly. He thus identified himself as the all-purpose factotum, handyman and keeper of order. Ridiculed and feared at the same time, the *Pedell* ensured the day-to-day functioning of any school. "There's far too many of you; we can't take you all," he shouted hoarsely, "and we'll give first place to them what was born here. You new guys better wait 'til we figure out what to do."

For a moment there was stunned silence, then the bolder of the refugee students started calling for the principal. Peter, angry and upset, shouted vehemently, "I'm not taking orders from the housekeeper!" All eyes turned to him as he muscled his way through the crowd to the principal's door. He knocked twice and entered without waiting for a reply. The surprised *Pedell* lunged to catch up with him and both stood in front of the fragile man who rose from his chair, his eyes bulging with shock and confusion.

[3] Housekeeper

"I respectfully request that all of us may register for classes today," Peter boomed in his post-puberty baritone.

The lanky young man towered over the principal, who was holding on to his desk with both hands, stuttering. "B-but...but... *Herr* Mayer has told you that there is no room for you people." Pulling at his goatee the old man looked helplessly at Mayer, whose massive head and bullneck turned bright red with rage.

"By the devil, who d' you think you are, Gypsy boy!" Mayer roared furiously. "We oughta send all you bastards home, nobody asked you to come here!"

Peter paled at the slur and whirled around to hiss at the *Pedell* between clenched teeth, "We've got every right to be here! We certainly didn't ask to come to this backwater of a town! But now that we are here, we expect to be treated like everyone else!" Several of the refugee teenagers had followed Peter into the principal's office, including Anton. They stood respectfully and watched in silence.

The frail man looked blankly at them, one by one, then turned to Mayer despairingly, as if to ask what to do next. The *Pedell* again took the stage, somewhat calmer now. "Perhaps we can double up on the classes, though the professors sure won't be happy about that," he said hesitantly. Then he addressed the principal officiously. "*Herr Oberstudiendirektor*, let's take down the names so we know how many of them there is."

"That's exactly what I was going to say, *Herr* Mayer! Why don't you arrange that!" Niederholzer threw himself into a posture of authority and squeaked, "Young gentlemen . . and young ladies"—he had spotted two or three girls in the crowd—"*Herr* Mayer will take all your names and addresses, and we'll attempt to make some arrangements for classes to begin next week." He turned and slumped in his chair, exhausted.

Anton added his name to the list with the others and followed Peter outside into the bright sunshine. "That was brave of you, Peter," he said with undisguised admiration. Peter gave him a wide grin, obviously pleased with himself. His breezy, self-assured manner impressed Anton who had not yet overcome his inherent shyness. Peter seemed so much more worldly and mature, although they were the same age. Clearly his new friend had learned from the experience of disruption to take matters into his own hands and ignore conventional deference to authority. Anton's introspection and Peter's flamboyance would make a good basis on which to build a friendship.

Classes did begin a week later, and Anton and Peter found themselves in a crowded room with forty other students; about a dozen were refugees from the Sudetenland and from other parts of Germany. The rest were local or from nearby villages and towns. After all the ups and downs of displacement, the orderly routine of attending classes again seemed unreal and even confining to Anton, and he brooded about his ambivalent feelings. On the one hand he cared about doing well—something the Wildert brothers had always been proud of—while on the other he found it difficult to concentrate and to develop a sense of belonging. Peter admitted to having similar qualms, but his innate aggressiveness helped him adjust to the new situation much faster than Anton.

The collection of teachers at the school was made up of characters that could have sprung from the pages of a satire about preparatory school education. One or two were in their prime, but the others, often quirky and absent-minded, were close to or past retirement. Yet somehow instruction carried on and the majority of the students were serious about learning. They shared a few old books, wrote notes and assignments on scraps of coarse paper, and made the most of what knowledge the often tired and dejected teachers imparted. Like everything else, school materials and textbooks were in short supply, a gap the teachers bridged only to a small degree by the laborious dictation of basic concepts for the class to write down.

Anton and the other refugees found they had more in common with each other than with the local students. They spoke with their own distinct regional accents, but more importantly, they lived at much different levels of comfort. In more carefree days such mingling of backgrounds would have been full of exploration and shared adventure. Under the dreary conditions of late 1946 even schoolchildren were immersed in the daily struggle to exist, queuing up for basic needs or scouring the countryside for farmers interested in bartering food. The refugee youths were particularly close to these concerns, and friendships were invariably colored by such differences.

Anton remembered his own first encounters with eastern refugees during the last year of the war. When they spoke of their suffering and of their past and present problems, he had listened without comprehending, only sensing the differences that divided them. It was difficult to understand the feelings of those who had become homeless and insecure. Now he was experiencing what it meant to be cast adrift among strangers.

Anton and his refugee friends lived every day with deprivations and indignities, and worst of all, the indifference of the local population. It was hard not to become resentful when being met with an obvious lack of interest and little understanding by the community. Maria often urged him not to let his relationships with local schoolmates be clouded by slights and ill feelings. She repeated over and over, "How do they know how we feel? How can they? How can we expect them to understand?" But there were also exceptions, and Anton struck up a solid friendship with Ferdinand, a thoughtful local boy, whose calm manner was unassuming and reassuring, and with whom he could share many of his thoughts.

Life for the Wilderts at the Blohmstett apartment was a long series of irritations and clashes, which in one incident escalated into the two women trading slaps in the face. Anton, upon hearing their shouts, rushed to his mother's defense; in trying to shield her from Hildegard Blohmstett's raging blows and scratches, he unintentionally bruised the woman's face. She was not really hurt and he thought with smug satisfaction that it was a small retribution when she had to conceal the black and blue mark with heavy makeup for a day or two.

Soon after school started, the American occupation forces began a program that provided a simple but nourishing hot soup or cooked cereals for the students at noon. The meal was free for those who could not afford to pay the nominal charge. Anton, Peter and the other refugees were especially glad to receive this vital supplement to their poor rations. Although many local students participated, some of those better off were disdainful and criticized the taste and quality of the food. This did not deter Anton and a few others from carrying part of their lunch ration home to share.

Although he welcomed and enjoyed the food, Anton felt uncomfortable about accepting charity in any form. He and many schoolmates could not afford to pay, and he suffered from hurt pride; his family had never had to accept such help before. When he talked it over with his mother she made him see that this was not the time to be proud about help which was offered to everyone, and that their precarious situation was not of their own making. In fact, they ran out of money a few weeks earlier and only the fortuitous next-day arrival of her funds sent by Martha enabled them to carry on.

As fall declined towards winter, conditions of everyday life worsened. The economy remained moribund, productive work became even more scarce, and the overcrowded cities and towns provided no more than a make do existence. Rations for food and fuel were tighter than ever, and stores and service establishments were stripped and barely functioning. Barter took on a heightened importance, leaving refugees who had little to trade at a severe disadvantage. What paper money there was among the population seemed almost useless, for there was little to buy. The effects of a prolonged minimal diet began to show in pallid faces and unhealthy bodies.

Maria and Anton carried on day after day as best they could, and the Blohmstetts continued to treat them with cold indifference, living openly far better than the Wilderts could even dream. Contact with the vonEckenbachs and the managers was rare and impersonal. Dr. Zimmermann did keep in touch sporadically, pleading preoccupation with work and the obligations of a houseful of relatives, but still extending occasional kindnesses. Maria made tentative human attachments and contacts at the refugee restaurant, and Anton enjoyed budding friendships with a number of his classmates.

When the first snow fell, the outlook for the future was as

bleak as the chill in the air and the leaden skies above. Although they tried to reassure each other, Maria's steadfast hope and brave talk that somehow things would turn out well began to lack conviction. Anton sensed that the faith that sustained them both during their crises was eroding under the ongoing stresses of their tenuous existence.

It was going to be a long, hard winter. Would there be a spring?

TWENTY-THREE

The New World

August 1950

Anton sat comfortably in the deep plush seat by the wide window of the elegant blue and gold *Wagon lits* sleeping car, watching the expanse of vineyards and fields of the Rhône valley fly past, accompanied by the softly cushioned rhythm of the speeding wheels. In the distance remnants of the ancient bridge at Avignon braved the river's swirling waters, reminders of a glorious past, of Popes, pomp and power. The sleek train leaned smoothly into the next curve. Anton hummed the charming little song he remembered from his French course at Schlossberg. *"Sur le pont... d'Avignon... on y danse... "* In those days he would never have dreamed that today, in August 1950, he would glimpse the famous bridge on his way to the French Riviera. Maria, elated and proud as never before, had seen him off in Frankfurt, the very station where four years earlier she almost died under the wheels of a train.

There was the girl at Schlossberg who bade him a tearful goodbye, happy for him that he had the chance to attend a university in America, but also instinctively fearing that Anton might not want to return to the town's provincial atmosphere after he had seen and tasted more of the wide world. Margarete was a local girl and had been his friend for the past two years, a good companion for the striving refugee boy. But he had given no thought to a steady attachment—there was so much to see, to learn, to experience.

What a whirl the past nine months had been! Anton was still unable to grasp the reality of his good fortune. Since the trauma and aftermath of the expulsion and the refugee existence at

Schlossberg, his life had taken unexpected and positive turns. Within his reach now lay the possibility of a more stable and normal life, something that seemed unattainable only a few short years ago. An education at Munich University was assured; his good grades entitled him to admission, and there was even the prospect of financial assistance for his years of study. He was certain he wanted to become a journalist. Now he was riding in a crack express train en route to Cannes where he was to board a ship for a year's study in the United States together with five hundred other students from all parts of western Germany.

As he leaned back in his lavish compartment—the luxury train had been taken over by the Americans when it fell into their hands after being used by the German high command—Anton gazed into the distance, reflecting on a kaleidoscope of vivid memories, on developments in his life he could never have foreseen when he and his family left the villa in Aussig. He saw images of the past appear as if superimposed on the scenery outside the gleaming window.

In his graduation year the Schlossberg preparatory school nominated him for a one-year scholarship for university study in America, sponsored by the U. S. State Department. Schools all over West Germany proposed one nominee, and from these a final five hundred students were chosen after extensive tests and interviews. The program began the previous year when a local student from Schlossberg was nominated and won a scholarship to go to America. He wrote glowing letters to his parents and to the school about his experiences at a southern university, and the townsfolk felt privileged and pleased that one of their own received this rare opportunity.

When his English instructor mentioned to Maria that Anton would be the next candidate to be proposed for the honor, she was torn between motherly pride and dread of separation, but Anton was beside himself with joy. After consultation with the city council—Kastner included—the faculty's nomination became final and Anton hurled himself into the special tests and interviews.

He waited longingly to hear about the scholarship and almost gave up hope when the New Year came and passed. Undaunted, he kept up his studies for the critical final exams while also working hard at his part-time job as a roving reporter for the regional newspaper. At last, in February, the official letter arrived with the news that he had indeed been selected, pending the successful conclusion of his studies in June. Spurred on by this incentive Anton charged through the work of the last semester and the government-run final exams, finishing first in a class of twenty-nine.

The refugee community welcomed Anton's nomination as a clear sign that the distinction between indigenous residents and postwar newcomers was beginning to fade and that an integrated sense of belonging might become possible. Performance seemed now to be recognized on equal terms—although in fact there had been some maneuvering to nominate another Sudeten student who, besides having good qualifications, was better connected to the emerging political power structure of the Sudeten community. But in the end everyone accepted Anton as the candidate of choice, and the award of the scholarship became good news for the whole town.

Still lost in reverie Anton mused about the tortuous path he and his mother had taken to arrive at this high point of his life. The winter of 1946–47 had turned out to be a test of stamina. Malnutrition, illness and cold living quarters took numerous casualties among the refugees, especially the older people. Life moved at a snail's pace; for many subsistence was possible only through an occasional pittance of money or staples doled out by the Refugee Office. Hundreds of additional Sudeten expellees came to Schlossberg; they were crowded into the old castle in camp-like conditions, occupying the ice-cold and shabby halls in communal closeness for lack of better shelter.

The following year brought little improvement in living conditions, although the more enterprising residents began restarting their businesses and even founded new ones, often based on salvaging materials from the ever present rubble and scrap. Still the queues at stores and offices were endless, and money had practically no value. Barter continued to be the only means of obtaining scarce food, fuel, tobacco, and clothing. Many caches of goods remained stored away in hiding places, of course, and some aid also trickled in through official channels. Anyone with access to such sources enjoyed a considerable advantage, and black-market profiteers thrived in a climate that attracted nimble and shady characters like flies to a carcass.

The Wilderts and most of their fellow refugees were hardly touched by this subculture. They survived by the occasional barter of things they themselves could hardly spare, and sometimes the charitable instincts of farmers made them willing to part, for money, with some milk, butter or eggs. While always short of funds, the Wilderts managed to live on their refugee allowances and a small monthly token payment which the vonEckenbachs finally granted Maria.

For everyone the turning point came with the sweeping currency reform of 1948, suddenly executed with a bold stroke by the Military Governments in western Germany under strong American influence. Overnight, forty new Deutsche Marks were issued to every citizen, while simultaneously the old currency was declared null and void. All future claims and obligations were revalued on the basis of one new mark for ten old marks. An additional twenty marks were issued to everyone some weeks later. Refugees lost little in the drastic exchange as savings accounts and insurance claims had already been blocked or canceled after their expulsion. Locals often suffered considerable monetary losses, but the goods which merchants had hoarded for so long immediately became valuable with the new, sound currency.

Anton recalled how stores in Schlossberg suddenly displayed merchandise not seen for years, obviously brought out of hidden storage and modestly priced in the new currency. He and his fellow students followed and discussed the exciting developments during the days of the currency reform, hour by hour, sensing that this surprise gamble for economic rejuvenation held hope for them all. Economic activity indeed rebounded as if someone waved a magic wand. For the first time since the collapse there was real value in the workers' wages and in business profits. The United States provided extensive assistance which finally took hold in this enterprising climate and helped to create work in both reconstruction and productive endeavors. Most important, there now was an incentive for individuals to strive and progress.

Anton sensed the positive forces emerging in the spirit of the people around him, and he himself felt more purpose and hope in the struggle for his education. He reached out in new directions, exchanging correspondence with a Camp Fire Girl in Des Moines, Iowa; the excitement of receiving the first letter from America would always stay with him. He also took part in a youth program sponsored by the American occupation forces which provided reading matter, sports equipment, and meeting rooms for German teenagers. The enterprising German ex-sergeant in charge of the activities took groups of young people on outings and weekend excursions to the Alps, and Anton and his friends loved to go on these inexpensive trips. It didn't matter that they traveled on the platforms of canvas-covered trucks. They sang to their hearts' delight, hiked and swam, enjoyed the grand scenery and shared simple meals.

The Wilderts still lived in a single room but in a different part of town, having managed a move through a risky but successful circumvention of the official strictures. Their room was now more comfortably furnished with several pieces of furniture lent them by Dr. Zimmermann. Although cramped, it had become a home base where the striving boy studied and pursued his interests. From bartered spare parts Anton built a simple radio that seemed to work as well as the prewar sets in other peoples' homes, and he lived with his mother in an atmosphere of sharing, achieving small improvements in material well-being, and growing in maturity gradually but steadily.

They had no great expectations, but gratefully welcomed every small step ahead that made their frugal existence more agreeable. Nannerl appeared one day from Munich for a joyful reunion, having searched for the Wilderts for more than a year, and, after spending many hours savoring memories they remained in regular contact. Maria also corresponded from time to time with *Frau* Winkler from the corner house in Aussig, who had settled near Stuttgart, warmly reminiscing and sharing their current experiences. Margot stayed in touch, maintaining Maria's link to a better past, and continued to advise and encourage Maria in her letters.

Anton chuckled with merriment when he suddenly recalled how they had boldly moved to their new quarters in town one New Year's Eve in defiance of the housing authorities. Some months before the Blohmstetts left Schlossberg, having separated after stormy battles in the apartment about Hildegard's alliances with both American officers and local men, who were the source of the couple's elevated standard of living.

The authorities allotted the Blohmstett apartment to a Sudeten banker, his wife and adult son. The Wilderts' initial joy about sharing the crowded space with people of similar background and experience soon wore off when the relationship turned sour. The couple did everything they could to drive the Wilderts out, particularly the shrewish wife, whose hilarious facial contortions Anton loved to mimic when telling the story later.

Officials reacted to repeated appeals for a change in rooms with bureaucratic apathy. When Maria fortuitously learned from a friend of a vacancy several streets away she energetically took matters in her own hands. Late on the last day of December Dr. Zimmermann gleefully sent the company's delivery wagon to move the Wilderts to their new address, glad to help Maria in her struggle against officious bureaucrats with whom he himself wished to settle a few scores. By the time the New Year rang in they were installed in their new room. The authorities were completely surprised when they found out two days later. After some fruitless bluster they meekly yielded to the accomplished coup. To Anton it had been a real adventure and, for once, a resounding victory over bureaucracy.

Anton loved to write. When he submitted a story to the regional newspaper about one of the alpine excursions with the youth group, the editor published it and offered him part-time reporting work with small but welcome monetary compensation. He assigned Anton to prepare a series of feature stories about civic institutions and services, ranging from the municipal archives to the electric power plant. He became adept at interviewing people in authority, including the mayor and other key officials, businessmen, and professional people. When the rebuilt bridge over the Danube was dedicated he did an exhaustive report not only on the ceremonies, but also on the planning and construction for the project.

Movie reviews followed, giving him the chance to see all the new movies in town free of charge while taking along his girlfriend. The films were mostly American releases of the thirties and forties, with German subtitles, and he was able to test his English while gazing wistfully at the Hollywood version of the Good Life. After the shows Margarete strolled with him to the quiet editorial offices in the old part of town, and Anton pounded his reactions and insights into an ancient typewriter. While she sat with him they argued and discussed his points until he was ready to pass the copy to the typesetters. Then they walked home hand in hand.

These journalistic endeavors yielded needed extra income to the Wilderts, paying for such luxuries as a new bicycle. His work gave Anton a growing confidence in himself and brought a sense of approval and belonging he had not known since his former life was shattered.

He found it exciting to make his opinion public and to see his words in print. It was an even greater thrill when people he respected commented favorably on his reviews, including the proprietress of the movie house, who even agreed with some of his more scathing critiques. During the last year he produced a regular weekly column under his byline; the subjects ranged from humorous interpretations of local happenings to seasonal topics and attempts at commentary. His material was well accepted by the paper's readers. When his departure to the United States was imminent, the editor, treating him like a colleague, asked that he continue his column, "Anton Wildert Writes," by sending periodic impressions of his experiences in the New World.

As he watched the landscape of southern France, Anton already thought of the points he would make in describing the beginning of the trip—ranging from the interesting and fun-filled preparatory sessions at a mansion on Starnberg Lake near Munich to the luxurious mode of his train journey.

"Toulon, Toulon!" the loudspeaker blared at the picturesque Mediterranean station. The train slowed smoothly for a brief stop. Anton and Hans, his traveling companion from Augsburg, pulled down the window, letting in the balmy sea air.

"Look, Hans, palm trees!" Anton gestured to the swaying fronds beside the whitewashed arches of the Toulon train depot. "This is so wonderful, I've never seen a real one!" It would not be far to Cannes, their destination.

After gliding out of the station the train wound its way through picturesque rocky bays and coves of the peaceful Mediterranean sea, white beaches flashing, the sun glistening on the gentle waves. The students crowded the seaward windows, fascinated with the glorious southern landscape, where barren soil changed to emerald green park grounds and back to rocky expanses, shaded by palms and cypresses, and framed by the azure sea. It looked like a fairy tale land to northern eyes.

From the Cannes station they took a shuttle to the quiet harbor, where motor launches brought them to a small white steamer anchored well out at sea. The lettering on the stern of the gently swaying ship read "S.S. Brasil." Though it was a well-worn vintage vessel that had even been sunk once, the ship seemed magical to the excited Anton. After a happy investigation of the decks and facilities the young travelers settled into their quarters. As the evening sun sank into the western sea, the "S.S. Brasil" hoisted anchor and set course for Gibraltar, Lisbon, the Azores and New York.

Anton was serene and happy as seldom before. He plunged into the many shipboard activities and savored the Italian food, a new experience for him. When the ship passed landmarks like the rock of Gibraltar, or wound its slow way into the vast harbor of Lisbon he busily used his prize possession, a new Kodak camera, snapping shot after shot in excited efforts to preserve the happiest memories of this idyllic adventure.

They went ashore to tour ancient Lisbon, where Anton found the ornate architecture and the temperamental people fascinating. Back on board they watched the European continent fade from view. A brief stop at the Azores brought the excitement of young divers submerging for coins tossed from the deck and the noisy trade for tropical fruit offered by shouting vendors in bobbing boats.

The Atlantic crossing proceeded leisurely and Anton relaxed with his new friends, taking in the sun and dancing into the night. He felt carefree and happy. Then a major hurricane forced the ship to change course. The vast storm brought on leaden skies, howling winds and mountainous waves; the small steamer was tossed around like a log. For a while Anton tried to brave the rolling and pitching, but soon like everyone else he lay prostrate in his bunk, suffering miserably until the waves subsided.

In the early morning hours they neared New York harbor, gliding through smooth, glassy waters. They crowded the railing on the upper deck, everyone trying to be the first to glimpse the Statue of Liberty. The rising sun broke through the swirling morning mists, and suddenly brilliant shafts of light illuminated the famous statue. Anton's heart leaped at the sight; in wild elation he flung his arms around the girl standing next to him, planting a kiss on her mouth. Arm in arm they watched the drama of the New York skyline emerge from the fog and mist, starkly powerful and grandiose. The sun angled brightly through the low clouds, outlining the massive, looming skyscrapers.

Even though the awe-inspiring spectacle of the New World before him was alien in its vast proportions and impersonal grandeur, Anton instinctively felt he found a new beginning—that in fact he had come home. He realized his scholarship covered only one year, that he was expected to return to Germany, but at this moment it seemed to him that he saw a glimpse of his destiny. He did not know why he felt this way, except that his heart and soul yearned for a new future. The larger-than-life dimensions of the city intrigued and excited him—already he sensed the contrast when reflecting on the confined world of rivalries and hatreds from which he came.

After the gangway was lowered the students jostled onto the pier and were herded before customs and immigration officers in the arrival hall. Anton's understanding of English had never been challenged more than when suddenly confronted with the examiners' unadulterated Brooklynese. Humbled by the strange sounds he reverted to sign language, but all went well and soon the happy crowd spilled onto the noisy streets of Manhattan, throbbing with life, raw with contrasts.

The students arrived at Columbia University to receive a few days' counseling before departing individually for universities all over the country. Anton and his friends explored sights of the pulsating metropolis with youthful vigor. American students from the dormitory joined them on these excursions, sharing in their joy of discovery. It was a carefree time and Anton's vigorous enthusiasm knew no bounds.

Anton was issued his train ticket to travel across the continent. The university that granted his scholarship was in the far west, and the trip would take three days. After hearty and spirited good-byes to counselors and friends he found himself in the cavernous expanse of Grand Central Station ready to board the westbound streamliner. The diversity, scale and tempo of life in the New World awed him, and the immense station seemed a fitting grand finale to his vision of New York.

After boarding the stainless steel coach he nestled into his reclining seat, impressed by the space and comfort surrounding him. How different this was from the dreary boxcar that carried him across the German border just four years before, he thought. Anton hardly noticed the train's movement when the heavy carriage began to glide smoothly through the underground. When it emerged in daylight and gathered speed the sleek streamliner gave Anton a mobile vantage point from which to view the many-faceted images of America. His first stop was Washington, D. C., where he spent a few hours roaming the Capitol, the Mall and the expanse of Pennsylvania Avenue. He still had not adjusted to the vast dimensions of everything he saw, the sleek automobiles, the immense buildings, and so much space. He felt he could breathe freely, there was elbowroom, and opportunity.

The streamliner moved him through a vivid panorama of impressions of the New World. He saw the ugliness of city slums, the raw industrial might of the country firmly planted in smoky towns, and the vast green landscape of rural America, open and inviting. During a brief stopover he glimpsed the vibrancy of Chicago and its glamorous lake front.

Anton found the rolling prairies of the Midwest astounding in their endless expanse from horizon to horizon. His crowded homeland diminished even more before these dimensions, facts which he had learned in school but could not grasp until they appeared before his very eyes. In Des Moines he met his pen pal Gloria and spent a happy afternoon with her and her family. They talked and laughed, reminiscing about their letters and what the faraway touch of friendship meant to them both.

Anton was vibrant with elation when the train began to traverse the rugged grandeur of the Rockies and the western deserts. He sat riveted to his window seat, absorbed in the bizarre shapes and colors of the rock strata, the lonely expanse of barren soil stubby with sagebrush, and the myriad tints of light and shadow. The drama of the crimson sun setting over a vast and varied wilderness exceeded in raw beauty anything he had ever seen. Anton remembered the stories he read as a boy about cowboys and indians and the make-believe games he and his friends played. He recalled the yearning he always felt to see for himself some day that great unfenced land, the vast spaces so full of mystique and drama. And here he was, traveling in cool comfort through that very world!

Anton began to jot down notes for his next column, deciding that this engrossing train journey would be his first topic. He looked up and listened joyfully whenever the wailing, melancholy howl of the throbbing steam locomotive echoed in the dusky canyons. He knew this haunting sound would always remain with him, touching an inner part of him, a key to unlocking bittersweet memories, an invitation to yearning and hope. A new life was beginning, founded on many small miracles that had become interwoven in a mysterious pattern.

His good fortune beckoned him, and he was eager to follow.

TWENTY-FOUR

California Reflection

June 1995

A tall man in his sixties strode briskly along the sun-drenched sidewalk of San Francisco's California Street past the ornate facades of towering office buildings that exuded the prosperity of the early twentieth century. At the Montgomery Street intersection he stopped for the red light, enjoying the view up the busy slope toward the crest of Nob Hill where wisps of ocean fog hastened east in the pale blue sky, fading gently in the warm rays of the mid-morning sun. A clattering, clanging cable car crawled unhurriedly up the steep incline, passengers clinging cheerfully to its sides, hanging on amidst the jostle of automobiles trying to dodge the antique conveyance.

Halfway up the slope the deep red brick facade of Old St. Mary's stood dwarfed by the sleek new office towers that had begun to crowd the hill in recent years. Its square steeple, proud in the brilliant sun, proclaimed in gilded letters: "Son, observe the time and fly from evil." The graceful pagoda roofs of Chinatown flanking the quaint edifice blended in ecumenical harmony with the ornate wrought iron cross atop the oldest church in the city. A colorful crowd of well-dressed office workers, dotted with the diverse characters of this crossroad city of the Pacific, scrambled though the intersection. It was a bustling scene, a beautiful setting that lifted the spirit.

Anton Wildert climbed the steep sidewalk until he reached the church. He ascended the worn stone steps and passed through the arched brick portal into the quiet interior, faintly fragrant with incense. He often used the sanctuary as a peaceful haven, if only to say a brief prayer before the statue of St. Anthony, his patron saint and the saint of miracles. Old St. Mary's was still almost empty at this hour. Anton loved the simple, bright Italianate cheerfulness of the small church; its white altar surmounted by a large painting of the Madonna and Child reminded him of the copy of an Italian master's work that used to hang in his grandmother's bedroom. The melodic bells of the clock tower struck eleven. Anton sat down in one of the pews near the statue of St. Anthony, the small alcove bright with muted sunshine. He came on this June day in 1995 to say a prayer for his mother Maria who had passed away on this date ten years before.

Maria joined him in the United States while he was still a student and observed his career develop, first teaching at Harvard University, then joining a large San Francisco corporation, and more recently his decision to practice as an independent consultant. Before Maria's final illness she also witnessed his happy marriage to Julie Meadows, an English widow, whom he met by fortunate coincidence on his fifty-first birthday. Julie and her two grown daughters, Elizabeth and Louise, brought him the fullness and joy of family companionship after long years of almost exclusive immersion in his work. Over the years Anton began to think that finding true love and friendship would elude him forever; now he often gave thanks for what he considered the most wonderful miracle of his life.

Anton's mind was alive with memories, reaching back further and further. He reflected on the many twists and turns in his life, beginning with the experiences of his boyhood that at an early age thrust him into the cauldron of European history in the making. By this time he had acquired a conscious ability to see these events in a greater perspective. Time and maturity began to mellow the raw emotions that so often tormented him not only in his dreams. He was at peace.

The echoing footsteps of a worshiper stirred Anton out of his reverie. He glanced at his watch and realized his mind had wandered for half an hour. He wiped his brow as if to brush away the kaleidoscope of memories, rose, and lit three candles on the tray before St. Anthony's statue. His head bowed, he stood in silence and thought lovingly of Maria, Friedrich and Johann. Feeling a deep sense of gratitude he turned, walked along the rows of pews and left by the main door after casting back one more glance at the familiar painting above the altar.

Refreshed and ready to face the daily concerns of his work he stepped lightly into the street and jumped on the clanging cable car, hanging on to its side for the noisy ride down the long slope to the financial district.

TWENTY-FIVE

Epilogue

The extinction of the Sudetenland at a cost of over three million refugees and a quarter million dead is an historical fact—passed over and forgotten in the struggle to rebuild the world after the defeat of Hitler and his Axis partners. Yet the basic causes that led to the 1938 crisis and its ultimate tragic ending cannot be ignored. Beyond the fate of its many victims, the Sudeten episode is but one more example of lack of statesmanship in settling the status of a small territory or a minority population within a larger nation. The lesson is as valid today as it was half a century ago.

The "final solution" of the Sudeten problem was deadly fruit that grew from seeds of moral weakness and blind nationalism, sown in the fertile soil of ethnic discontent at three historical turning points: The peace arrangements at the end of World War I, the crises leading to World War II, and the political realignment of Europe after World War II.

Had the leaders responsible during these various times practiced moral courage, consistent with their stated ideals, world history might have taken a different turn. But as these leaders made their decisions they brushed aside the elementary right of people to determine their own fate. The stroke of a pen altered boundaries and national alignments; no one sought the advice or consent of those whose vital interests were involved because their numbers and their territory were small.

Unfortunately, the story of the Sudetenland has many parallels in past history and in current events. Suppression of people's rights in the name of political expediency or nationalistic fervor still occurs in today's world. But as has been shown again and again, the eventual consequences may far exceed the bounds of the initial offense. Like ripples on a pond the effects spread beyond the point of impact and can become a wave of dislocation, suffering and death. What seem like minor and isolated injustices may in the end exact a grievous toll on mankind. The Sudeten dispute brought about the creation of a country disparate in ethnic makeup, the opportunity for a dictator to take one more provocative step affecting the fate of the world at a critical time and, ultimately, the tragic expulsion of millions.

At issue is basic morality and justice—the morality of political decisions made by leaders of individual governments or alliances that may, temporarily, have the upper hand. To the shortsighted, "might makes right," but the wise know that injustice cannot endure. Morality lapses when statesmen yield to the temptation to resolve political or territorial disputes by shortchanging the rights of regional populations, whether out of ignorance, through neglect, or by intent. Such leaders violate morality when they exploit a temporary state of confusion and misrepresent facts about minorities and their territories to bring about a *faît accompli* in the eyes of the world. Morality is impaled when the innocent and helpless are made to suffer for the mistakes or transgressions of national leaders, or of those in their midst who are truly guilty under moral and temporal law. The guilt from wanton revenge is just as insidious as the guilt from any earlier offense. The convenient guise of national retribution cannot be used to justify cruelty and deprivation, for morality must transcend political boundaries, nationalism, and expediency.

Will the nations of this world some day heed the wisdom of their philosophers and the moral guidance of their prophets? Will mankind muster the courage to respect human and territorial rights? When will the world's leaders and citizens break the vicious cycle of violation, retribution, and counter-retribution?

Nearing the close of the twentieth century we should ask ourselves if the inhabitants of this planet are forever condemned to repeat the mistakes of the past, to reap the bitter harvest of evil deeds rooted in misguided motives. Must generation after generation of innocent people suffer? When will we adhere in spirit and deed to the lofty ideals we so proudly proclaim in our institutions and memorials?

What will the answer be as we begin the Third Millennium?

Erich A. Helfert

Erich Anton Helfert was born in the Sudetenland. He came to the United States as a student in 1950, graduated from the University of Nevada and received an MBA and Doctorate from the Harvard Business School. After serving on the Harvard Business School faculty for eight years, Dr. Helfert joined Crown Zellerbach Corporation in San Francisco, where over the next twenty years he held management positions including Vice President, Corporate Planning. Since 1985 he has been engaged in management consulting and executive development with major corporations nationwide, and he and his wife Anne live in the San Francisco Bay area.

Dr. Helfert gained early writing experience as a journalist and correspondent, and has published extensively in the field of finance. His best-seller *Techniques of Financial Analysis* is in its ninth edition and has been translated into seven languages. *Valley of the Shadow* is his first literary work.